CHINA CHANGES FACE

CHINA CHANGES FACE

The Road from Revolution 1949–1989

JOHN GITTINGS

Oxford   New York

OXFORD UNIVERSITY PRESS

1989

Oxford University Press, Walton Street, Oxford OX2 6DP

Oxford New York Toronto
Delhi Bombay Calcutta Madras Karachi
Petaling Jaya Singapore Hong Kong Tokyo
Nairobi Dar es Salaam Cape Town
Melbourne Auckland

and associated companies in
Berlin Ibadan

Oxford is a trade mark of Oxford University Press

British Library Cataloguing in Publication Data
Gittings, John 1938–
China changes face: the road from revolution, 1949–1989
1. China, 1949–
I. Title.
951.05
ISBN 0–19–215887–2

Library of Congress Cataloging in Publication Data
Gittings, John.
China changes face: the road from revolution, 1949–1989 / John Gittings.
p. cm Bibliography: p. Includes index.
1. China—History—1949– I. Title.
951.05—dc 19 DS777.55.G534 1989 88–30854
ISBN 0–19–215887–2

Typeset by Latimer Trend & Company Ltd.
Printed in Great Britain by
Biddles Ltd.
Guildford and King's Lynn

ACKNOWLEDGEMENTS

I am grateful above all to Aelfthryth Gittings, Kay Clay, and Robert Gittings, who have given me heart-warming support as well as offering helpful comments. I have benefited from the critical opinions of many friends including Harriet Evans, Kan Shioyun, Helen Lackner, Cyril Lin, Robin Munro, and Peter Nolan. The graphics owe much to my work with Anna Merton and the Chinese Visual Aids Project at the Polytechnic of Central London. Students, both English and Chinese, at the PCL School of Languages and in China, helped me by their own experiences and insights to keep abreast of Chinese post-Mao changes. (The future, as Chairman Mao said, lies with them.) I owe a deep intellectual debt to the Chinese scholars of the 1980s who are ready to ask difficult questions about their country's past and future. I hope that they will find the answers, and that those in China—often young and hardly known—who have suffered for asking even more difficult questions will find their freedom.

CONTENTS

LIST OF ILLUSTRATIONS

1. Urban poverty before Liberation. Woodcut by Shi Zhishi, 1948, *Zhongguo banhua ji* [*Collection of Chinese woodcuts*] (Shanghai: Zung Kwang Publishing Co., 1948).

2. Rural poverty before Liberation. Woodcut by Xi Ya, 1948. *Zhongguo banhua ji.*

3. A village cadre listens to poor peasants, and helps them dig a well. North-west China Party Propaganda Department. *Gongchandangyuan biaozhun de baxiang tongsu jianghua* [*Eight Popular Lectures for a Model Communist*], (Xian: North-west People's Press, 1952).

4. Mechanization in a rural co-operative. Woodcut by Gu Hong, 1954. *Shinian lai banhua xuanji, 1949–59* [*Selection of woodcuts from the past ten years*] (Shanghai: People's Arts Press, 1959).

5. Village youth present the wives of soldiers with honorific titles. Papercut, Hebei, 1954. *Folk-arts of New China* (Beijing: Foreign Languages Press, 1954).

6. Peasants light firecrackers in Great Leap euphoria. Woodcut by Gu Yuan, 1958. *Shinian lai banhua xuanji.*

7. Construction team building a dam during the Great Leap. Woodcut by Li Hua, 1959. *Zhongguo xinxing banhua wushinian xuanji, xia 1950–81* [*Selection of new Chinese prints of the past 50 years, ii.*] (Shanghai: People's Arts Press, 1981).

8. Themes of study and modernization are revived after the Great Leap. Woodcut by Huang Xinbo, 1961. *Zhongguo xinxing banhua wushinian xuanji.*

9. Young Red Guard at work. Papercut, c.1967.

10. Worker, peasant, and soldier raise Mao's essays on high. Papercut, c.1967.

11. A student sent to the countryside examines medicinal herbs. From papercut series on 'new women', c.1973.

12. A bus driver cleans her windscreen, with a copy of *Red Flag*

CHRONOLOGICAL GUIDE, 1949–89

1949: Liberation. China is at last at peace after the CIVIL WAR between Communists and Nationalists (1946–9), which followed close after the ANTI-JAPANESE WAR (1937–45), and concludes with CHIANG KAI-SHEK's flight to Taiwan. Mao proclaims the PEOPLE'S REPUBLIC OF CHINA on Tiananmen Square, 1 October 1949. 'The Chinese people have stood up. . . . We have friends all over the world!'

February 1950: Sino-Soviet Alliance. The US has rejected diplomatic relations and trade with China unless it refrains from alliance with the Soviet Union. Mao refuses to be neutral—there is 'no middle road'. Two months of tough negotiations with Stalin produce the SINO-SOVIET TREATY OF ALLIANCE AND MUTUAL ASSISTANCE.

1950–2: Land Reform. Land and tools are taken from the landlords and rich peasants and redistributed, completing the process begun during the civil war in the communist areas. Several hundred thousand are executed after STRUGGLE MEETINGS, others are left with a share of land. The 1950 MARRIAGE LAW condemns the 'feudal system'. Peasants are encouraged to join MUTUAL-AID TEAMS, sharing manpower and tools in the busy season.

Economic rehabilitation. Unemployment, prostitution, and inflation are tamed in the towns, banditry suppressed in the north-west and south-west, railways and irrigation works restored and extended, communist 'cadres' replace corrupt local officials, a nation-wide food distribution system and public health network begin to be built, all in spite of . . .

June 1950–July 1953: Korean War. China is obliged to intervene in Korea just as it embarks on 'peaceful reconstruction' at home, when US forces, retaliating against the North, approach the China–Korea border. (Mao is supposed to have paced the floor for three days and nights before deciding.) The US imposes an economic blockade, and 'interdicts' the TAIWAN STRAITS to prevent the People's Republic from recovering Taiwan. China is excluded from the UNITED NATIONS and forced into greater dependence upon Moscow.

1953–6: Building a 'normal' society. The mood becomes more stolidly socialist in the Soviet style. FIRST FIVE-YEAR PLAN (1953–7) emphasizes heavy industry, with a 'command economy' and low investment in agriculture. First NATIONAL PEOPLE'S CONGRESS (1954) adopts state constitution; EIGHTH COMMUNIST PARTY CONGRESS (1956) pronounces end of 'class struggle' and hardly mentions Mao's name. The PEOPLE'S LIBERATION ARMY becomes a conscript army with ranks, medals, and sliding pay scale. After STALIN'S DEATH (February 1953), more equal relationship with Soviet Union. In talks with the US after the BANDUNG NON-ALIGNED CONFERENCE (April 1955), China's offer of trade, cultural exchanges, foreign ministers' conference, etc. is rejected.

1955–7: Mao explores a new road. Mao, against the trend of 'normalization', encourages rural activists to speed up establishment of AGRICULTURAL CO-OPERATIVES (1955) in which land becomes collective and income is distributed according to labour. Mao denies the need to wait for MECHANIZATION. The Chinese peasants are like a 'sheet of white paper' on which one can write beautiful words of socialism. In the HUNDRED FLOWERS MOVEMENT (1956–7) Mao first invites intellectuals to speak out against Party bureaucracy, but then endorses Party crack-down, worried by the example of protests in Hungary and Poland. Thousands sent to countryside in ANTI-RIGHTIST CAMPAIGN (1957). Mao begins to criticize post-Stalin Soviet leadership for 'leaving the socialist path'.

1958–61: Great Leap Forward—and back. The goal is to speed up the TRANSITION TO COMMUNISM, and overcome the THREE GREAT DIFFERENCES (between mental and manual labour, city and countryside, worker and peasant). Agricultural Co-operatives merged into PEOPLE'S COMMUNES with unsuccessful experiments in communal eating, rural steel-smelting, etc. Simultaneous 'Leap ahead' is called for in industry. Normal production is disrupted by unrealistic policies and bad weather. There is local famine and widespread hardship leading to millions of premature deaths. China opposes Soviet *détente* policy towards US; Moscow withdraws aid and SINO-SOVIET

DISPUTE becomes open. China develops economic policy of SELF-RELIANCE, becomes a nuclear power without outside help. People's communes are subdivided into brigades and teams, most functions assigned to the lowest team (village) level.

1959–65: The first 'inner-Party' struggle. At LUSHAN PLENUM (July 1959), Minister of Defence PENG DEHUAI criticizes the Great Leap, is denounced by Mao as 'anti-Party', and is replaced by LIN BIAO. In 1962 Head of State LIU SHAOQI speaks in favour of PENG's rehabilitation. A play by Beijing's deputy mayor WU HAN, *Hai Rui Dismissed from Office*, makes a veiled attack on Mao's dismissal of Peng. At TENTH PLENUM Mao responds with warning, 'Never forget class struggle', claiming that China like the Soviet Union faces danger of 'revisionism'. JIANG QING (Madame Mao) encourages radical Shanghai scholars ZHANG CHUNQIAO and YAO WENYUAN to launch a counter-attack on WU HAN's play. Mao's LITTLE RED BOOK is prepared and circulated in armed forces by LIN BIAO. SOCIALIST EDUCATION MOVEMENT (1964–5) targets alleged revival of capitalism in countryside.

1966–8: The first Cultural Revolution. Radical attack on WU HAN (see above) leads to overthrow of Beijing Communist Party leadership in May 1966. LIU SHAOQI and other leaders try to contain growth of RED GUARD movement in Beijing colleges, but Mao urges them to rebel against those Party leaders 'taking the capitalist road'. ELEVENTH PLENUM (August 1966) endorses 16-POINT DECISION on Cultural Revolution, demotes LIU SHAOQI. Millions of Red Guards attend Beijing rallies, denounce officials as bureaucrats, ransack 'bourgeois' homes, travel around China to 'exchange experiences'. CHEN BODA leads Party's CULTURAL REVOLUTION GROUP with JIANG QING as deputy. LIN BIAO proclaimed as Mao's 'chosen successor'. Early in 1967 pro-Mao rebel groups encouraged to 'seize power' from Party bureaucrats, but are split by factional quarrels. In the WUHAN INCIDENT the ultra-left attacks Premier ZHOU ENLAI and armed forces. Reaction against indiscipline and violence leads to disbandment of Red Guards under army supervision.

1968–76: The second Cultural Revolution. By September 1968, REVOLUTIONARY COMMITTEES set up for all provinces, and at lower levels of government, also in schools, factories, etc. By

1976 twelve million students have gone DOWN TO THE COUNTRY-
SIDE. Colleges reopen with policy of OPEN-DOOR SCHOOLING and
'political criteria' for admission. In industry, cadres and workers
partially exchange functions in the TWO PARTICIPATIONS; campaigns are launched against material incentives. People's communes improve land in campaigns for CAPITAL CONSTRUCTION:
some 'RAISE LEVEL OF OWNERSHIP' from team to brigade:
BAREFOOT DOCTORS and MEDICAL CO-OPERATIVE SCHEMES
spread.

February 1972: The Nixon Visit. US President Richard Nixon
visits Beijing acknowledging Chinese position that Taiwan is
part of China. China enters the UN and is soon recognized by
two-thirds of its members. With new opportunities, Chinese
trade doubles from 1965 to 1973. Large-scale imports of western
technology begin.

1971–6: The second 'inner-Party' struggle. September 1971,
death of LIN BIAO in plane over Outer Mongolian airspace;
ZHOU ENLAI restores state administration; 1973 return of DENG
XIAOPING to become Zhou's deputy, rise of WANG HONGWEN at
NINTH PARTY CONGRESS; ultra-left launch CRITICIZE CONFU-
CIUS AND LIN BIAO CAMPAIGN (directed against Zhou). January
1975, NATIONAL PEOPLE'S CONGRESS, Zhou announces FOUR
MODERNIZATIONS; anti-revisionist polemics by ZHANG CHUN-
QIAO and YAO WENYUAN. Summer 1975, DENG XIAOPING calls
for industrial and educational reform. January 1976, death of
ZHOU ENLAI. 5 April, TIANANMEN DEMONSTRATION leads to
Deng's dismissal, HUA GUOFENG appointed Acting Premier.
9 September, death of MAO. 6 October, Gang of Four arrested.

1977–84: Rejection of Cultural Revolution. 1977, HUA GUOFENG
elaborates FOUR MODERNIZATIONS policy to take China to THE
YEAR 2000. December 1978, THIRD PLENUM 'readjusts' policy,
calls for SEEKING TRUTH FROM FACTS. 1979, DEMOCRACY WALL
and UNOFFICIAL MAGAZINES briefly encouraged; higher living
standards emphasized, peasants paid more for produce, free
markets opened in towns. 1980–3, RURAL RESPONSIBILITY SYS-
TEM allowing land to be managed by individual households
spreads to 90 per cent of rural population. July 1981, RESOLU-
TION ON QUESTIONS OF PARTY HISTORY condemns Cultural
Revolution and Mao's 'mistakes'; HUA GUOFENG replaced by

Hu YAOBANG. October 1984, DECISION ON REFORM OF ECO-
NOMIC STRUCTURE extends reform to urban sector.

1983–8: Rethinking versus reaction. October 1983, campaign
against SPIRITUAL POLLUTION. December 1984, Hu YAOBANG
encourages RETHINKING OF MARXISM. September 1985, CHEN
YUN warns against excessive reform. Spring–summer 1986,
reform-minded scholars argue for REFORM OF POLITICAL STRUC-
TURE. December 1986, STUDENT DEMONSTRATIONS. January
1987, resignation of Hu YAOBANG; conservative/leftist revival
led by DENG LIQUN. October 1987, ZHAO ZIYANG confirmed
as Secretary-General at THIRTEENTH PARTY CONGRESS, calls for
DEEPENING THE REFORM and OPENING THE DOOR WIDER. March
1988, LI PENG becomes Premier at SEVENTH NATIONAL PEOPLE'S
CONGRESS.

1979–   : Open Door policy. 1979, China signs trade agreement
with US, first law allowing Chinese–foreign JOINT VENTURES.
1980, China gains EEC most-favoured nation status, foreign oil
companies begin offshore prospecting, China rejoins IMF and
World Bank. Early to mid-1980s, SPECIAL ECONOMIC ZONES,
OPEN CITIES, and COASTAL PROVINCES gain increasing autonomy
to attract foreign investment and manufacture. 1987, Hainan
declared a new province with special status; Zhao Ziyang calls
entire seaboard China's 'gold coast' and key to future; Chinese
arms sales expand to Gulf and Middle East.

1988–   : New turning-point? PRICE REFORM postponed at
September 1988 Central Committee as INFLATION tops 20 per
cent. Another campaign launched against Party CORRUPTION.
Agriculture fails to meet GRAIN OUTPUT target of 400 million
tons. Demonstrations in TIBET (October 1987; March 1988) are
suppressed by force with civilian casualties. But SINO-SOVIET
RELATIONS look forward to possible summit meeting, and
tension over KAMPUCHEA eases. China prepares to celebrate 40TH
ANNIVERSARY OF THE PEOPLE'S REPUBLIC (1 October 1989).

CHINA CHANGES FACE

CHAPTER ONE

After the Revolution

THE TWO ROADS

If the Japanese scientist, in order to help mankind vanquish syphilis, had the patience to test six hundred and five preparations before he developed a six hundred and sixth which met definite requirements, then those who want to solve a more difficult problem, namely, to vanquish capitalism, must have the perseverance to try hundreds and thousands of new methods, means, and weapons of struggle in order to elaborate the most suitable of them. (Lenin, June 1919)

After a period following the Transition to Ownership by the Whole People, the Productive Forces of Society will be expanded even more greatly; the Products of Society will become extremely Abundant; Communist Ideology, Consciousness, and Moral Character of the entire people will be raised immensely, and Education will be Universal and raised to a Higher Level. (Red Flag, 1 Sept. 1958)

For a period in the past, the tune for Communism was deafening. This tune may have been loud, but it was unfortunately divorced from reality. It made the masses suffer and really discouraged them. (People's Daily, 18 Nov. 1987)

Actually up till now we have had no theory, correct or incorrect, that could tell us what our future will be like. We used to say 'socialism'. Now we say 'Chinese-style socialism'. What is 'Chinese-style socialism'? Just a name.
(Fang Lizhi, dissident scholar, 1985)

China has changed. Forty years after the revolution it has become apparent quite suddenly that China is now a completely

different place from the People's Republic of Chairman Mao
Zedong (Mao Tse-tung). As their country continues to be
transformed around them, the Chinese are still trying to adjust—
particularly those who remember the nearly three decades (1949–
76) of Self-reliance and Hard Struggle while Mao was alive.
Outside China, it is almost as hard to keep up with and evaluate
the new face presented by a country which in the 1970s appeared
to offer the Third World a distinctive model of 'revolutionary
socialist' development. Mao's successors now say that his road
was the wrong one for China, let alone for other countries, and
that they are not at all sure what socialism means, let alone
communism. In just one decade most of China's cities and
coastal regions have already joined the modern world of advanced technology and global communications, and are providing goods and labour for the international market. Political
change is slower—the combined legacy of Confucius and Mao
remains considerable. But the argument for democracy within
the Communist Party and even for a multi-party system can be
heard frequently and the Party 'conservatives' are steadily losing
ground. As reform gathers momentum elsewhere in the 'socialist
world', and particularly in the Soviet rethinking led by Gorbachev, the Chinese experiment learns from other countries' experiences, and is studied by them in turn.

One of the most remarkable changes of the 1980s in China
was announced quietly a year before the fortieth anniversary by
the State Statistical Bureau. China was no longer a nation of
peasants. As late as 1980 four out of every five Chinese had still
lived in the countryside—800 million out of the total population
of a billion by that date. The Bureau revealed that in the years
1980 to 1986 the proportion of urban population in China had
increased from 20.6 per cent to 37.1 per cent of the total. In
numbers, this meant an increase from about 210 million to nearly
400 million. This development, said the Bureau with careful
balance, was both 'gratifying and worrying'. It was gratifying
because the urbanization of China meant that it was becoming a
more developed country. It was worrying because another 180
million people had become food consumers rather than food
producers, creating new pressures on the supply of grain, meat,
and vegetables as well as upon the physical and social fabric of
China's cities and towns.

An equally remarkable shift took place in the late 1980s in the field of theory. Mao Zedong, the architect of the 'Chinese road to revolution' and of the attempt to find a Chinese path to socialism after 1949, was now criticized for not having gone abroad in his youth to study 'modern capitalism'. The relationship between socialism and capitalism was now described not as the 'class struggle' which according to Mao had to be pursued until one side won and the other lost, but as a learning process on both sides. 'It now seems that modern capitalism still has considerable room for development', said Xu Jiatun (head of the Chinese Communist Party in Hong Kong), describing it as 'a great invention of human civilization'. The distinguished Chinese economist Xue Muqiao called for greater understanding of the capitalist countries, which had changed for the better both in their domestic and foreign policies. There were no longer two rival blocs in the world. There was only one global market in which all participated, and socialism and capitalism should 'mutually rely on and co-operate with each other'. Another scholar reflected a widespread rejection of the old belief that socialism was a well-defined model which must lead inevitably to communism. 'Socialism is not a cake that can be ordered,' said Li Honglin, 'and it has no fixed pattern.'

To the ordinary Chinese family of the 1980s, however—and particularly in urban China—these questions of doctrine were of little interest. Life for many people had improved considerably at first, particularly for large numbers of peasants who were allowed to farm the land independently and were paid more for their produce. City dwellers, especially those able to take advantage of the new economic freedoms, still suffered from overcrowding and inadequate services, but had more variety in their food and a widening choice of consumer goods. (China was to become the world's largest manufacturer of washing machines and colour TVs.) But before long China had run into the familiar problem of rising prices caused by a combination of excess demand, inadequate supplies, and the attempt to reform a price structure which had been geared to a low-wage high-subsidy economy. From the mid-1980s onwards, Deng Xiaoping's drive to create 'market socialism' in China, loosening state control and diluting price restrictions while the peasants earned more for their produce, had created unheard-of inflation. The slim pamphlets of the 1970s, handed out to every foreign visitor, with the title 'Why China has no inflation' were now an anachronism. The official figures for inflation were 9 per cent in 1987, and 11 per cent in 1988. Urban dwellers insisted that food costs were rising at well over 20 per cent. In May 1988 long queues formed outside state stores in Nanjing selling basic staples such as rice and vegetable oil—the first to be seen, older Chinese recalled, since before the 1949 Liberation. Those with money to save queued instead outside luxury goods stores selling foreign colour TVs, French perfume, refrigerators, motor cycles, and alcohol. These were believed to be a better investment than putting one's savings in the bank. Government ministers in Beijing toured food stores, listening to consumer complaints that new subsidies to city dwellers were of little help in cushioning the effect of higher prices. Deng Xiaoping admitted that the escalation in prices was the main concern of most people. But, he insisted, 'we have to stick with the policy of reform. We cannot stand still, otherwise there would be no solution.'

While those on fixed salaries, such as teachers and civil servants (if they remained honest) suffered from inflation, many people engaged in private business or living off their wits were thriving. Some did extremely well. *Beijing Review* published a lead article with the title 'Private businesses produce million-aires'. It would have been inconceivable just a few years ago, it observed correctly, for socialist China to have millionaires, but now the ranks of those who had become 'rich through indivi-dual work'—that is, as private entrepreneurs—were expanding quickly. The article admitted that private business did not hesitate to siphon off talent from the collective sector, and that tax evasion was also a problem, but no reform could be 'free of its bad side'. Much more worrying and apparently impervious to correction was the growth of corruption within the Communist Party itself. The *People's Daily* complained of officials who 'disregard Party discipline and state law, ride roughshod over the people, seek personal gain and act wantonly'. Such cases were by no means rare, it said, and had seriously undermined the Party and government's prestige.

During the Cultural Revolution, Mao had accused the Soviet leaders of restoring capitalism in their country and of practising 'social imperialism' abroad. When China in the 1970s mended its relations with the United States and began its economic reforms, it was Moscow's turn to accuse Beijing of collaborating with imperialism and destroying socialism. By the late 1980s, in spite of outstanding differences over a few foreign policy issues (particularly Indo-China), the Soviet Union and China were on the same wavelength for the first time in forty years. Soviet delegations visited China to study the Special Economic Zones on the seaboard and the reform of Chinese agriculture. One adviser to Mikhail Gorbachev, Fedor Burlatsky, reported back that China's rural reforms had produced 'a colossal effect both for the development of productive forces and for the raising of living standards', and were 'not only socialist but an efficient socialist form' from which the Soviet Union should learn. The Chinese now said that the Soviet Union was a socialist country and that their anti-Soviet polemics of the 1960s had been mistaken. When the Soviet party rehabilitated Bukharin, who had defended the Soviet peasant against Stalin's collectivization, China welcomed the move and said that many of his ideas were accepted in Beijing. And when Gorbachev pressed ahead with 'perestroika'—the restructuring of the Soviet economy—Premier Zhao Ziyang commented that the question of reform was 'one of the major currents . . . of the socialist bloc' (ever since the Sino-Soviet split, the Chinese had denied that such a bloc existed), and wished the Soviet Union 'success in its pursuit'.

Asked about China's own reform, Zhao singled out as its most significant feature the newest Special Economic Zone on the southern island of Hainan, and plans to 'open up' the provinces of Guangdong and Fujian even more extensively to the outside world. No change was more noticeable than the comprehensive flinging open of the door to foreign trade and investment, and the leadership's high expectations that this would transform the whole Chinese economy. Foreign manufacturers were urged to take advantage of lower wages along the coastal seaboard, from the far north to the southern border with Vietnam. China, by now the world's fifth largest oil producer, also offered new terms to attract more foreign oil companies to prospect in its offshore waters, although little had been found in the early 1980s. Untapped reserves, it was claimed, still lay in the interior. The Tarim basin in the north-west, a desert area the size of France, was thought to possess reserves almost as large as those of Kuwait.

The influx of foreign business, tourism, news, and fashion also brought more worrying social change for the Chinese leadership, which waged an intermittent and unsuccessful battle to inoculate young people against the 'harmful aspects of capitalism'. In May 1988 the Chinese Education Committee introduced new regulations on dress and behaviour: secondary school students should have an 'orderly appearance' and should avoid trashy or pornographic literature, unhealthy songs, cigarettes and alcohol, and bars and discos, as well as high heels, jewellery, and make-up in the classroom. A few days later the problem was highlighted when a break-dancing party (also banned) in Beijing led to a riot between police and students in the streets. The increasing diversity, for better or worse, in Chinese society was illustrated by two other reports. There was a big increase in marriages in 1986—half a million more than the previous year—while the average age at which young people married fell from 23.8 years in 1984 to 22 years. (The recommended age of 27 for men and 25 for women was now totally ignored.) The divorce rate was also rising, with half a million granted in 1986. Figures were published in 1988 on the problem of begging. There were estimated to be 670,000 beggars in the country, some driven from the countryside by natural disasters, but many now taking up begging as a profession. At the Beijing railway station twenty-five vagrants had been found dead in the previous fifteen months. The Minister for Civil Affairs admitted that the combined effect of the new economic reforms and 'opening up to the outside world' was widening the gap between rich and poor, and that his Ministry was faced with 'new risks and dangers'.

December 1988 should have seen a triumphant celebration of the tenth anniversary of Deng Xiaoping's reforms. Instead there was talk for the first time of a crisis. The changes had got out of hand: inflation was running at over 20 per cent, and in September the Party was forced to throttle back proposed price reform. Corruption was openly acknowledged to be rife, and central economic control of the provinces had seriously weakened. Social ills—rising crime, falling educational standards, bribery, prostitution—were widely discussed. This freedom of discussion was at least a hopeful sign. But political debate was muffled, especially by comparison with Gorbachev's *glasnost*. The growing possibility of a Sino-Soviet summit illustrated how China's problems were now much more internal than external, although Tibet lay somewhere in between. There had been some improvement after years of Han Chinese oppression, but the loosening of control and the influence of 'open-door' tourism only encouraged dissent. The bloodily suppressed demonstrations in Lhasa of October 1987 and March 1988 reflected very badly on China. The Dalai Lama still sought to restrain young Tibetan activists, and proposed negotiations falling short of a demand for full independence. Behind all these difficulties lay a more fundamental political malaise. Secretary-General Zhao Ziyang seemed in summer 1988 to have lost ground to the more cautious but colourless Premier Li Peng. There was a feeling that China was losing its way, led by a Party which had forfeited popular confidence. It could no longer be assumed that the succession would be smooth after Deng Xiaoping. The 40th anniversary of the People's Republic was a reminder that each previous decade had seen a new direction, and that the present course might not be immutable either.

Why has China changed, and could it have happened any other way? The verdict of the post-Mao leader (and Mao's former colleague), Deng Xiaoping, and his group of enthusiastic reformers headed by the Communist Party's Secretary-General Zhao Ziyang, is very clear. In human terms, they say, the main responsibility for the past lay with Mao, who was misled by foolish and evil advisers in his final years, particularly by his Minister of Defence Lin Biao and his own wife Jiang Qing, who headed the ultra-leftist Gang of Four. The 'Resolution on questions in Party history since 1949', adopted by the Party Central Committee in 1981 after long and difficult discussion, admits that part of the responsibility belongs to Mao's colleagues, and provides some explanation for the cult of Mao in terms of the influence of Stalinism and China's own tradition of feudal obedience to authority. But it relies heavily on the argument that Mao committed 'errors', and that these were inflated into 'crimes' by those around him.

By the late 1980s there was less emphasis on the role of personalities and a greater effort to provide a theoretical explanation

which would account for present as well as past policies. China
had been led astray for over three decades, it was now argued, by
the dream of 'communism in the not-too-distant future' which
inspired the economic chaos of the Great Leap Forward (1958–
60) and led on to the political struggles and disasters of the
Cultural Revolution (1966–76). 'We have finally come back from
heaven to earth', announced the *People's Daily* after the Thirteenth Party Congress in 1987, which confirmed the new course
of full-scale Reform—a word which has now virtually replaced
Socialism. 'Earth' is the new doctrine which says that China is
only at a vaguely defined 'initial stage of socialism' which will
persist into the middle of the next century. It rejects most of the
economic and political theories of the past decades, and is
prepared to adopt many phenomena previously condemned as
belonging to capitalism, including what amounts to private
ownership of land, a stock exchange, widening the differentials between the lower and higher paid to reward 'ability'
and 'initiative', and encouraging private enterprise on a
large scale.

The alternative explanation is that which Mao himself would
undoubtedly offer if he were still alive, and it would insist that
it is the present road which is leading the Chinese people astray.
Socialist society, wrote Mao in the last of his polemics against
the Soviet Union in 1964, will last for a very long historical
period, during which 'the struggle goes on between the road of
socialism and the road of capitalism'. Two years later he
launched the Cultural Revolution against 'those in power who
are taking the capitalist road'. Perhaps only a small number of
those who supported him then and were later labelled as the
ultra-left would say that China is definitely embarked today
upon that road. These would include Mao's widow Jiang Qing
who remains reportedly unrepentant in prison where she has been
serving a life sentence (commuted from death) since 1981. Yet
the spread of the 'get rich first' ethic, the growth of corruption,
the craving for foreign imports, and the rising inflation which
were all features of the late 1980s did alarm a considerable
number of senior Party members—perhaps 15 to 20 per cent of
those holding posts in the hierarchy—who should be labelled
'conservative' rather than 'ultra-left'. They were still strong
enough to stage two reactions against the reform policies, in the

campaigns against 'spiritual pollution' (1983) and 'bourgeois liberalism' (1987).

A more substantial conservative reaction, which might revive some of Mao's views on the need for more self-reliant and explicitly socialist policies, could still be provoked by political uncertainty (perhaps following the death of Deng Xiaoping) or by economic recession. It would be strongly tinged with national-istic reaction against the growing influx of foreign consumer values, along lines already briefly aired during the 1987 anti-bourgeois liberalism campaign. The reformers at that time were accused not of having descended from heaven to earth but of being deluded by new gods. In the words of one conservative polemicist, '[They] hold that only capitalism can save China, that the capitalist world is a "paradise on earth" and that there is no future or hope for socialism. . . .'

The stark alternatives presented by these two interpretations have been mirrored in western attitudes towards China in the 1980s. For obvious reasons Western governments and business communities were glad to see China edge apparently closer to capitalism. China's willingness to open its doors to foreign investment and loans and the encouragement of a domestic market economy have earned it particular praise. In effect, China has legitimized the advice which the international financial community, led by the World Bank, presses upon those Third World countries seeking to protect their economies from foreign penetration. (In the past, some of them thought to see a very different sort of model being offered by Mao's China.) 'The fading of the men who fought their way to power four decades ago,' said a *Times* editorial after the 1982 Party congress, 'has coincided with the advance of modern communications and the penetration of Western economic wealth to bring China to the threshold of a new age.' A small number of Western critics still believe, however, that the 'self-reliant' approach of the Maoist period, in spite of being more seriously flawed than its foreign admirers admitted at the time, still offered a serious attempt to provide a socialist road to development, and that Mao was right to warn of the dangers of 'capitalist restoration'.

Neither of these opposing views really explains what has happened in China since 1949. This book is not intended to demonstrate either that Mao led his people astray to pursue a deceptive Utopia or that Deng has since betrayed China to capitalism. There is some truth in a moderate version of both theses. Without Mao's powerful and idiosyncratic pull upon Chinese political culture, the extremes of the Great Leap and the Cultural Revolution could probably have been avoided. Deng (and particularly his lieutenant Zhao Ziyang) has sanctioned not just the opening of the door to Western trade—this had already begun in the early 1970s when Mao was still in charge, largely as a result of the US initiative to mend relations with Beijing—but has virtually allowed the door to be taken off its hinges. But both theories ignore the changing context which would in any case have shaped Chinese policies along roughly the lines which were adopted. Thus, China's weakness in both economic and defence terms in the 1950s and 1960s, coupled with the hostility of the West, would have made it extremely dangerous to contemplate any diminution of national self-reliance and centralized planning. Conversely, the much greater strength and economic diversification of China in the 1980s meant that such policies now imposed fetters upon development instead of offering protection. Other factors which need to be considered include:

● The heady effect of revolutionary victory, which encouraged the communists to believe that they could solve peacetime problems by similar guerrilla methods, and gave them the prestige to attempt to do so.

● A political style containing elements of both traditional feudalism and modern Stalinism, coupled with a low level of political awareness among the rank and file.

● A Utopian view of the communist goal, unaccompanied by any clear strategy of how to get there.

● The sheer size of China's economic and social problems, which could only be tackled with an attitude of revolutionary optimism.

● The warping effect of China's enforced isolation from the Western world and initial dependence upon the Soviet Union.

● The real achievements nevertheless scored in raising living standards generally and preparing the ground for post-Mao economic modernization.

● The explosive impact of the Cultural Revolution in politicizing Chinese youth—though not in the direction intended by Mao—and alienating public opinion generally from the Party.

● The impact of the global economy upon China once the door had been opened by President Nixon.

● The general trend among state socialist countries in the late 1980s to re-examine the orthodox theory of centralized planning and state power.

Both in spite of and because of these internal and external constraints, China from 1949 until Mao's death was a purposeful society in which a quarter of mankind knew in theory where it was heading. Disagreements over the route to be taken were resolved at the highest level without public discussion and there was only one possible 'correct line' at any one time. The superiority of the people's communes, Mao said in 1958, was that they were 'both Big and Public'. Even those of his colleagues who dissented from the Great Leap Forward did not quarrel with the proposition that a socialist society must mean the development of larger productive units with a higher degree of public ownership. It was this feature, allied with a steady increase in moral and intellectual 'consciousness', which would enable the nation to progress along a predetermined path, becoming increasingly prosperous along the way. That path was the socialist 'transition', and at the end of it lay the goal of 'communism'. The only leader who sometimes expressed doubts was, perversely, Mao himself—and only to a small audience. It was also assumed by the time of his death that some considerable progress had been made along the transition, though the Great Leap claim that communism was only a few years distant had to be discarded.

The disastrous effects of the Cultural Revolution and the subsequent reversal of many of Mao's policies destroyed the certainties of previous dogma. In many respects this was a very beneficial development. To paraphrase Marx, Chinese political theory could at last begin to move from the 'realm of necessity' to the 'realm of freedom'. But the result was to cripple concepts which had been used to mobilize the Chinese population for several decades. Loss of doctrinal certainty also removed an important cohesive force within the Communist Party. At first the immediate succession to Mao, represented by Chairman Hua Guofeng, sought to retain the main ideological thrust of the past twenty years, claiming that it had been distorted by the Gang of Four. But Hua's 'moderate Maoists' were then ousted by Deng

Xiaoping's 'modernizers'. Socialism now acquired a more limited and utilitarian meaning, as a system which, in Deng Xiaoping's words, was better able than capitalism to 'satisfy the people's material and cultural needs'. But it became increasingly unclear what was meant by socialism, especially after the decision that China was only at its 'initial stage' (and that this stage was specific to China, rather than a general feature of other socialist societies). While older Marxist scholars attempted to redefine the concept, many younger ones concentrated on economic reform mainly on the basis of contemporary Western thinking. The fact that China had 'skipped' the capitalist stage, once claimed by Mao to be an advantage, because it had thus avoided the creation of an entrenched bourgeois class, was now admitted to have weakened the basis for socialism. Although no one said so publicly, some people doubted whether China had really begun on the socialist road at all, or was ready for it.

The Communist Party's prestige was also now a thin shadow of that which it enjoyed generally in the first decade after the 1949 Liberation. The troubles of the Cultural Revolution could not simply be blamed upon a small handful of conspirators—the so-called Gang of Four. In the familiar phrase, 'It takes more than one cold day to produce ice three inches thick.' The ice had begun to form in the late 1950s when many intellectuals were alienated by the Anti-Rightist Campaign, followed by the Great Leap Forward which led to chaos for millions of peasants and deprivation for most urban dwellers. In retrospect, what is surprising is how many people continued to trust the leadership even after these events. The Cultural Revolution dealt a final blow, bewildering many of the older generation while mobilizing youth towards egalitarian goals which were soon frustrated. The efforts of Mao's successors to restore confidence in the Party were undercut by their own internal feuding and by the growth of corruption fed by new economic opportunities for enrichment. By the late 1980s, popular attitudes towards the Party ranged from the sceptical to the cynical.

A random questioning by the writer of popular attitudes towards the Party on the eve of the 1987 Thirteenth Party Congress produced the following range. The most positive view, from a non-Party scientist, was the pragmatic one that 'Better or worse, there is no alternative to the Party. Without it, China would fall apart.' Others argued that 'The top leadership are sincere, though the task may be too great', pointing to the low calibre of rank-and-file cadres (officials) and the enormous scale of China's economic and social problems as reasons for scepticism. Motives for joining the Party were now usually suspect, even among many who did so. 'Quite frankly, I am only joining in order to get the leadership to approve my project', explained a university researcher. Many ordinary people openly said they were uninterested in politics, and at best were prepared to judge the Party by results. 'If they can keep prices down and solve the housing shortage, I have nothing against them!' said a Beijing taxi-driver. Others shared the emphatic view of a Shanghai factory-worker: 'Nowadays we hate the Party!'

Forty years after the revolution succeeded, China was at last able to discuss the fundamental question 'What happens *after* the revolution?' without its hands being hopelessly tied by economic backwardness and external isolation, but ironically this point had only been reached after a process which undermined popular faith among most of the population in any sort of socialist ideology. China was now closer than ever before to the sort of Great Debate which should accompany all serious social experiment. Yet the question for the 1990s is not what sort of socialism can China achieve, but whether the word still means anything at all.

A *note about labels*

Party Secretary General Zhao Ziyang in an affable press conference with foreign journalists after the 1987 Congress denied that he and his colleagues could be divided into 'conservatives' and 'reformers'. 'Why is it', he asked reprovingly, 'that when there is some difference of views you take it as something remarkable?' The labels applied to the leadership during the Cultural Revolution have similarly been denied in the past, although they are now used as standard definitions in Chinese accounts of that period. Privately, Chinese who are involved in politics today speak quite openly about factions and feuds among the high-ups and of their frequently opportunistic use of ideology. I make no apology for using such labels. Ideology is a genuine force; so is the pursuit of power, and scholars like myself who were sympathetic to China in its years of isolation helped no one by trying to soften the contours of factionalism. But the labels are admittedly confusing. Here I shall use:

Ultra-left: Those both in the leadership and at lower levels who in the late 1960s carried to an extreme Mao's views on (*a*) the necessity for class struggle, and (*b*) putting 'politics in command', in a manner which was both dogmatic and profoundly undemocratic.

Mainstream Maoist: Those who accepted the self-reliant and basically egalitarian view of society which began to take shape, however sketchily, in the 1970s before Mao's death.

Reformers: Those who put the economic modernization of China in first place, and in the decade after Mao's death developed a radically new strategy stressing the 'open door' and structural reform of the economy. Many reform-minded scholars moved towards the view that these reforms will not succeed without radical political reform.

Conservatives: Those who parted company with the reformers in the mid-1980s, favouring more cautious policies which maintained centralized control, and feared a complete erosion of conventional 'socialist ethics'. Confusingly but quite logically, their position overlapped at times with a revival of ultra-leftism.

Dissenters: Mostly young students and workers, first politicized by the Cultural Revolution, active in the Democracy Movement, and suppressed in the early 1980s. Many became political prisoners, and some were still detained by 1989. Dissent among scholars and intellectuals has been more restrained, with most preferring to explore the limits from within the system.

CHAPTER TWO

Search for Socialism

FROM LIBERATION TO UTOPIA

Scene: A village somewhere in north China, 1952.

Party Secretary Wang left the old Taoist temple where the village council had been installed, and walked out into the fields where the peasants were working late on their newly distributed plots of land. Under the chestnut trees on the hillside, next to a few graves, there was still enough light to sit and read. Today he had organized the Poor Peasants to start digging a new well, and he had personally gone down the shaft to shift the largest stones. Chairman Mao said that every Party cadre should Plunge Deep into Construction and play an Exemplary Role among the Masses.

But Party cadres were also expected never to lose sight of the long-term goal—communism. Now, at the end of the working day, there was just time for half an hour of self-study. Secretary Wang took a creased pamphlet out of his pocket, and squatted down with his back against a pile of brushwood. The contents were simply arranged for the barely literate reader. The main text was written in large characters, setting out the eight main tasks of the model Party member. Each sentence was followed by a longer explanation in smaller type—just like the old commentaries on Confucius and the classics. Wang found his place at a line drawing of Stalin, surrounded by factory chimneys and other signs of material progress, and began to read:

The final aim of the Chinese Communist Party
is to establish communism in China

Socialism is only the first step towards communism. In this stage, those who don't work don't eat, and the system is 'From each according to his ability, to each according to his work.' But when communism has been attained, class distinctions will disappear. Production will develop greatly. Both agriculture and industry will have been electrified and mechanized. One person will be able to support several tens of people with his work, or several hundreds—or even several thousands. The working people will have a high cultural and technical level. The differences between workers, peasants, and intellectuals will have disappeared. Everyone's needs will be fully satisfied, and the system will be based on 'From each according to his ability, to each according to his needs.'

The textbook went on to say that when communism was reached, the state itself would be abolished, including the government, the law courts, the army, and the police. Imperialism would have been defeated, everyone would live as one big family, and there would be Great Harmony in the World. Secretary Wang found this rather puzzling—especially the bit about the state withering away. Besides, it was getting too dark to read, and the storekeeper in the village below had promised him a special bottle of liquor, not available across the counter. With a little belch of anticipation, he set off down the track.

The Communist vision

Between the ultimate vision of communism and the immediate tasks of rebuilding the Chinese nation, shattered after nearly four decades of internal strife and external war, lay a vast theoretical void which the Chinese communist leadership made no attempt to fill for nearly a decade. There was no shortage of theory on the subject of the revolution which had just been successful. 'The Way of Mao Zedong' was advertised (much to Stalin's irritation) as the right path not only for the Chinese revolution but for all the other 'colonial and semi-colonial countries', especially in Asia, which still had to throw off their burdens of 'feudalism and imperialism'. But the path ahead remained undefined. There was not the slightest echo of the lively debate on the role of the state, the Party, and the army which had followed the Soviet revolution, and to which Lenin had contributed passionately and extensively. Mao showed no signs of even having read Lenin's *The State and Revolution*, in which the Soviet leader discussed the means by which the state apparatus would 'wither away' during the transition to communism (although the text was a prescribed document for study by all Party cadres). In this long essay—the most Utopian of his writings—Lenin expounded (according to the historian E. H. Carr) 'his vision of a society in which, after the destruction of the bourgeois state and the ending of class antagonisms, the coercive functions of the state would wither away . . .'. He also argued in some detail how the bureaucratic and coercive functions of the state could be replaced quite speedily by the voluntary participation of its citizens in running their own affairs, and forecast that this might be achieved 'in ten years or perhaps more'.

The other classic texts on the subject of the transition to communism, Marx's *Critique of the Gotha Programme* (1875) and Engels's *Anti-Dühring* (1878), are also ignored by Mao in his *Selected Works*. Mao did predict the eventual withering away of the state, and with it the Communist Party, in his 'On the People's Democratic Dictatorship', published three months before Liberation. But he did so briefly and polemically, and without beginning to raise any of the questions about the transition to communism which had so exercised Lenin at the time of October Revolution.

Communists the world over are wiser than the bourgeoisie, they understand the laws governing the existence and development of things, they understand dialectics, and they can see further. The bourgeoisie does not welcome this truth because it does not want to be overthrown . . . But for the working class, the labouring people, and the Communist Party the question is not one of being overthrown, but of working hard to create the conditions in which classes, state power, and political parties will die out very naturally and mankind will enter the realm of Great Harmony.

It was characteristic of Mao to use a traditional term, which dated back to the fourth-century BC philosopher Mozi, the *da tong* or Great Harmony, as a euphemism for communism. The term had been adapted by the late-nineteenth-century reformer Kang Youwei to serve his own argument attempting to persuade the Manchu emperor to work towards an age of Great Harmony by promoting reform. Mao's purpose in using it was not to speculate on the future withering away of the state, but to stress the present need for unconditional leadership by the Chinese Communist Party, and to mock the defeated Nationalists for being unwilling to accept their own much more imminent demise. There was some confusion as to what he meant by Great Harmony. Some texts (including the one read by Secretary Wang on the hillside, quoted above) explained it as 'world communism'. A later footnote in Mao's *Selected Works* offered a less internationalist definition, loosely embracing both Marx and Mozi: 'It refers to a society based on public ownership, free from class exploitation and oppression—a lofty ideal long cherished by the Chinese people. Here the realm of Great Harmony means communist society.'

The 'Common Programme' adopted in September 1949, which served as China's constitution until the first National People's Congress was held in 1954, did not even mention the word 'socialism'. Premier Zhou Enlai (Chou En-lai) explained that it would be 'proved to the entire people through practice', and therefore did not need to be put into writing. Mao told the drafters of the Common Programme that China would only enter the socialist stage some time in the future, 'unhurriedly and with proper arrangements when our economy and culture are flourishing, when conditions are ripe, and the transition has been fully considered and endorsed by the whole nation'.

Mao's reticence can partly be explained by political caution. The Common Programme was adopted by the Chinese People's Political Consultative Conference, a non-Party body through which the communists were seeking to mobilize the middle-of-the-road political forces which had long ago written off Chiang Kai-shek and were prepared to give the new regime a chance. The Communist Party needed the support of the 'national bourgeoisie'—the factory owners, businessmen, and intelligentsia of the urban areas—although they could already dispense with the rural landlords. But Mao after all did not hesitate to proclaim that communism was the ultimate goal, nor that in foreign policy the new Chinese government intended to 'lean to one side' (that is, to enter into an alliance with the Soviet Union). The most compelling reason for uncertainty was that Mao and his colleagues simply had not thought about the future. 'Mao was very practical', a Chinese political scientist has explained. 'At that time China was still in the period of New Democracy which lasted in theory until 1956. And if Mao did not think about the theory of socialism, then no one else would.'

If China had already been reasonably well developed and the international environment had been less threatening, this lack of theoretical clarity could have resulted in a long period of gradual change (as seemed at first to be the case). But China's circumstances encouraged impatience and innovation. The combination of a well-defined end (communism) and an ill-defined means (socialism) would have a profound effect upon the politics of the next four decades. The Utopian objective created a constant pressure to find new and better means of making progress towards it. It was necessary, then, to reshape theory in order to justify changes in practice. At any one time there was only one correct 'line' which supposedly reflected a universal truth or 'law'. Yet in reality the underlying doctrine had to be improvised to meet changing political needs. Socialism changed its meaning, as this chapter will demonstrate, no less than seven times between 1949 and 1989, and in doing so became increasingly less credible to the majority of the Chinese people.

Peach-blossom socialism

Socialism meant something very simple at first. The two mountains of feudalism and imperialism, described by Mao in his famous adaptation of the parable of the Old Man who Moved Mountains, had been levelled by the revolution. Now it was time to 'revive the nation'—a phrase familiar from the earlier twentieth century—and to bring about the social and economic well-being which it had been denied by nearly forty years of warlord struggles, war with Japan, and civil war. 'We promote socialism', said Mao—not yet concerned with more complex definitions—'because we want to develop our country, develop a national economy and culture that is better than the system of private ownership, and to ensure our national independence.' People were proud of China and confident about their future. The mood was conveyed by Soong Ching Ling, widow of Sun Yat-Sen, in a triumphant statement published on the first anniversary of the liberation of Shanghai:

This has been a year of learning. We have learned about ourselves. We have learned about our city. We have learned about our future ... We have discovered that the Chinese people have a mountain of strength, bursting vitality, and a genius that can competently meet any problem and overcome any difficulty . . . We are going to bring prosperity to our city and to China, the likes of which our long history has never recorded . . .

In the backstreets of Shanghai, socialism had a more practical meaning in the sanitation campaigns which were launched to clean up the rubbish and the drains. Lanes and neighbourhoods competed for red pennants in the Sanitation Campaign. The Family Women's Organization got to work:

We'll get some powdered lime to sprinkle around the drains and damp and shaded places and along the house walls and fences. We've already contracted with a plumber to clean the drains twice a month and we'll share the cost . . . Besides cleaning up all places—where [rats] can nest, we should use traps and bait to catch them. Then we'll send them to the police station. We get credited with every rat we turn into the police.

The mood was above all one of getting things done which had been obstructed in the past by the heavy burden of oppression, extortion, and ignorance. Simple improvements led to rapid and visible progress in many areas. The mortality rate fell from 25 per thousand before 1949 to 17 in 1952 (and 10.8 by 1957) mostly as a result of simple sanitation measures. Those who knew Shanghai's factories before the revolution were astounded to find labour regulations enforced, machines protected with guards, exits cleared of rubbish, and anti-dust fans installed. 'In the old days the machines came first', explained a worker, 'and we were their servants. Now we are the masters, we make them work for us.' The 505 kilometre-long railway from Chongqing to Chengdu, planned for over forty years without a start being made, was completed within two years. Civil servants retained from the old regime knew they had to work conscientiously to keep their jobs. Others were replaced by new officials who made up for lack of experience by enthusiasm to 'serve the people', taking up their posts wherever they were assigned. The county magistrate no longer prayed in front of the City Temple God for rain: he mounted his bicycle and rode to meetings, listening to the people who asked for electricity, piped water, a new cinema.

In the countryside the vast majority of peasants benefited from redistribution of land and worked hard to improve it. There were stories of peasants who went out to their land in the middle of the night to check if it was still there. These innocent expectations of future material wealth were attached to the new idea of socialism. Chin Chaoyang, a young writer eager to record the optimism of the peasants among whom he had worked before Liberation, reports the words of a fruit-grower describing the benefits of the new co-operative which was now organized in his district:

Now at last the people in the whole of our mountain district were getting firmly rooted. The roots that they were growing were the roots of socialism! And socialism means that our mountain district will be clothed with trees, that peach-blossom and pear-blossom will cover the hillsides. Lumber-mills will spring up in our district, and a railway too, and our trees will be sprayed with insecticide from aeroplanes, and we will have a big water reservoir! . . .

Can we cover more and more of the mountains in the whole district with green trees, and make the streams clearer each year? Can we make the soil more fertile, and make the faces of the people in every village glow with good health? Can we make this mountain district of ours advance steadily on the path to socialism? If you ask me, I tell you it can be done! We have heart, and we have hands! It can be done!

Socialism Soviet style

The vision thus conjured up, expressed in hundreds of woodcuts and oil paintings showing the first tractor being welcomed by joyous villagers, was based on the experience of the only state to call itself 'socialist' so far—the Soviet Union. 'The Communist Party of the Soviet Union is our very best teacher', Mao had already written in his 1949 essay, 'and we must learn from it.' Only a few years earlier Mao and some of his colleagues had been tempted by a very different vision of a post-war China seeking Western—particularly American—technology and investment. Their invitation, extended to American visitors, including some US diplomats, was part of an unsuccessful effort to win US neutrality during the 1946–9 civil war. Even in spring 1949 the new communist government made private approaches to continue diplomatic relations with Washington. But the 'loss of China' had by now become a political issue, and Washington would only deal with a China that refrained from close relations with the Soviet Union. In spite of Mao's differences with Stalin, the Soviet Union on balance was still preferred if China had to choose sides. (The opportunity for an opening to the West would not recur for another twenty-five years, when President Richard Nixon visited Beijing.) Cut off from Western trade and finance by American containment—a deliberate policy of isolation which began before the Korean War but intensified as a result of it—the Chinese were soon obliged to rely on the Soviet Union for credits, equipment, and education. During the 1950s, at least ten thousand Soviet advisers (some estimates suggest up to twenty thousand) worked in China, and more than eighty thousand Chinese engineers and researchers were trained in the Soviet Union. Knowledge of policy differences with Moscow was confined to the highest levels: the general public was expected to respond without reservation to Mao Zedong's call in February 1953 for 'a great nation-wide upsurge of learning from the Soviet Union in order to build up our country'. Only two years later Mao would hint that not everything about the Soviet Union was worth learning, but for the time being socialism meant the Soviet Union, as the head of the Chinese Publications Administration explained:

Without the moral and material assistance of the Soviet Union, the nation-wide victory of the Chinese revolution would have been inconceivable, so it is not surprising that there is an upsurge of interest all over the country to study the Soviet Union and her advanced socialist experience ... Since we are on the threshold of large-scale economic construction and a readjustment of curricula is under way in our universities, we now stand in urgent need of large numbers of translated works that introduce us to advanced Soviet scientific theory and technique and which will take the place of the stale and outworn texts cribbed from bourgeois writers and scholars which in the old days were used for the education of Chinese students.

It was China's misfortune to catch the Soviet model in its last and intellectually most stultified years of Stalinism. The theoretical debates of the early 1920s in the Bolshevik Party about the nature of the transition to communism had long ago been reduced to bland assertions that the Soviet Union was well on the way. At the end of 1953 Stalin's successors appointed a new ambassador to China, the philosopher P. F. Yudin whom they hoped would strike an ideological chord with Mao. (The Chinese later said scornfully that the appointment had brought to Beijing someone who might be better able to 'study Mao Zedong's Thought'.) Yudin's work on the transition to communism was already a familiar source-book, making it sound reassuringly simple. All that was required for the Soviet Union, he wrote in *On the Nature of Soviet Society* (1950) was to complete the nation's main economic task: 'To overcome and outstrip the principal capitalist countries in the main items of industrial production.' These had already been defined (by Stalin in 1946) with what Yudin called 'scientific precision': 50 million tons annually of pig iron, 60 million tons of steel, 500 million tons of coal, and 60 million tons of oil. 'Once the productive forces reach this level of development', concluded Yudin, 'it will then be possible to pass over to communism in the USSR. This task will be carried out by further developing heavy industry, especially the iron and steel, machine-building, and chemical industries and power supply . . .' China also set specific tasks in the First Five-Year Plan (1953–7 but only fully worked out in 1955): Lenin had said that the foundation of socialism was 'large industrial development', and heavy industry was to be allocated 58 per cent of total investment in the Plan (actually a larger proportion than the 49 per cent allocated in the first Soviet Plan of 1928–33), while state investment in agriculture at 8 per cent was less than half the Soviet figure (19 per cent).

The pressure to 'be modern and Soviet' was overwhelming for a while after the ending of the Korean War and not unwelcome to many young Party cadres searching for a way to overcome China's economic backwardness. With China set on its feet again, the Soviet emphasis upon heavy industry as the key to development of light industry and then agriculture, and as the prerequisite for socialism, seemed to guarantee results of an impressively tangible nature. It made good sense too, when translated into terms which could be understood by the Chinese peasant. Wide publicity was given to the remark of an 85-year-old peasant on viewing his first Stalin-80 tractor, that 'Twenty oxen ploughing for a day can't do as much as this iron ox in one shift.' The distinguished economist Chen Hanseng, author of several famous studies of Western economic penetration and rural backwardness before the war, produced an imaginative historical argument to demonstrate the need for giving priority to heavy industry:

In many lands, where agriculture was ruined by war, pestilence, or depopulation, it perished for lack of large-scale mechanical means to restore it. That was the cause of the downfall of the Babylonians in Iraq, the Incas in Peru, the Mayas and Aztecs in Mexico, and the Uighur civilization in our southern Sinkiang [Xinjiang] province. The development of heavy industry and modern engineering—plus socialism—makes it possible to reclaim vast areas of wasteland. This has been shown in the Soviet Union, and it means much to us because we have huge tracts of unused land.

China's main task, wrote Chen, was to build a heavy industry which would enable it to become a semi-industrial nation by 1957, the end of the First Five-Year Plan. It would then be 'well on the way to socialism'.

The gradual road

To make political progress towards socialism in China conditional on economic advance was not merely a response to Soviet dogma. The country was exhausted after four years of civil war preceded by eight years of war against Japan and, before that, over two decades of internal instability. As the American writer William Hinton recalls, after 1949 the prospect of a prolonged stage of New Democracy—collaboration between the Communist Party and all social forces prepared to accept its leadership—was 'consensus politics' in Beijing. In the rural areas where the revolutionary process of land reform was still in progress, the consensus was only reached after three years (1950–2) of frequently savage struggle in which the poor peasants settled scores with their oppressors, landlords and their agents who had often raped and killed on behalf of the Japanese or Guomindang. Some 700,000 of them now paid the price. But once the redistribution of land was completed, the Party encouraged only the most cautious social reorganization in setting up 'mutual-aid teams' and, later on, low-level co-operatives. In urban life, the mixed economy extending from state to private ownership was intended to persist for many years. The reality was sometimes different, partly because of a new siege mentality brought about by foreign isolation and the pressure of the Korean War. But after that war was concluded, the general mood was peaceful as the Chinese people enjoyed the absence of conflict for the first time in their modern history. Chinese leaders now restated their gradualist view of the transition: before any further radical change in the 'relations of production'—for example, setting up rural co-operatives on a large scale and completely abolishing private commerce—the level of the 'productive forces', particularly the country's industrial base and the mechanization of agriculture, should be greatly raised.* This process, said the head of state, Liu Shaoqi, at the Eighth Party Congress in September 1956, would take between five and ten more years. The Congress's resolution stated that socialism had been basically established in China, that class struggle now belonged mostly to the past, and that the main contradiction was between the people's aspirations for a better life and their material backwardness.

Of course, our people still have to struggle to liberate Taiwan, to complete the socialist transformation [of industry and trade] and to eradicate finally the system of exploitation. We must also continue to struggle to purge the remnant forces of counter-revolution . . . Nevertheless, our main internal contradiction is now between the people's demand to build an advanced industrial state and the reality of our backward agriculture. It is between the people's need for rapid economic and cultural development and the actual situation where our economy and culture cannot satisfy their demands.

Liu Shaoqi also spoke approvingly of the need to 'enlist the services of the bourgeois and petty-bourgeois intellectuals in building socialism', and he proposed that political movements and 'struggles' should be phased out and replaced by a well-defined legal code. Meanwhile, Deng Xiaoping, the Party's General Secretary, made a tactful speech taking its cue from the

* The 'productive forces' comprise the 'means of production'—land and farm implements, machinery, and plant—and human labour itself together with the 'human resources' (like housing and hospitals) which will make that labour more productive. The 'relations of production' refer to the sets of relationships between the producer and the productive system, including (i) ownership (private, collective, or state), (ii) distribution of rewards (i.e. pay, share-out of produce, and so on), and (iii) management or 'human relations' (how production is planned and work organized and assigned). The 'productive forces' and the 'relations of production' together form the 'material base' available to a given society. That society's political complexion, as well as its vital resources of education and culture, form the 'superstructure', which thus includes political parties, armed forces, police, and civil service.

de-Stalinization under way in Khrushchev's Soviet Union to condemn the 'cult of the individual', although he still argued that 'love for the leader' who had been chosen by the Party was acceptable. More to the point, the Thought of Mao Zedong was dropped from the new Party Constitution. Mao probably accepted the need to depersonalize his leadership in view of what was happening in Eastern Europe, although many years later in the Cultural Revolution Liu and Deng would be charged with sabotaging his Thought. On the pace of change, Mao was ambivalent, and we shall see that he had already moved to speed up rural co-operativization. But there is no evidence that he opposed the demotion of class struggle. Within a few months, he had launched the Hundred Flowers campaign to encourage non-Party criticism of the bureaucracy with a speech (February 1957) which in its original version implied that class struggle had come to an end. 'Now we have entered a different kind of battle . . .', he said. 'When class struggle is over, we declare war on nature.'

The mid-1950s would later be regarded as golden years, characterized by a high degree of social harmony and shared enthusiasm for the future. This was true of everyday life as well as broad policy, as the British journalist Alan Winnington, one of the very few foreign residents at the time, recalled:

Beijing was vivid, kaleidoscopic, optimistic. If you went into the clay-walled *hutongs* where its real life pulsed, the city's ordinary activity was an exciting pageant, bright with the genius by which the Chinese can make the simplest everyday things attractive.

Makers of everything, sellers of everything announced their presence and their wares and services: the taps of second-hand dealers, the clash of knife grinders, trumpet calls, and whistles were all part of the daily scene. Moslem priests went round to slaughter sheep in the ordained manner. Falcons sat hooded on their owners' wrists. Women gossiped as they stitched shoes, spun noodles, cooked wonderful simple meals on home-made clay stoves in a single pan. At every corner there was something delectable to eat, costing pennies. Life had vastly improved since those days when we had marched in as liberators.

Poor is beautiful

Yet the inner compulsion of a still-revolutionary process must be to fulfil its goals in the shortest possible time. Gradualism was grounded more in caution than in theory, and it had no effective defence against the politics of optimism, especially when the leading optimist was Mao. Preoccupied in the early 1950s by the Korean War and China's edgy relations with the Soviet Union, Mao had left pronouncements on socialism and the economy to the head of state, Liu Shaoqi. Returning to the subject, Mao looked carefully at the countryside where the pressures from below for 'continuing the revolution' were far greater than in urban China. Where Mao chose to intervene, he would always prevail. Early in 1955 a group of Party officials who visited Confucius's birthplace at Qufu—a pleasant spot with ancient cypress trees and a comfortable guesthouse—but failed to take in a neighbouring rural co-operative received a pointed reprimand from Mao:

[Confucius] didn't care much about the economic aspects of the life of the people . . . Now the people in his home town have set up socialist co-operatives. After three years of co-operation, the economic and cultural life of the people, who were poor and destitute for over two thousand years, has begun to change. This demonstrates that the socialism of our time has indeed no parallel in history. Socialism is infinitely superior to the Confucian 'classics'. I would like to suggest to those interested in visiting the Temple and Tomb of Confucius that on their way they might well go and have a look at the co-operative . . .

Mao now launched a full-scale propaganda campaign, going over the heads of his Politburo colleagues to speed up the establishment of 'socialist' agricultural co-operatives in which all the land, tools, and other means of production were collectively owned and the profits were shared on the basis of work-points, not according to the amount of land or equipment originally put into the collective. Poorer peasants who had gained less from the original land reform generally supported the pooling of labour and resources in the new co-operatives. Less poor 'middle' peasants and the rich were naturally more dubious. The Party's own Rural Work Department was sceptical, and Mao accused it of 'tottering along like a woman with bound feet'. Reports of local success stories were edited by Mao with sharp comments on the obstructionism of local cadres, and circulated to the delegates of a full Central Committee meeting in October 1955 which endorsed the speed-up. Mao the journalist proudly told the delegates that he had spent 'eleven days behind my closed study door' making his editorial selection, and—with another dig at Confucius—that he had travelled more widely in spirit than had the sage in his wanderings.

Though the theory was not yet fully spelt out, Mao had already begun to break with the orthodox view that the 'productive forces' must be fully developed before further change could be made in the 'relations of production'. For agriculture this view—later attributed to Liu Shaoqi—meant 'mechanization before co-operation'. Mao argued on the contrary that only co-operation could provide the collective infrastructure and produce the surpluses necessary for mechanization. He also contested the belief that the peasants were not sufficiently educated to run co-operatives. Perhaps not at first, but co-operatives would provide both the framework for communal literacy classes and the incentive (through the need to keep collective accounts) for education. Underlying Mao's advocacy was the belief that the 'socialist enthusiasm' of ordinary peasants was itself a potential productive force waiting to be unleashed. Mao dramatized his faith in the masses with a phrase soon to become famous. China suffered, he said, from being poor, but poor people possessed the advantage of 'wanting revolution'. China suffered too from being 'blank' (uneducated), but this too had its advantage. Holding up a sheet of paper, on one side of which he had scribbled some notes, Mao turned it over dramatically. On the other, blank, side fine words could be written (and fine pictures drawn, he added later). Although twenty years later the co-operatives campaign was judged to have been 'over-hasty', for many peasants at the time, especially the younger ones, it opened up the possibility of translating the vision of socialist plenty into a reality where the peasants played their part rather than passively waiting for urban industrialization. The novelist Zhou Libo put their enthusiasm into the character of a young secretary of the Youth League in a mountain village in southern China with big plans for the future:

> After the co-operative is established, I'm going to propose that we do away with all the ridges between the fields, and make small plots into large ones. With large fields, the Iron Buffalo [tractor] can go into the water ...
>
> When we've built a reservoir, all the dry fields in the village will be irrigated, and even after paying tax we shan't be able to eat all the grain we grow. We'll send the surplus grain to help feed the workers in

industry. Won't that be wonderful! Then they, all smiles, will come in their jeeps to the countryside, and say to us, 'Hello, peasant-brothers, would you like to have electric light here?' 'Yes, paraffin lamps are really too inconvenient and wasteful.' 'Very well, we'll install it. Do you want the telephone?' 'Yes, we want that as well' . . .

With electric light, telephone, lorries, and tractors, we shall live more comfortably than they do in the city, because we have the beautiful landscape and the fresh air. There'll be flowers all the year round and wild fruit, more than we can eat . . .

Another later element of Maoist theory was also implicit in the collectivization campaign—the fear that failure to move ahead in restructuring social and production relations would increase the danger of a move backwards. Land reform, Mao maintained, had led to 'a vast sea of ownership by individual peasants' which, unless quickly raised to the co-operative level, would polarize the countryside, as the better-off peasants strove to get rich while the poorer fell into debt. There was merit in the argument, but it was overstated and expressed in language which hinted at political storms far ahead. Mao talked of a 'foul atmosphere' which was now being dispelled by a tidal wave of popular enthusiasm 'sweeping away all demons and monsters' (a familiar Red Guard slogan ten years later). Political work was 'the lifeblood of economic work', and hard struggle would be needed to oppose 'spontaneous tendencies towards capitalism'.

Great Leap socialism

Although the 1955 co-operatives movement led directly to the establishment of the people's communes in the Great Leap Forward of 1958, this had not been planned. Mao expected the co-operatives to develop in time directly into state-owned farms rather than collectively owned communes (essentially, agglomerations of many individual co-operatives). Both the structure of the new communes and the theoretical basis for them were at first improvised, indicating that in spite of later criticism there was a genuine degree of spontaneity in their origins. The starting-point was a vast campaign for water conservancy and land improvement in the slack 1957 winter season, for which co-operatives joined forces with their neighbours. It was an impressive effort: by January 1958, said the Chinese press, one out of every six people was out 'digging the fields and hacking the hills'. The defects of this crash campaign, which included not only shoddy construction but disastrous effects upon water tables and soil cohesion, were as yet unperceived. A modernized folk-song from Shandong, one of hundreds published at the time, conveys something of the mood:

A Girl's Reply
We were under the trees when I asked with a sigh:
'You still won't take up with a sweetheart, now why?'
Her cheeks became flushed with a mantle of red
And after some light-hearted banter she said:
'I won't be a wife till the hills are reclaimed,
I won't leave my home till the river's been tamed.
Green hills and green water for bride-chair I'll take,
For my dowry the orchards and fields that we'll make.'

Romantic poems were not uncommon in the new style, and were not always as trite as might be expected. The following example was written by a worker at the Liaoyang Textile Mill:

The Girl Checker
The dark eyes of the girl checker are sharp:
Not a single defect in warp and woof escapes them.
Some I know are afraid of these eyes
But still more are fascinated!
I send her the cloth I have woven myself,
And my heart that can stand any test.
I hope she will take the keenest look at them
With her beautiful eyes!

Henan province in the north took the lead, claiming to have doubled its irrigated acreage, and under the leadership of its first Party Secretary Wu Zhipu (a student of Mao's thirty years before) its agricultural co-operatives began to merge forces, at first spontaneously and then as a party-guided experiment. In the first issue of a new theoretical journal, *Red Flag*, Mao Zedong leapt into a bold generalization based on the achievements of a Henan co-operative which had 'removed the threat of flood and drought' from its land. 'Throughout the country', wrote Mao, 'the spirit of communism is surging forward. Political consciousness among the masses is rising rapidly. Backward sections among the masses have roused themselves energetically to catch up with the more advanced . . .' Reiterating his 'Poor and Blank' thesis, Mao said that Heaven was sending down 'talented men of every kind' who emerged from the ranks of the masses. The quote was from a poem by Gong Zizhen of the Qing dynasty:

> Let thunderbolts rouse the universe to life.
> Alas that ten thousand horses should stand mute!
> I urge Heaven to bestir itself anew
> And send down talented men of every kind.

The *People's Daily* ran a new feature called 'Greatness from small beginnings', introducing the lives and work of Chinese and foreign inventors who had contributed to science in spite of their lack of formal education. The Chinese peasant personified the spirit of new China as a whole, now expressed in the rejection of the Soviet economic model, and the determination to 'catch up and overtake' the Western world by very different means.

Though the mood was clear, the theory was improvised. Mao did not use the term 'commune' in his first *Red Flag* note. He spoke instead of a 'large, public community' (*da gong she*). The phrase 'large and public' (*yi da er gong*) would become a standard description of the advantages of the commune, Maoist both in its brevity and ambiguity. The actual term 'people's commune' was first used two issues later by Chen Boda, editor of *Red Flag*, Mao's close ideological adviser and later head of the Cultural Revolution Group. Chen envisaged the setting up of agri-industrial co-operatives which would break down the historic barriers between town and countryside and between mental and manual labour. Foreshadowing the 'all-round' approach of the Great Leap, which soon led to the mostly useless smelting of steel in rural backyard furnaces, Chen wrote under the heading 'Brand-new society, brand-new man'. Mao endorsed the 'all-round' approach after a provincial tour in August 1958. 'It is better to run people's communes', he pronounced. 'Their advantages lie in that they can merge industry, agriculture, trade, culture and education, and military affairs into one entity, and make it easier for leadership.' The agro-industrial co-operative had become the new basic unit of social organization; urban society too was supposed to be organized into communes in the first wave of Great Leap enthusiasm. This notion of the 'many-handed peasant' is caught in a photograph from Shucheng

County in Anhui. The local peasants are packed on to a parade
ground in front of a thatched village with low wooded hills
behind. Four large cartoons are displayed on posts among them,
showing: a small blast furnace; a resolute peasant; a student
clutching two books marked respectively 'Marxism-Leninism'
and 'College Graduate' in one hand and the atomic symbol in
the other hand; and a militiaman with rifle and broad-brimmed
hat.

The improvization of theory led at first in some interesting
directions. A *Red Flag* editorial described the commune 'not
only as the primary unit of our present society but the primary
unit of the future communist society'. This implied a rejection of
the hitherto orthodox progression from collective to state ownership. The commune enthusiasts spoke instead of a transition
from collective to 'by the whole people' ownership. The latter
phrase was not (as in the Soviet Union and previously in China)
interchangeable with state ownership, but suggested instead a
continuation into communism of self-management by the community. *Red Flag* also briefly revived the notion of the withering
away of state power: 'The function of the state will only be to
deal with aggression from external enemies; it will no longer play
an internal role.' (Even this external function would be modified
by the communes' new military role in which a greatly expanded
People's Militia would play a vital part in national defence.) Yet
the theoretical uncertainties of the Great Leap and the people's
communes prompted no great debate. The only argument was
with the Soviet leader Nikita Khrushchev, who mocked the
whole affair, accusing the Chinese of 'skipping over a stage' and
indulging in 'egalitarianism'. Mao had vaguely proposed that
every Chinese province should have its own *Red Flag*, with
licence to publish on 'all matters under the sun'. In reality Mao's
ad hoc pronouncements in the central journal rapidly became
dogma which precluded real discussion among the party rank
and file, let alone among the 'masses'. The only debate which
did take place was a deeply divisive one within the upper ranks
of the leadership, as the Great Leap veered from enthusiastic
excess to demoralizing disaster. Disillusion began to spread
within the Party, where some wondered if the leadership really
knew where it was heading. News of the disgrace of the Minister
of Defence Peng Dehuai, who had criticized the Great Leap,

spread with the announcement of his replacement by Lin Biao in October 1959. Many local cadres, obliged to meet impossible targets, either alienated the peasants by dragooning them into collective work or offended their superiors by refusing to falsify the figures. A sense of losing the way filtered through to the non-Party masses as well, though there was still a fund of great enthusiasm. A character in Wang Meng's short story 'The Barber's Tale' recalls the mood:

In the late fifties we celebrated the construction of new factories, electric power stations, bridges, and the victory of the socialist reformation. But at the same time many unusual things happened. One day we'd hear that a certain high-ranking person was a wolf in sheep's clothing; the next that one-fourth of China's arable land would be growing flowers. Or that China would realize communism very soon. Incredible announcements, conferences, and deeds were all too frequent.

Rethinking the transition

The early 1960s were a time for reflection, as Mao contemplated both the collapse of the Great Leap Forward and the worsening of the Sino-Soviet dispute. With Chen Boda beside him, Mao retired to his study. First he picked up the latest edition of a standard Soviet textbook on political economy, and wrote a set of critical reading notes which were then circulated among cadres (but not published until long after his death). In these notes Mao provided retrospective justification for the Great Leap, filling out his instinctive view that the poor and the blank could more easily achieve the transition to socialism. There were a few insights too into the flawed political relationships which had been concealed by the formal apparatus of the socialist state—privilege, nepotism, and the dictatorial behaviour of Party cadres. The *Notes* (1961–2) were still mainly concerned with ways and means of raising the level of social ownership and collective work (the relations of production) in order to stimulate economic growth (the productive forces). But as this attempt to hoist China into communism by a rapid advance in productivity failed, and met with opposition both at home and abroad, Mao broodingly turned away from the 'material base' to focus on the 'superstructure' of politics and culture. With the assistance of

Chen Boda and a large team of researchers, Mao produced a series of fluent anti-Soviet polemics (the *Nine Critiques*, 1963–4) which concluded with the claim that capitalism had been restored in the Soviet Union under Khrushchev's leadership. It followed that in China too it was essential to be on one's guard.

In an important passage of the *Notes*, Mao challenged Lenin's statement that 'The more backward the country, the more difficult is the transition from capitalism to socialism.' On the contrary:

Actually, the transition is less difficult the more backward the economy is, for the poorer they are the more people want revolution . . . Countries of the East, such as China and Russia, had been backward and poor, but now not only have their social systems moved well ahead of those of the West, but so does the rate of development of productive forces. In the development of the capitalist countries too, the backward overtake the advanced as America overtook England, and as Germany later overtook England early in the twentieth century.

But what was the nature of this transition? In the Soviet textbook (and in Stalin's 1952 essay 'Economic Problems of Socialism in the USSR', on which Mao had also commented), socialism was a relatively well-defined system with its own economic laws. Its society was unified except for a few malevolent forces and free from internal contradictions. Its economy was proceeding smoothly to the point where the productive forces would be sufficiently developed for the breakthrough to communism to be achieved. Cultural levels were rising steadily; so was the growth of 'communist consciousness'. Mao took exception to the orderliness of this view, and now drew together the threads of the alternative perspective which he had begun to construct patchily in the 1950s. First, contradictions not only persisted in a socialist society but were the 'motive force for social development'. This was true both in human terms, where the tension between the backward and advanced could be harnessed to mobilize popular enthusiasm, and in economic terms, where it was a mistake to believe that there could or should be a perfectly planned balance. Mao wrote of the 'wave-like advance of the development of socialist production' which could never be 'perfectly linear and free from dips' (the setback after the Great Leap was one of those dips). Planning was the attempt to regulate the 'objective laws of imbalance', but if a perfect balance was achieved then there could be no progress. 'Balance is relative,' wrote Mao, 'imbalance absolute. This is a universal law which I am convinced applies to socialist society.'

Mao's second theoretical innovation was to spell out the need for developing the social organization of production *ahead of* the productive forces. (Although this had been done during the Great Leap, Chinese theorists had continued to pretend that orthodoxy was still being observed, claiming that the productive forces were far more developed than they were in reality, and therefore that it was the relations of production which were belatedly catching up.) Mao now deployed exactly the reverse argument as another universal law: 'We must first alter the relations of production', he wrote, 'before we can possibly develop social productive forces on a grand scale.' After all, the revolution itself had not waited for China to reach a higher level of productivity before embarking on its transformation of society. The revolution started with Marxist-Leninist propaganda to win over public opinion, then destroyed the old political superstructure and thus created a new set of production relations. Only then was it possible to set in motion a revolution in technology. Moreover, just as in the revolution, material incentives were not an adequate form of motivation. People still had to be inspired to work for socialism. Over-reliance on incentives, Mao argued, was a futile attempt to 'beat capitalism at its own game'.

[The textbook] should put stress on hard and bitter struggles, expanded reproduction, and the future of communism. It cannot emphasise personal material interests, and lead people into the private pursuit of 'a wife, a dacha, a car, a piano, and a TV set'.

A third, much less well-articulated, area of theoretical innovation in Mao's musings of the early 1960s was his attempt to identify some of the social tensions which persisted in spite of the formal labels of state ownership and government 'by the people'. He wrote in the *Notes* that 'much remains to be written about human relations in the course of labour, e.g. concerning the need for the leadership to adopt egalitarian attitudes and to change certain [restrictive] regulations and established practices'. If industrial cadres did not change their attitudes, Mao continued, then the workers would never look on the factory as their own. 'Do not think that under socialism creative co-operation between the workers and the leadership of the enterprises will emerge all by itself without the need to work at it.' Mao also touched on the emergence of new vested interests in the state socialist system, particularly among cadres. Village cadres, for example, would be reluctant to surrender their power when their production brigades were eventually merged into larger communal units. Among the ordinary peasants, those who earned more under the system of differential work-points would object to a loss of earnings when a more egalitarian system of sharing out the proceeds of labour was adopted. 'The human animal is queer indeed', Mao pondered. 'No sooner do people gain some superiority than they assume airs . . . it would be dangerous to ignore this.' Mao also noted the emergence of a new form of privilege which would only be generally recognized after his death:

The children of our cadres are a cause of discouragement. They lack experience of life and of society, yet their airs are considerable and they have a great sense of superiority. They have to be educated not to rely on their parents or martyrs of the past but entirely on themselves.

The rethinking of the early 1960s should have led to a much broader discussion on how to move forward. But theory was the exclusive preserve of Mao and his closest colleagues, who were if anything further to the left than he. (Chen Boda wrote an article early on in the Great Leap calling for the abolition of 'commodity production' and the 'law of value'. Mao criticized him at the 1959 Beidaihe conference for advocating what would have amounted to the creation of a society where prices had no meaning.) The only serious theoretical challenge came from Sun Yefang, director of the Institute of Economic Studies, who advocated a return to farming on a family basis and more attention to the 'law of value' so that costs could be properly compared. In 1960–1 the commune system was modified, restoring the basic-level village or 'team' (*shengchan dui*) as the main unit for planning and production, restricting the role of the intermediate-level 'brigades' (*da dui*), and reducing the size of many communes by creating new ones. These reforms were more a response to events than to argument. The political scientist Su Shaozhi, one of the most independent thinkers of the 1980s, has recalled how willingly he and his colleagues in the 1960s followed the changing line: 'What I wrote then was often explanation of policies or interpretation or elaboration of talks by Party and government leaders, fettered by personality cult.' Su describes how he wrote an article explaining why the basic accounting unit in the people's communes should be the *dui* or 'brigade', according to the official formula at the time. He then learnt that the word *dui* in the formula now referred to the 'team'—and promptly wrote another article explaining why this was more appropriate. Sun Yefang became the target of a criticism campaign organized by the Party's Central Propaganda Department.

Return to class struggle

The Great Leap Forward had taken for granted the enthusiasm for socialism of all but a tiny percentage of the population, and it charted a future road along what was still an essentially materialist path. The attempt to hoist China into communism by a rapid elevation of collective ownership and productivity failed. Convinced that China's enemies within were far more numerous than had been thought Mao turned away from the 'material base' of production and producers to the intellectual and bureaucratic 'superstructure' of politics and culture, which he regarded as lukewarm if not hostile to continuing the revolution. His conviction was strengthened by events in the Soviet Union where, he believed, the leadership had now abandoned not only the 'sword of Stalin' but the 'sword of Lenin'. Nine research groups were set up to compile volumes of material to prepare the *Nine Critiques* against the Soviet Union which were then produced by smaller writing teams and edited by Mao or his closest colleagues. (The drafts were approved by Deng Xiaoping—an embarrassment which meant that by the late 1980s no satisfactory reappraisal of the critiques had yet been made public in Beijing.) The research group on 'war and peace' alone produced five large books summarizing the views of Marx, Engels, and Lenin, of Mao himself, of the 'revisionist' Soviet Union, and of the 'imperialists' and Yugoslavia.

Khrushchev's crude attempts to force China into line by withdrawing Soviet aid and manœuvring against Mao in the international communist movement brought the dispute into the open. The origins of the dispute were primarily concerned with international diplomacy. Tension between China and the Soviet Union was to be expected as China emerged from its dependence of the early 1950s. Mao strongly opposed the Soviet search for *détente* with the US (which was hardly in China's interest since it could only further isolate Peking) and complained of lukewarm Soviet diplomatic support. Soviet reluctance to help China become an independent nuclear power enraged the Chinese. But Mao, with his own recent memories of heavy-handed Soviet guidance, also reacted sharply to Khrushchev's disapproval of the Great Leap, and regarded Soviet society as a model of what he sought to avoid. He saw in the Soviet Union a privileged stratum of bureaucrats which, although already in existence under Stalin, had since degenerated to become a 'new bourgeoisie'.

The members of this privileged stratum have converted the function of serving the masses into the privilege of dominating them. They are abusing their powers over the means of production and of livelihood for the private benefit of their small clique. The members of this privileged stratum appropriate the fruits of the Soviet people's labour and pocket incomes that are dozens or even a hundred times those of the average Soviet worker and peasant. They not only secure high incomes in the form of high salaries, high rewards, high royalties, and a great variety of personal subsidies, but also use their privileged position to appropriate public property by graft and bribery. Completely divorced from the working people of the Soviet Union, they live the parasitical and decadent life of the bourgeoisie.

Mao regarded Khrushchev as leader of a 'revisionist clique' which had rejected Marx and Lenin along with Stalin and was now paving the way for the 'restoration of capitalism'. Not far below the surface of Mao's anti-Soviet critique lay his growing dislike of China's own bureaucracy (which he believed had largely sabotaged the Great Leap) and mistrust of most of his own colleagues, whom he also suspected of 'revisionism'. Already in 1962 Mao had responded to their veiled criticisms of the Great Leap by producing a new call to action, 'Never forget class struggle!', at the Tenth Party Plenum in September. The more moderate economic policies in 1960–1 were now condemned for 'painting the picture too black', encouraging the peasants to 'go it alone', and seeking to 'reverse the verdict' on

Peng Dehuai and other 'anti-Party' figures. The opposition of the bourgeoisie was more than a remnant from the past. As long as the transition to socialism continued, the opportunity existed for 'new bourgeois elements to be produced'. The struggle was protracted, and one could not even be certain about its outcome. What one should do was to 'talk about class struggle every year, every month, and every day'. The external and domestic stimuli to Mao's rethinking of theory had now converged, and the ninth *Critique* concluded with a fifteen-point statement on 'how to prevent the restoration of capitalism' which was intended to apply as much to China as to the Soviet Union:

Socialist society covers a very long historical period. Classes and class struggle continue to exist in this society, and the struggle still goes on between the road of socialism and the road of capitalism. The socialist revolution on the economic front (in the ownership of the means of production) is insufficient by itself and cannot be consolidated. There must also be a thorough socialist revolution on the political and ideological fronts. Here a very long period of time is needed to decide 'who will win' in the struggle between socialism and capitalism. Several decades won't do it; success requires anywhere from one to several centuries.

Mao had now arrived at the Stalinist conclusion that the class struggle would intensify rather than diminish as the socialist transition progressed further. Like the waves of the sea, it might be calm at one time but turbulent at another, and it was this struggle that would decide the fate of a socialist society. (After his death, the 1981 Party Resolution would censure him above all for having 'widened and absolutized the class struggle' at the 1962 Tenth Plenum.) Mao's response was less Stalinist. The solution, the fifteen points went on to explain, was to 'train and bring up millions of successors who will carry on the cause of proletarian revolution'. It was they who would do battle with the 'capitalist-roaders' who, unless checked, might one day cause China to 'change colour' and 'become revisionist or even fascist'.

Basing themselves on the changes in the Soviet Union, the imperialist prophets are pinning their hopes of 'peaceful evolution' on the third or fourth generation of the Chinese Party. We must shatter these imperialist prophecies. From our highest organization down to the grass-roots, we must everywhere give constant attention to the training and upbringing of successors to the revolutionary cause.

Early in 1965 Mao wrote in a document setting out guidelines for the 'Socialist Education Movement', which was designed to clean up the countryside, that the chief target was to be 'those Party persons in power taking the capitalist road'. The ground was now prepared for the Cultural Revolution—not a straightforward purge (although many were arrested and allowed to die if not actually executed) but a much more complex affair which mobilized millions of activists to defend one man at the top and his version of the road to communism.

CHAPTER THREE

Leadership from Above

MAOISM, CENTRALISM, AND INTRIGUE

It had been a heated argument in the Hall of Embracing Benevolence, built by the Empress Dowager for five million silver dollars after the Boxer Rebellion. For two days (14 and 16 Feb. 1967) the new Cultural Revolutionary leaders wrangled with the old guard. Did the Cultural Revolution need the Communist Party's leadership? Should veteran cadres be overthrown? Should the struggle by Red Guards and Rebels be extended into the armed forces? In the afternoon of the second session, the Minister of Agriculture Tan Zhenlin put on his coat, picked up his documents, and prepared to walk out:

Tan: You lot carry on, I'm going. Chop my head off, put me in jail, expel me from the Party, I'll still go on fighting!

Foreign Minister Chen Yi: No, don't go, Stay and fight them here!

Yu Qiuli (in charge of planning): What a way to treat old cadres! If the Planning Committee does not apologize, I won't criticize myself!

Li Xiannian: Now they've made it a nationwide confession [for old cadres]!

Tan: I never cried before but I've cried three times. Only I can't find anywhere to cry in private, because of my secretaries and children.

Li: I've cried a lot too.

Tan: Just look at my record from the Red Army on Mt Jinggangshan right up to now. When have I ever opposed Chairman Mao?

The ultra-left leader Zhang Chunqiao hurried to Jiang Qing with a report on the proceedings, which she conveyed swiftly to Mao. Two days later Mao convened the Politburo and bitterly denounced the veteran protesters. Seven more sessions were held to criticize them for seeking to 'restore' (capitalism) and 'reverse' (the verdicts on Peng Dehuai and other disgraced officials). The Politburo then ceased to meet at all.

Origins of the cult

In January 1965 Mao, by his own account, took the decision that Liu Shaoqi must be removed from office, and in the same month he was interviewed by the American journalist Edgar Snow, an old friend from their first meeting at Mao's revolutionary base in 1936. Snow had noticed a marked increase in the glorification of Mao since his last visit in 1960. At the climax of a performance of the song-and-dance pageant *The East is Red*, Snow saw a portrait of Mao copied from a photograph taken by him in 1936, blown up to about thirty feet high. 'It gave me a mixed feeling of pride of craftsmanship and uneasy recollection of similar extravaganzas of worship of Joseph Stalin seen during wartime years in Russia.' He put the question to Mao when they met again: was there a basis for the Soviet criticism that a cult of personality was now being fostered in China?

Mao replied that perhaps there was. It was said that Stalin had been the centre of a cult of personality, and that Khrushchev had none at all. The Chinese people, critics said, had some feelings or practices of this kind. There might be some good reasons for some more. Probably he concluded, Khrushchev, fell because he had no cult of personality at all.

Almost unobserved (for Snow did not grasp the significance of what Mao was saying—he had to be reminded of it when he met the Chairman again five years later) Mao had demolished the alibis offered on his behalf for the cult. He was not unaware of its extent, nor was it enlarged against his will by sycophantic followers. It served a precise political purpose at a time when he was preparing to launch the Cultural Revolution. (Yan Jiaqi, author of China's first scholarly account of the Cultural Revolution, begins the whole tale with Mao's remark to Snow.) It had served a similar purpose in support of Mao's leadership for more than two decades.

Mao Zedong was a hero to many millions of Chinese, but more particularly he was a hero to himself. This dimension of his self-image became more pronounced as he grew older. The heroes of the revolution in his early poems were 'the soldiery of heaven' (*tianbing*), the Chinese workers and peasants who soared through the high clouds punishing the corrupt and the bad. By the 1960s there was only one hero: the wonder working

Monkey King celebrated in the classic novel *Journey to the West*. Monkey, wrote Mao in a 1961 poem much quoted later by Red Guards in the Cultural Revolution, 'wrathfully swung his massive cudgel, and the jade-like firmament was cleared of dust.' Mao was once observed by the American writer Robert Payne watching an episode from the *Water Margin* epic on the stage in wartime Yanan. There was no doubt in anyone's mind, wrote Payne, that this drama of peasant heroism in the Song dynasty was a morality play: the leader of the peasant forces in his dragon-painted gown represented Mao, and the white-faced feudal landlord represented Chiang Kai-shek. As for the real Mao, enjoying the performance from the front row of the audience, he had 'deliberately or undeliberately modelled himself on the old Chinese heroes', believing that democracy and socialism were 'the essential aims of heroism' in the modern age. Edgar Snow was also convinced that Mao modelled himself on the peasant chieftains of the *Water Margin*. 'He certainly believed in his own star and destiny to rule.'

Mao saw himself as the commanding officer of the Chinese revolution, just as he recognized Stalin as playing the same role for the world revolution. Without a Stalin, he asked in 1939, who would give orders? Who would be the good commander and ensure that the soldiers of the revolution were properly looked after? Many years later, while acknowledging Stalin's 'mistakes' and the hard bargain which he had driven with China in the 1950 negotiations, Mao still insisted that the revolution needed its heroic leader as well as its collective leadership. In his 1958 speech, 'On the problem of Stalin', Mao argued that a cult of the individual—or at least of the 'correct side' of an individual—was justified in so far as such a person 'represents the truth'. Marx, Engels, Lenin, and 'the correct side of Stalin' all held truth in their hands, so why should they not be revered? Party historians have since described the effect of Mao's formulation upon his own cult: 'Some Party comrades developed a confused understanding of this question. Even at the Chengdu Conference [in 1958, where Mao spoke on the Stalin problem] some responsible cadres raised the slogan: Believe in the Chairman to the point of blind faith, obey the Chairman to the point of following him blindly.'

The official view, which describes how Mao's cult escalated in the 1960s until he 'became arrogant' (in the words of the 1981 resolution on Party history) and led China into the Cultural Revolution, glosses over or ignores the early appearance of the Mao myth during the authentic revolution of the 1940s. This had soon elevated 'Mao Zedong Thought' to the guiding doctrine which laid down 'the correct path in the entire course of China's liberation movement—past, present and future . . .' The triumph of Mao's Thought came at the end of the 'rectification campaign' (1941–2) in which Mao destroyed the influence of the Moscow-trained 'returned students' faction, defining the characteristics of the Chinese revolution as the 'sinification of Marxism'. It also coincided with the reduction of Soviet interest in China to its lowest point, as Moscow became overwhelmingly preoccupied by war with Germany. To some extent the myth of Mao also responded to a not dissimilar effort on the Chinese Nationalist side to promote its cause through Chiang Kai-shek's ghost-written book *China's Destiny*. The need to promote Mao's own thought was accepted by most of his colleagues and particularly by Liu Shaoqi, whose hagiographic speech in July 1943 first introduced the concept to the public. (Liu's involvement has since become an embarrassment to Chinese historians.) Liu again took the lead at the long-delayed Seventh Party Congress held in April 1945, calling Mao 'not only the greatest revolutionary and statesman in Chinese history, but also the greatest theoretician and scientist . . .'. Visiting Yanan in 1946, the American journalist Theodore White observed that, although Mao was supposed to be first among equals, 'his will was perhaps even more dominant in the Communist Party than Chiang's in the Guomindang. At public meetings it was not unusual for other members of the Political Bureau, men of great rank themselves, to make ostentatious notes on Mao's free-running speeches as if drinking from the fountain of knowledge.'

Limits of Great Democracy

Was Mao's semi-feudal relationship with his colleagues in some way offset by a greater concern than theirs for popular democracy? During the Cultural Revolution this was a popular explanation of Western sympathizers who argued that Mao had turned to the 'masses' in order to clip the wings of Party bureaucracy. Mao did combine an autocratic style of leadership with a 'mass line' which sometimes paid more attention to popular opinion than many of his colleagues allowed. However, it was never a question of submitting problems to arbitration by the masses, but at the most of allowing them to 'make suggestions' (*ti yijian*, a phrase which implies a carefully restrained element of criticism). Mao demonstrated the limits of this approach in discussing the 'suggestions' which were offered on the draft new Constitution in 1954.

They are of three kinds. The first consists of suggestions that are incorrect. The second consists of suggestions that are not so much wrong as unsuitable and that had better not be adopted . . . The third consists of those suggestions that have been adopted. These are of course very good and necessary.

An anecdote told by Mao to the second session of the Eighth Central Committee reveals both his concern for what he called 'great democracy' to combat growing bureaucracy, and the limits which he placed on it. Several years previously, he said, an airfield was to be built somewhere in Henan province, but no proper arrangements had been made to provide alternative accommodation for the peasants displaced by it. 'So the local people set up three lines of defence: the first line was composed of children, the second of women, and the third of able-bodied young men. All who went there to do the surveying were driven away and the peasants won out in the end.' What Mao meant by winning was simply that the authorities were compelled to give 'satisfactory explanations' to the peasants. They were then relocated, and the airfield was built according to plan.

Mao grew increasingly concerned by the problem of state–people mediation when events in the Soviet Union and Eastern Europe, echoed to a lesser extent in China, showed just how wide the gap could grow. It was in this context that Mao in 1956–7 advocated 'democratic methods' to resolve what he now defined as 'contradictions among the people'. Such contradictions were not 'among the people' in the sense that they expressed the rival demands of different interest groups whose relative strengths should be weighed and adjudicated by the government. They were, rather, those differences between the ruling stratum and the ordinary people which were judged (by the former) to be relatively benign and open to discussion—

although always on the assumption that it was the leadership which held the correct view. Mao was chiefly concerned in such situations to ensure that the leadership used persuasion and education rather than coercive measures to enforce its policies, on the pragmatic grounds that 'regulations alone will not work'.

In a revealing comment during the Great Leap on the experiences of a village which had persisted in running the (often unpopular) communal dining-halls, Mao quoted from Sun Yat-sen: if men with 'foresight and vision' carried out that which conformed to the 'heavenly truth' (*tianli*) and answered the people's desires (*renqing*) then the cause would not fail. But how could one establish what the people really wanted? In a crucial argument in defence of the Great Leap Forward in 1959, Mao used statistical sophistry to convert the minority who did support the communization of the countryside into an absolute majority:

At least 30 per cent of them [the peasants] are activists, another 30 per cent are pessimists and landlords, rich peasants, counter-revolutionaries, bad elements, bureaucrats, middle peasants and some poor peasants, and the remaining 40 per cent will follow the main stream. How many people are 30 per cent? It's 150 million people. They want to run communes and mess-halls, undertake large-scale co-operation and are very enthusiastic ... For the followers of the main stream, it does not matter whether these programmes are carried out or not. Those who are not willing to carry on constitute 30 per cent. In short 30 per cent plus 40 per cent is 70 per cent [in favour of the Great Leap, if it is handled correctly] (speech of 23 July 1959).

The Great Leap demonstrated Mao's growing unwillingness to 'listen to opinions' unless they conformed to his definition of what was correct. Peng Dehuai, Minister of Defence and a blunt critic at the Lushan Plenum (July 1959) of unrealistic targets and the exaggerated 'wind of communism', sought to offer his views in a private letter to Mao. The Chairman—always a master tactician of inner-party manœuvring—had the document circulated as a 'Letter of Opinion', and then denounced it as a 'programme of an anti-Party nature'. Mao (or perhaps those closest to him) insisted that Peng had formed a 'Military Club' which constituted an anti-Party clique, maintaining this definition even though Peng sought to have the letter withdrawn and made a self-criticism. Two months later Peng was replaced as

Minister of Defence by Lin Biao (later to become Mao's 'chosen successor' and chief sycophant in the Cultural Revolution). The political thread of internal Party struggle which would be publicly unravelled in the Cultural Revolution can thus be traced precisely to Mao's obstinacy in the Peng Dehuai affair. Liu Shaoqi and Deng Xiaoping did not support Peng at the time, but by advocating more cautious policies later they retrospectively, and for Mao woundingly, validated his critique of the Great Leap. Liu spoke out in favour of Peng's rehabilitation in 1962, when Peng himself sent Mao an 80,000-character letter of justification. A group of Party intellectuals in the capital wrote veiled attacks on Peng's dismissal, including the famous play *Hai Rui Dismissed from Office* by the writer and deputy mayor of Beijing, Wu Han. These became the first targets of the literary polemics written by the ultra-left group now congregating around Mao, with which the Cultural Revolution was launched. The political chain led directly first to the mayor of Beijing, Peng Zhen, who had sought to protect Wu Han, and then to Liu Shaoqi, who sent 'work teams' of Party cadres to try to silence the first Red Guard agitators. A separate thread of connections leading back to Peng Dehuai was unravelled in the People's Liberation Army, where Lin Biao first disposed of the Chief of Staff Luo Ruiqing, and then neutralized most of the military leaders of his generation.

Discipline and dissent

Mao's growing authoritarianism was assisted by the preference of his colleagues, most of whom were to suffer in the Cultural Revolution, for discipline at the expense of democracy. The Party's highly vertical structure had been taught by Soviet advisers in the 1920s (who also helped the Guomindang establish a similar model). Soviet manuals on Party discipline were required reading. As Liu Shaoqi wrote in his famous 1941 lecture, 'On Inner-Party Struggle', the Chinese had the advantage of being able to take the Soviet CPSU as its 'living example', and 'the majority of our Party members can recite from memory the organizational principles of the Bolshevik Party'. On the eve of Liberation Mao had called on the People's Liberation Army, which would provide large numbers of cadres for civilian life, to turn itself into 'a great school', and urged the party to behave modestly, shunning the 'sugar-coated bullets of the bourgeoisie' by which it would be tempted. Yet these provisos were outweighed by the belief that the Party's right to rule had been validated beyond further question by the sacrifices of the revolution. In his classic text, 'How to be a Good Communist', Liu Shaoqi quoted approvingly from the philosopher Mengzi (Mencius): 'When Heaven is about to confer a great office on any man, it first exercises his mind with suffering, and his sinews and bones with toil.' The members of the Communist Party, he continued, now faced 'the unprecedentedly "great office" of changing the world'. This Confucian belief in the 'superior man' dovetailed neatly with the Leninist concept of the 'vanguard party' and the Stalinist example of the 'great leader'.

The emphasis upon unity masked the reality of chronic disunity. The history of the Party had been punctuated by damaging internal conflicts which were designated as 'struggles between two lines [sets of policies]'. Political handbooks listed these in chronological order, starting with the 'line struggle against Chen Duxiu's rightist opportunism' in 1924 (Chen was the founder of the Party). The eleventh 'line struggle' would be designated briefly as that against Deng Xiaoping's 'right deviationism' in 1976, soon to be replaced by the struggle against the Gang of Four's 'anti-Party clique'. These episodes only increased the pressure for conformity. The Party Constitution contained provisions for 'inner-Party democracy' including the right (variously worded at different times) to appeal to higher authorities. Those who did so ran the risk of being identified as oppositionists. As the wartime Constitution warned, care should be taken that this right would not open the way for 'any conspirator, renegade or factionalist to utilize the principle of democracy to injure or divide the activities of the Party'.

Lower-level Party cadres were thus always under pressure to validate policies decided above by demonstrating that they worked below among the 'masses'. Mao himself acknowledged this danger during the Great Leap, yet deterred honest reporting by his own treatment of the Peng Dehuai opposition. Many writers of the late 1950s were labelled as 'rightists' precisely because they identified this harmful practice. The novelist Wang Meng made his name—and was exiled to the countryside—after publishing a short story in which complaints about a domineering factory director are answered with the warning to 'respect the leadership and strengthen unity'. The journalist Liu Binyan wrote a fictionalized report, 'On the Bridge Site', showing how a disaster was caused while officials waited for 'higher instructions' instead of taking decisions during an emergency. Liu too was labelled a rightist. So was the young engineer who dared to make decisions on his own and provided the model for Liu's story.

In 1956 the Party had held its Eighth Congress after an interval of eleven years since the Seventh. The delay could be explained by civil war and the struggle for post-war reconstruction, and the congress seemed to mark the completion of a return to normal Party life. The main congress speeches were published in full. Central Committee meetings were then held at least once a year until the Tenth in 1962. There followed a prolonged gap until the highly irregular Eleventh in August 1966, which officially launched the Cultural Revolution. The Ninth Congress, which should have been convened in 1960 at the required four-year interval, did not meet until 1969. This progressive 'abnormalization' of Party activity reflected Mao's increasing suspicion of the bureaucracy and preference for operating through *ad hoc* meetings such as 'working conferences' of provincial and national officials. His colleagues, led by Liu Shaoqi and Deng Xiaoping, did not clamour for a resumption of internal democracy, but seemed happy to manipulate the system from within. Their policy differences with Mao were confined to the highest level, and they made no attempt to mobilize the Party rank and file. Mao was a better tactician in Party warfare, as he had been in guerrilla warfare. While circumventing the Party's democratic rules, he targeted the Party bureaucracy for his criticism, appealing to the less privileged and more resentful cadres. In December 1963 he wrote that 'large numbers of fine comrades are frustrated by those comrades who are highly placed with fat emoluments and live in style, who are conceited and complacent and are only too glad to stick to the beaten track, and who are addicted to bourgeois metaphysics; in other words, these fine comrades are frustrated by the bureaucrats'. Provocatively, he argued on another occasion that

There are always people who feel themselves oppressed; junior officials, students, workers, peasants, and soldiers who don't like big-shots oppressing them. That's why they want revolutions. Will contradictions no longer be seen ten thousand years from now on? Why not? They will still be seen.

But cadres within the Party in the early 1960s who sought to criticize bureaucracy were likely to harm their promotion prospects and to attract negative reports in their personnel files. In extreme cases they were sent to prison or to mental hospitals. Many denunciations of higher officials in the Cultural Revolution were fuelled by the real resentment of their juniors. Whole government ministries would be taken over by 'rebel' cadres who published exposés of the bureaucratic style and the privileged existence of their superiors. This happened most notoriously in the Ministry of Foreign Affairs, where the young chargé d'affaires from the embassy in Indonesia, Yao Tengshan, gained temporary power by denouncing the 'shameless behaviour' of Liu Shaoqi and his wife on their 1963 visit to Indonesia. 'Rebel' junior diplomats, interpreters, and trainees seized truckloads of classified documents and published exposés in Red Guard magazines. Senior diplomats were accused of revelling in foreign luxuries: 'They prefer everything foreign, even including foreign-made paper napkins ... Many ... are known to have brought back dozens of trunks of foreign merchandise, such as radios, television and stereo sets, tape recorders, cameras ... in addition to sizeable bank balances.'

Anatomy of ultra-left

Many people supported the ideals of the Cultural Revolution with a genuine conviction that they belonged to the 'true left' which was working for the creation of a 'socialist new man'. Their commitment was fatally tarnished by the usurpation of power at the apex of the Party by leaders who combined ultra-left rhetoric with an autocratic style and the acceptance of luxurious privilege. Though labelled retrospectively as the Gang of Four, the ultra-left was a more complicated phenomenon with its own internal divisions. It included serious though dogmatically inclined theorists; others who rose from the Party ranks through opportunism or zeal; and a few thugs and criminals.

The Gang of Four was a shorthand expression, originally

used by Mao in a private memorandum, which only became common after his death. Three of the group, Jiang Qing (Mao's wife), the Shanghai-based Party leader Zhang Chunqiao, and the polemicist Yao Wenyuan, had worked closely together to foment the Cultural Revolution. They were sometimes known contemptuously as the 'ten-eyed three' (because two of them, Jiang and Zhang, wore glasses). The fourth, Wang Hongwen, was an ex-worker from Shanghai, promoted to high Party office in 1973 in order to bring new blood into the leadership. A much larger group of ultra-leftists was briefly active in 1966–8, working through the Cultural Revolutionary Group with Chen Boda, Mao's intellectual confidant, as its head (and Jiang Qing as a deputy leader). Most of this group discredited itself in 1967 by openly attacking Premier Zhou Enlai and by seeking to stir up revolution within the armed forces. Chen himself was denounced in late 1970 as a 'sham Marxist political swindler'. His disgrace was followed by the much more sensational exposure of Mao's 'chosen successor' Lin Biao, Minister of Defence since 1960, in September 1971, when his alleged plot to assassinate Mao was exposed and he died in an aircrash while fleeing the country. Jiang Qing herself, although closely involved with the discredited groups, managed on each occasion to distance herself sufficiently to retain her influence, although this dwindled considerably in 1971–3. The period 1974–6 then saw a second struggle between a new ultra-left coalition, now owing total allegiance to her group, and the moderate forces led by Zhou Enlai and his *de facto* deputy, Deng Xiaoping, who was rehabilitated in 1973.

Mao was well aware of the dubious quality of the ultra-left forces on which he relied to launch the Cultural Revolution, but regarded them as a lesser evil than the Party bureaucracy. Transcripts of meetings show his impatience at sycophantic interjections by Lin Biao. Mao objected to a speech by Lin (18 May 1966) warning against a *coup d'état* and flattering Mao as a 'genius' of modern Marxism–Leninism. In a letter written in July 1966 and published internally in September 1972, Mao had already told Jiang Qing not to become 'dizzy with success', but to keep in mind her 'weak points, shortcomings, and mistakes'. But, he added, his criticisms could not be made public because it would mean 'pouring cold water on the leftists'. He added prophetically that they might not be published until after his death, when the rightists would probably 'use my words to hold high the black banner'.

Although Jiang Qing enjoyed lavish material privileges as the Chairman's wife, she resented the disapproval of his colleagues which had excluded her from active political life since Liberation. (It was said that they only approved her marriage with Mao in 1938 on condition that she should refrain from political activity.) When Mao showed his growing concern with class struggle and the reform of the superstructure—the world of politics and culture—she seized the chance. In March 1967, speaking to a group of Red Guards, Jiang gave a revealing account, which has so far escaped the attention of her biographers, of her ascent to power, claiming that it was she who from the early 1950s had encouraged Mao to criticize 'revisionist' tendencies in literature and art. Though Jiang's account was self-serving, it illustrates that even Mao's wife needed to secure his validation (although at first it seems to have been half-hearted) for her actions. Jiang's concern, verging on an obsession, with the reappearance of 'feudal' culture from the past meshed with Mao's own fear that the cultural superstructure had been taken over by his opponents.

In the last seventeen years [since 1949] there have been some good or fairly good works in literature and art reflecting the Workers, Peasants, and Soldiers. But most things were Famous, Foreign, or Fabled, or else they distorted the people's real image. As for education, it all seemed to belong to Them, plus a whole lot of stuff from the Soviet Union. So in literature and art we produced some Old Artists, and in education we produced even more intellectuals than before who were completely Cut off from the People, Proletariat and Production. Without the Cultural Revolution, who would ever manage to change things? They wouldn't budge if you hit them!

I thought it very funny then, all those Hong Kong films we were getting stuffed with, so I did my very best to shove them away. But They said something like 'Oh, we must pay attention to the needs of the National Bourgeoisie'. I really was on my own then! You can't have Peaceful Coexistence in this area of ideology. You Co-exist, and They'll Corrupt you.

Jiang Qing then launched a sidelong barb at Zhou Enlai (who appears to have been at the same meeting with her). It was

Zhou, she said, who argued that China should subsidize the patriotic films made in Hong Kong 'as long as they're not anti-communist'. She then revealed that while she was 'ill for several years' the doctor advised her to 'Participate in Cultural Life', apparently as a form of therapy. She soon discovered that there were some Big Questions in Literature and Art, with mostly 'bourgeois and feudal stuff' on the stage and the screen.

I think it was in 1962 that a whole heap of Hong Kong, imperialist and revisionist films appeared. And so many new opera companies! I'm a great fan of Beijing Opera although I know it's been on the decline. Well, they used the Ministry of Culture to set them up everywhere— even down in Fujian there was more than a dozen! So everywhere you could see Lords and Ladies on the stage! I come from Shandong, and when I was a child they used to call the Hebei Clapper style the 'Big Opera'. I went to investigate and found that the Big Opera was now mostly Beijing. There were forty-five Beijing Opera companies, not counting illegal ones and amateurs. Shanghai opera had also spread all over the country in the same funny way. But they never put on stage the Rich Achievements of our People, or the Long March, or the Red Army, or the Anti-Japanese War. They never put on all those heroic things. Films had the same problem. So I gradually became aware of this problem. In 1962 I talked about it with four ministers or deputies from Propaganda and Culture, but they wouldn't listen to me.

Jiang Qing then explained how she and her confederates 'took a big risk' in preparing the article by Yao Wenyuan (which eventually launched the Cultural Revolution) without Mao's approval. She gathered some information on the 'Problems' in literature and art, but did not show it to her husband because he was 'too tired'. She admitted that Mao at first rejected her criticism of the play by Wu Han which allegedly was a covert defence of Peng Dehuai. But she relied on a tortuous interpretation of Mao's response to claim she was justified in pursuing the matter further.

. . . the Chairman turned me down. He said he wanted to read it [Wu Han's play] and that we should protect some of the historians like Wu Han. I only realized later that this was Mayor Peng Zhen's idea; he said I was completely negative about the world of history, which was actually a distortion of what I thought. So I said to the Chairman, 'Can I stick to my opinion?' And the Chairman said 'Stick to it if you like'. At that time Peng Zhen was doing everything to protect Wu Han. The

Chairman must have seen it all clearly but he didn't speak out. It was because he allowed me to stick to my views that I felt entitled to organize that article and keep it a secret.

The loyal opposition

Control of the Cultural Revolution in the first 'Red Guard' period (1966–8) was vested in a special group, run by Chen Boda with Jiang Qing as adviser, and responsible only to the Politburo's much smaller Standing Committee. Zhou Enlai's authority in the Cultural Revolution was based on a decision taken when it began that he should be 'in charge of the daily work of the Politburo and . . . of handling the routine affairs of the Party, government, and army'. The distinction was vital: Zhou could explain and interpret policy but he could not initiate it, nor is there any evidence that he sought to. His overriding concerns were to keep the state apparatus functioning and to save as many senior figures as possible from victimization. Legalisms were still vital amid the chaos. After receiving a note from Mao asking him to intervene on behalf of an old friend, Zhou felt entitled to draw up a 'protection list' of senior officials who should be saved from the Red Guards. An article mourning Zhou's death bore the title: 'A towering huge tree guards China heroically.' Many stories tell of his efforts—not all successful—to mitigate the worst consequences of Red Guard violence and Gang of Four vendettas. (Sometimes Zhou's countermanding order arrived too late, and when an investigation had been ordered only Mao could authorize release from prison.)

Yet Zhou gave the impression at the time to all of those who met him of being firmly convinced by the basic theory behind the Cultural Revolution, while struggling to protect it from manipulation by the ultra-left. Deng Xiaoping later tried to give an explanation for this. Premier Zhou, he said, 'was in an extremely difficult position then, and he said and did many things that he would have wished not to. But the people forgive him because, had he not done and said those things, he himself would not have been able to survive and play the neutralizing role he did, which reduced losses. He succeeded in protecting quite a number of people.' Ten years after Zhou's death, the *People's Daily* for the first time admitted that he might have meant some of the things that he said. Zhou's understanding of the Cultural

Revolution, it explained, was 'restricted by historical conditions'. Since its 'true nature' had not yet been revealed, he still hoped that the movement would produce 'good results'.

Respect for Mao remained an important factor for many of his colleagues. Zhou's semi-official biographers explain that 'Mao had been right so many times before. If he decided that the Cultural Revolution was good for the Party and the country . . . Zhou went along without much question.' When it seemed to be leading to disaster, Zhou's first reaction was to reproach himself for failing to understand Mao's underlying strategy. Yet Zhou did not believe in Mao unconditionally. Mao should not be regarded, he had said in a speech on the eve of the 1949 Liberation, as a demi-god or a leader impossible to emulate— that would amount to isolating him from his people. Mao was 'a people's leader born of the experience and lessons of a history of several thousand years, of the revolutionary movements of the last hundred years, and of direct struggle over the last thirty years'. Young people should follow Mao's own example and 'seek truth from facts'—a concept later to become the catchphrase for the post-Mao regime of Deng Xiaoping.

Other leaders were deterred more by respect for Mao's power than for his ideas. 'None of us could say this [criticize the rebels] to Chairman Mao', the veteran Marshal Xu Xiangqian was to observe. 'Influenced by the awesome power of Chairman Mao, none of us could do anything about it!' Their opposition in the early months of the Cultural Revolution was blustering and ill-organized. A sympathetic account of the famous 'February (1967) Revolt' of the senior marshals depicts little more than a bad-tempered wrangle over whether or not the Cultural Revolution should be extended into the armed forces. Marshal Ye Jianying is said to have struck the table with such force that he cracked one of the bones in his hand. 'We don't read books or newspapers,' he told Chen Boda sarcastically, 'and we don't understand the Principles of the Paris Commune. Please explain what they are! Can there be revolution without party leadership and without the army?' The ultra-left compiled a damaging dossier and promptly reported to Mao. It included verbatim remarks by the Minister of Agriculture Tan Zhenlin:

The masses, it's always the masses, what about Party leadership? It's all day long without the Party, the masses Liberating themselves,

Educating themselves, Making Revolution. What's it all about? It's
Metaphysics!

Your aim is just to overthrow the old cadres and clean them out one
by one. Once you've fixed all the old cadres, forty years of revolution
will be smashed like a broken family . . .

Jiang Qing wants to have me Rectified as a Counter-Revolutionary
—she said so to my face! [A leftist supporter objects that Jiang Qing
only wants to 'protect' Tan.] I don't want her to protect me! I work for
the Party, I don't work for her!

Protesting his loyalty to Mao, Tan wrote an ill-advised letter to
Lin Biao accusing Jiang Qing of being worse than the notorious
Tang empress Wu Zetian. Lin promptly showed the letter to
Mao, who summoned a special Politburo meeting to castigate
the dissenters. More than four years passed before Mao fully
relented, choosing to regard the 'February adverse current' as a
protest against Lin and Chen Boda, who by this time had been
disgraced.

Meanwhile Deng Xiaoping, the ultimate survivor in the
1966–76 power struggle, refrained from shouting across the table.
Named as the Number Two Person in Authority Taking the
Capitalist Road (Liu Shaoqi was Number One), he was insu-
lated from the savage treatment which led to Liu's death from
pneumonia in 1969. Deng had always had a complicated
relationship with Mao, which now may have saved him. In
1954–5 he had loyally conducted the purge of the Gao Gang–
Rao Shushi faction, and then actively led the 'rectification'
campaign against dissenting intellectuals which followed the
1956–7 Hundred Flowers liberalization. At the 1956 Party Congress Deng had criticized the cult of personality—ostensibly
referring to de-Stalinization in the Soviet Union—in terms which
Mao later resented. However, Deng (like Liu Shaoqi) kept quiet
at the Lushan Party Plenum in July 1959 when Mao rejected
criticism of the Great Leap Forward. (According to one version
Deng pleaded illness and left early, claiming he had injured his
leg playing ping-pong.) Mao respected Deng's talents. 'See that
little man there', he told Khrushchev in 1959, according to the
Soviet leader's memoirs, 'he is highly intelligent.' But later Mao
claimed that Deng had for years failed to keep him properly
informed as Chairman of the Party. 'He treated me like his dead
ancestor', Mao complained.

In October 1966 Deng made a prudent self-criticism which helped him to withdraw from the leadership struggle and sit out the worst of the Cultural Revolution. He acknowledged that together with Liu Shaoqi he represented the 'bourgeois line' and had tried to suppress the mass movement. 'What I need to do', he concluded ambiguously, 'is to reflect on my past actions . . . Though I have gone astray on the road of politics, with the radiance of Mao Zedong Thought lighting my forward path, I should have the fortitude to pick myself up and go on.' (Liu Shaoqi's 'confession' was more courageous—he maintained that everyone in the leadership, including Mao, was open to criticism.)

In matters concerning class struggle and struggle within the Party, I have consistently shown rightist tendencies . . . I have become accustomed to lording it over others and acting like someone special, rarely going down among the people or even making the effort to contact cadres and other leaders so as to understand their working situation and problems . . . Rarely did I ask for help or advice from other comrades or the people. Worse still is that I have rarely reported to and asked advice from the Chairman. Not only is this one of the main reasons for my errors, but it is also a serious breach of Party discipline. In late 1964, Chairman Mao criticized me for being a kingdom unto myself.

In 1971 Deng was working in a 'May Seventh Cadre School' when he heard about the death of Lin Biao. Correctly perceiving that this had altered the balance at the centre in Zhou Enlai's favour, he wrote to the Central Committee saying that he was eager to get involved in the campaign to 'criticize Lin Biao'. He hoped that the Party would give him some work while he remained in good health. Soon afterwards Mao attended the funeral of former Foreign Minister Chen Yi. He informed his widow that Chen had been a 'good man', that Lin Biao's purpose had been to overthrow all of their generation, and that the cases of Liu Shaoqi and Deng Xiaoping were not counter-revolutionary but belonged to the more benign category of 'contradictions among the people'. Zhou Enlai saw his chance, and arranged for Chen Yi's family to quietly spread Mao's words. In 1973 Deng was restored to his previous post of Vice Premier. There is a story that at the end of 1973, Mao sent Deng and the young Wang Hongwen, who had just 'helicoptered' to power, to make inspection tours of the country. On their return, Mao asked both men: 'After I die, what will happen in China?' Wang replied that 'The whole country will certainly follow Chairman Mao's revolutionary line and carry through the revolution to the end!' Deng replied that 'Civil war will break out and there will be confusion throughout the country!' Mao preferred Deng's reply, and appointed him Chief of Staff of the People's Liberation Army.

CHAPTER FOUR

The Rebel Alternative

FROM 1919 TO THE RED GUARDS

In the early 1960s, a very junior clerk called Chen Lining became convinced that the Head of State, Liu Shaoqi, was a 'revisionist' and traitor to Mao's line. He wrote—as the Party Constitution allowed him to—a letter to the Central Committee. The case was promptly referred back to Chen's superiors who locked him up, at first in prison and then in a mental hospital. Three years later his case came to the attention of the ultra-left intellectuals running the Party journal Red Flag *under the head of the Cultural Revolution Group, Chen Boda. Chen Lining was transferred first to a Beijing hospital and then—with a set of new clothing—back into society. He was sent on a lecture tour to tell the tale of his persecution. A hostile account later reported that:*

Thrusting forward his small belly and swaggering, he put on airs of a 'hero' and demogogically deceived the masses. This counter-revolutionary element delivered 48 reports to an audience of more than 200,000. Still more people heard the playing back of his recordings, and read the materials carefully forged for him. Each day many people called on him because they admired his 'fame' and two men [were appointed] to receive the visitors . . .

A play was written about Chen with the title 'Madman of the New Era'—a conscious echo of the famous story 'Diary of a Madman' written by Lu Xun in 1918 describing the alienation of a young man from China's semi-feudal society. The hero, thinly disguised, was given the name 'Chen Weidong' ('Chen Guards the East') and was played by Chen himself in some performances. It was said to have inspired 'even more brazen plays', including one called 'Angry Flames of a Madman' performed in Shijiazhuang by a Red Guard troupe called the Madman Commune.

Chen's fame was shortlived. The ultra-left Red Flag *leadership was disgraced for attempting to extend the targets of the Cultural Revolution to include the armed forces and Premier Zhou Enlai. Chen Boda abandoned the group to save his own position. Chen Lining was investigated after a performance of his play at a literary festival in Tianjin which had been banned by the army authorities. He was declared to be 'not a madman but a counter-revolutionary', and sent to jail, where he disappears forever from sight.*

Making trouble in Heaven

Order and disorder, obedience and rebellion, are recurring themes in Chinese political culture, sometimes opposed to each other but as often yoked together. In Mao's philosophy they assumed a quasi-Marxist dialectical relationship, as in the phrase 'There is no construction without destruction.' In his later years Mao was apt to put it more colloquially: 'Do not be afraid to make trouble', he advised Party members in 1959. 'The more trouble you make and the longer you make it the better. Confusion and trouble are always noteworthy. It can clear things up.'

For generations of Chinese the concept of trouble-making instantly recalls the tale of Monkey, the troublesome hero of the Ming dynasty novel *The Journey to the West* by Wu Chengen, who leads his master, the Monk Tripitaka, through countless dangers to bring back the holy word of Buddha. 'It is clear', wrote Arthur Waley in his translation, 'that Tripitaka stands for the ordinary man, blundering anxiously through the difficulties of life, while Monkey stands for the restless instability of genius.' Monkey began his career by 'making trouble in Heaven' —theme of many an opera, folk ballad, and comic book—but then adopted the Great Faith and distinguished himself by 'the subjugation of monsters and demons'. After many adventures in which more than once he saved his master from wandering into death or defeat, Monkey with his companions ascended into Heaven and was rewarded with the title of Buddha Victorious in Strife.

During the Cultural Revolution these metaphors of struggle became the everyday language of wall-posters and manifestos. The targets of the Red Guards were those monsters and demons—the 'capitalist-roaders'—who, lurking in the shadows behind foolish monk-like leaders who had lost the way, sought to subvert the quest for the Holy Sutras of communism. One of the earliest manifestos from the Red Guards at the secondary school attached to Qinghua University in Beijing ends with this triumphant claim:

Revolutionaries are Monkey Kings, their golden staffs are powerful, their supernatural powers far-reaching, and their magic omnipotent, for they possess Mao Zedong's great invincible Thought. We wield our golden rods, display our supernatural powers, and use our magic to turn the old world upside down, smash it into pieces, pulverize it, create chaos, and make a tremendous mess—the bigger the better! . . . Long Live the Revolutionary Rebel Spirit of the Proletariat!

Mao had evoked this spirit of rebellion in very similar terms throughout his political career—a spirit which, it must be emphasized, lay and still lies close to the surface of the well-regulated face of Chinese society. The deportment of the Confucian man, wrote Mao in an early essay on the importance of physical exercise (published fifty years before the Cultural Revolution), may be cultivated and pleasing, but the Chinese nation needs people who are 'savage and rude'. They should have the ability to 'leap on horseback and to shoot at the same time; to go from battle to battle; to shake the mountains by one's cries, and the colours of the sky by one's roars of anger'. This concept of revolutionary 'rudeness' evoked both the legendary Chinese generals who featured in romances such as *The Tale of Three Kingdoms* and the anonymous heroics of peasant rebellion. Scholars have debated how far in theoretical terms Mao credited the peasantry with a leading revolutionary role. But there is no doubt that he identified emotionally with their sufferings, and approved of the measures to which they were driven by oppression.

As a young man, Mao had tried to emulate China's first great historian Sima Qian, who in the second century BC chronicled the exploits of actors and beggars as well as kings and generals, by travelling through the countryside. In the summer vacation of 1916, Mao and a friend set out on a 'travel study' tour not only dressed as beggars but actually begging for their food. (Half a century later, the Red Guards were encouraged to travel across

China 'exchanging experiences' and 'learning from the peasants'.) 'Having seen for himself the tragic suffering of the peasants ...', wrote an official biographer of Mao, 'how could he remain calm? How could he bury his head in the library?'

Ten years later, Mao returned to his home province of Hunan as the Communist–Guomindang alliance came under strain on the eve of the Northern Expedition led by Chiang Kai-shek to unify China. Once again Mao shouldered his pack and set off for a month-long inspection tour of five counties near the provincial capital of Changsha. He found a thriving movement of 'peasant associations' which in the revolutionary atmosphere had seized village power and made life unendurable for the local gentry and rich landlords. They had stepped on the ivory beds of the landlords' daughters, said Mao, paraded the gentry in tall paper hats like criminals, and turned everything upside down. The report which Mao produced, *The Peasant Movement in Hunan*, defended the peasant associations against the complaints not only of the Guomindang but of urban communists whom they had alarmed by 'going too far'. The associations were largely led, said their critics, by the village riff-raff who 'go around in worn-out shoes, carry broken umbrellas, wear blue gowns and gamble'. Mao did not deny much of this—though he did explain that most of them had actually stopped gambling and given up banditry! In refuting the charge of 'going too far' Mao produced what remained until the end of his life his most famous revolutionary judgement:

A revolution is not the same as inviting people to dinner or writing an essay or painting a picture or embroidering a flower; it cannot be anything so refined, so calm and gentle, or so 'mild, kind, courteous, restrained and magnanimous' [as were the virtues of Confucius]. A revolution is an uprising, an act of violence whereby one class overthrows the authority of another... If the peasants do not use the maximum of their strength, they can never overthrow the deeply rooted, age-old authority of the landlords ... To right a wrong it is necessary to exceed the proper limit; the wrong cannot be righted without doing so ...

Peasant rebellion

Within a year after his report on the Hunan peasant movement,

Mao found himself on the wooded mountain slopes of Jinggangshan in south-east China, patching together a rag-tag army labelled 'Soviet', with mostly peasant recruits who included at least two groups of bandits. The united front between the Guomindang and the communists, which helped to unify China and liquidate most of its warlord regimes, had been broken by Chiang Kai-shek in a vicious blood-letting against the communists once they had served their purpose. At the time, Mao and the other surviving communist guerrillas seemed not so different from the outlawed scholar-officials of imperial times who had taken to the hills to mobilize peasant rebellion. The tale of the *Heroes of the Water Margin* (a favourite of the youthful Mao) contains many examples of educated gentry and minor officials who, victimized by corrupt authority, take to Mount Liangshan. Though the disaffected scholars might have formed only a tiny percentage of the rebels, their skills and leadership were essential. But like the 'social bandits' analysed by E. J. Hobsbawm in his study of primitive forms of social protest, the leaders of China's peasant revolts possessed an ideology well described by him as one of 'revolutionary traditionalism'. In the last analysis, writes one authority on rural rebellion, the Chinese revolts only served 'to confirm the Confucian theory of the Mandate of Heaven, consolidating the traditional political system by purging it when this became necessary'. The great Taiping Rebellion (1850–64), led by a would-be scholar who had been frustrated in the imperial examinations, produced a regime which professed support for elections and recall of officials, equal distribution of necessities, and equality between the sexes, but which rapidly established a pseudo-imperial hierarchy with fatally destructive internal divisions. The memory of the failure of this movement of 'social bandits' (a very similar Chinese term, *huifei* or 'bandits of society', was used at the time) was still fresh in Mao's rural China.

The Chinese communist leaders consciously set out not to take over the existing order but to establish a new one and disprove the old saying that 'He who fails becomes a bandit, he who succeeds becomes a king!' The Leninist concept of the vanguard Party was handily available; Mao attributed the previous failure of peasant rebellions largely to the lack of 'correct leadership' by an 'advanced political party'. Mao's insistence upon strict Party control over the revolutionary armed forces, enunciated early on in the Gutian Resolution (December 1929), has rightly been regarded as crucial. Yet there was a paradox: In rational terms the communists argued for the dominance of the educated vanguard (Liu Shaoqi wrote of 'the rather low cultural level of the masses of the Chinese peasantry and other sections of the people, except for the intelligentsia'), but mass radicalism based upon traditional revolutionary culture had an appeal which was hard to resist, especially by local cadres who feared the accusation of 'stifling the masses' initiative'.

After publication in October 1947 of the first serious land reform programme in the communist-held areas, many peasant associations were dominated by the poor, who settled scores not only with landlords but with those defined as 'rich' or merely 'middle' peasants. Party officials tended at first to support them, reasoning as Mao had argued in Hunan that the most poor must be the most revolutionary. 'Their life is most bitter', proclaimed the government of one communist-led area; 'they are oppressed and exploited and pushed around. Hence they are the most revolutionary . . . This is determined by life itself.' But this revolutionary spirit from below led to dangerous demands for a share in the Party's political and military power, as in this open letter from the peasant association in the Shanxi–Suiyuan border region:

We peasants have the right to supervise and reform all departments and organizations, all working groups, schools, factories, or publicly owned shops whether they belong to the Party, the government, army, or the people . . .

You have not only the right to examine all cadres and organizations, you have also the right to reform and improve all organizations. You can improve the peasants' organizations, revive their constitutions and qualifications for membership. Democracy must be fully developed . . . In this way, all Party, government, military, and public organizations can be firmly built.

Hence we suggest: bear your share of responsibility for the people's army. This is the peasants' own army . . . Military force must be in the hands of the peasants. The people's militia must be under the direct control of the peasants' associations so that it will really be the armed force which protects the peasants.

The 'excesses' of this movement were vigorously criticized by Mao in a whole series of policy directives (much later in the Cultural Revolution, Liu Shaoqi would be improbably criticized for the ultra-left line of this period). Mao again stressed the leadership of the Party and the need to involve a broad spread of society in the 'revolutionary united front'—but not to share power. There was no word of approval now for 'going too far'. Instead, Mao condemned 'serious errors' which included the indiscriminate use of violence against landlords and rich peasants, 'sweep-the-floor-out-the-door' confiscations, and an obsession with unearthing the landlords' hidden wealth. Yet the revolutionary spirit made excess almost unavoidable, and junior cadres could also object that their 'errors' had at first been encouraged from above, as William Hinton showed in *Fanshen*, his first-hand study of land reform in a Shanxi village. The local Party secretary Chen condemned 'absolute egalitarianism', arguing that even if every peasant was given an exactly equal share today, inequalities must re-emerge until communism was realized. It was wrong to say that Left was better than Right. But Chen himself was reminded that he had sent work-teams to carry out land reform with the instruction that 'If you can't find any poor peasants you had better not eat'—an invitation to leftist excess—and he was obliged to accept 'primary responsibility' for the errors. It would take another three decades until after Mao's death before the long-term effect of the Chinese revolution's rural-based bias towards 'adventurism' was generally acknowledged.

After Liberation, the 'poor' peasants became a political spearhead for rural change, first finding their tongues to denounce landlord power, and later persuading the better-off peasants, by argument and example of their own efforts, to join the new co-operatives of the mid-1950s. There were also daunting physical challenges. The great floods of 1954 were contained (in contrast to the devastation of the 1931 floods) by vast voluntary armies of collective flood-fighters. Mass campaigns for literacy and public health demanded the support of rural activists. Within ten years, most peasants had acquired a basic reading knowledge, although standards fell off again in the 1960s. Public sanitation greatly improved and endemic diseases such as schistosomiasis (which requires immense physical effort to eradicate the breeding-places of the snail carrier) were brought at least partially under control. The Great Leap Forward, while bewildering many peasants with its millenarian aims, did absorb the energy and mobilize the enthusiasm of a large activist minority.

During the hard years of 1960–1 when the Great Leap failed, millions of people died prematurely for lack of food. Nevertheless, underlying support for the collective principle persisted, and rural activists could still be found to lead the Socialist Education Movement (1962–4) in the countryside. Yet peasant rank-and-file enthusiasm was beginning to wane. Already in the early 1960s the Party had become concerned by a revival of the 'three evil tendencies' of 'capitalist' practices such as money-lending, 'feudalist' customs such as bride-sale, and 'extravagance' in the shape of lavish spending and local corruption. The scaling down of the people's communes after the Great Leap created a more sensible balance between collective and private interest, in which accounting and the organization of production were carried out usually at the level of the local village or 'team', and 'private plots' were allowed. However, the prestige of the Party had been seriously weakened, and away from the main towns and lines of communication there was still widespread hardship, while the social and economic fabric of rural life had been undermined. Gu Hua, in his novel *A Small Town Called Hibiscus* (1981), describes the dislocation caused to the rural market, hub of a previously thriving community:

In 1958, the year of the Great Leap Forward, as everyone had to smelt steel and boost production, the district and county governments restricted village markets and criticized capitalist trends; so that the Hibiscus markets were reduced from one every three days to one a week, finally to one a fortnight. By the time markets disappeared, it was said, they would have finished socialism and entered communism. But then Old Man Heaven played up and they had bad harvests, on top of which the imperialists, revisionists, and counter-revolutionaries made trouble. It wasn't so bad their failing to make the great leap into communism; but instead they came a great cropper, landing back in poverty with nothing but vegetable soup in the communal canteen, and nothing in the market but chaff, bracken-starch, the roots of vines and the like. China and all her people developed dropsy. Merchants stopped coming to the market, which was given over to gambling and prostitution. Fighting, stealing, and kidnapping spread . . . Then towards the end of 1961 the county government sent down instructions to change the fortnightly market into one every five days to facilitate trading. However, so much damage had been done that Hibiscus market could no longer attract all those merchants from far away.

The May Fourth spirit

Student rebellion was a much more modern strand in Chinese revolutionary tradition. Mao and other communist leaders had first been radicalized in the 'May Fourth Movement' which, in 1919, voiced youthful disillusion with the warlord take-over of the first Chinese republic, and particularly with China's humiliation at the hands of the great powers. Students in the 1920s were fired more by patriotism than by a particular ideology, but the betrayal of the nationalist revolution by Chiang Kai-shek in the 1930s drove many sympathetic young intellectuals closer to the communists. Hundreds made their own long march to Mao's north-west base at Yanan. Most were chastened by the rectification campaign in the early 1940s after a few had criticized the first emerging signs of Party bureaucracy and privilege. But by the late 1940s, the Party's defects were hugely overshadowed by the oppression of the Guomindang and its secret police operating on university campuses in nationalist-held China. In 1949 the great majority of intellectuals welcomed the prospect of a 'new China'. Their welcome was reciprocated by the Party, which urgently needed a stock of young educated people to provide teachers, administrators, and cadres for an entire country.

In the first years after Liberation many responded to the demand, accepting their 'job assignments' without question, and eagerly joining the Youth League and the Party. The writer Lu Wenfu catches their enthusiasm in his retrospective political parable, 'The Gourmet':

When my turn came [to be assigned] I made a mess of things . . . I didn't have any particular skills and couldn't even sing properly [the previous student has just been assigned to join a 'cultural troupe'].

The man asked impatiently, 'You don't know anything at all?'

'Yes, I do, I know how to buy special foods for people, and I know all the eating places in Suzhou.'

'Right, go to the commercial department. Suzhou is known for its food.'

'No, no, please, I hate eating.'

'You hate eating? All right. I'll tell the cook to starve you for three days. Then we'll discuss it again. Next . . .'

Alas, my future was settled amidst general mirth. But I wasn't depressed, nor would I think of disobeying orders!

There was a hunger for education: in Beijing the students would climb the trees to read their textbooks by the light of streetlamps. Thousands joined the Communist Youth League, hoping to prove themselves worthy candidates for eventual membership of the Party. But the strength of idealism gave their support a conditional character and the tradition of student protest revived at Beida (Beijing University) in the Hundred Flowers movement (1956–7). In retrospect, the most striking feature of their criticisms was that they anticipated by two decades the analysis of China put forward in the democracy movement of the late 1970s and partly adopted then by Party reformers. There was a 'Democracy Square' in 1957 at Beida. Most of its wall-posters— more than three hundred in one day alone—accepted the socialist goal but challenged its dogmatic distortion by the Party cadres and their routine adulation of all things Soviet. Rene Goldman, who was studying at Beida at the time, recalls how the Hundred Flowers movement briefly stimulated student enthusiasm. The walls were covered with slogans like 'Think Independently' and 'Storm the Fortress of Science', which allowed discussion of Western science. 'Their thirst for learning was admirable and they sometimes dreamed up fantastic plans of research.'

Students demanded a more liberal cultural and educational policy but almost no one advocated a change of regime. Khrushchev's secret speech on Stalin to the Soviet Twentieth Party Congress was translated into Chinese by students of the Beida Physics Department from the version published in the United States. Students in the department of history complained of being taught that the Russo-Swedish war was a 'just war' because it gave Russia an outlet on the Baltic Sea. Lin Xiling, a 23-year-old student training to become a cadre at the People's University, had previously defended Stalin. Now she argued in terms which would lead to a campaign against 'Lin Xilingism' in the rectification which followed the Hundred Flowers. Her analysis of the feudal elements in Chinese and Soviet state socialism also anticipated the arguments of the late 1970s:

The problem of Stalin is not the problem of Stalin the individual; the problem of Stalin could only arise in a country like the Soviet Union, because in the past it had been a feudal, imperialistic nation. China is the same, for there has been no tradition of bourgeois democracy. This could not happen in France. I believe that public ownership is better than private ownership, but I hold that the socialism we now have is not genuine socialism; or that if it is, our socialism is not typical. Genuine socialism should be very democratic, but ours is undemocratic. I venture to say that our society is a socialist one erected on a feudal foundation; it is not typical socialism, and we must struggle for genuine socialism!

The analogy between Stalin and Mao now came close to the surface. Student speakers quoted the figure of 770,000 deaths during the land reform and other campaigns of the early 1950s from Mao's own 'secret speech', which had launched the Hundred Flowers and was only published in a revised version after the rectification began. The Party and its leader, they argued, belonged in Marxist terms to a backward political 'superstructure' which had not kept pace with the socialization of the country's economic 'base'. Mao had argued in his speech that 'contradictions among the people' which persisted under socialism could, if not correctly handled by the Party, become 'antagonistic'. Lin Xiling responded that such contradictions were those between 'the leadership and the led', and reflected an objective law that all ruling classes have their limitations. 'Men in different positions', she said, 'have different points of view. He who was the ruled before but who has now climbed to the ruling position (from worker to head of a factory) speaks a different language; everything has changed.'

This early flowering of a student democracy movement was soon extinguished, and left no visible mark as the policies of rectification and the Great Leap led to the beginnings of the 'revolution in education' which would culminate in the Cultural Revolution. Admission policies shifted to favour students from peasant and working-class families. Students helped with revived enthusiasm to build the Ming Tombs Reservoir, and joined the campaign to set up blast furnaces for steel in the suburban communes of Beijing. The educational institution, announced the president of Qinghua University, should become 'not just a school, but at the same time a research institute, factory, designing institute, and building concern.' But some officials soon became concerned at the effect upon educational standards and at the haphazard results of the 'half-work half-study' campaign. The new President of Beida, Lu Ping, warned that 'lofty revolutionary ambitions' should be combined with 'the good academic tradition of learning with realism and perseverance'. He expressed alarm at the number of injuries to Beida literature students who had been sent to work in primitive coal-mines west of Beijing. In 1963 all the students were brought back from work assignments, and examinations were reintroduced. Anyone who failed in two subjects had to withdraw from college and was assigned to be a secondary school teacher— frequently back in the countryside. Many of these came from the same poor 'worker-peasant' background which had been preferred during earlier student enrolment. Staff promotion once again encouraged those with ability in teaching or research, while political activity declined. These shifts in policy reflected growing divisions in China's educational establishments which provided much of the social basis for student activism in the Cultural Revolution. The Beida lecturer Yue Daiyun has described the realignment of Beida's three constituent groups in her remarkable memoir of this period:

One group was composed of those already established as faculty members and administrators before Liberation, people educated under the old system ... A second group was composed of people like me, who were educated largely after Liberation, who often had participated enthusiastically in the underground movement, but who had been influenced by the older generation of intellectuals and shared some of their ideals. The third group was composed of workers, peasants, and soldiers, many of whom had worked in the 'red', or rural, areas of the country during the revolution, people who had come to Beida after Liberation to receive an education and stayed on as teachers and Party cadres. It was this group that Chairman Mao had hoped would change the character of the universities.

These tensions now began to be manipulated by rival groups in the national leadership—the 'behind-the-scenes backers' as they would become known in the Cultural Revolution. In 1964 an investigatory 'work-team', sent to Beida by Mao's security chief Kang Sheng, condemned the University as a 'reactionary fortress' under Lu Ping. Within months a rival team had been sent to Beida by the mayor of Beijing, Peng Zhen, and the head of the city's Party Committee, Deng Tuo (both would be among the first targets of the Cultural Revolution in 1966). This team called a conference at the International Hotel in the centre of Beijing, busing nearly three hundred faculty members—both supporters and critics of Lu Ping—for discussions which lasted seven months and (it was later claimed) cost 200,000 yuan (£50,000) in hotel bills. The pro-Mao radical delegation to this conference was led by Nie Yuanzi, a former cadre from one of the post-war revolutionary bases who had become Party secretary of the Beida Philosophy Department. It was Nie's wall-poster attacking Lu Ping on 25 May 1966 which was to launch the Red Guard movement. Mao, it was said, soon 'heard about it'—not surprisingly, since it was probably instigated by people close to him. Describing it as 'the first Marxist-Leninist big-character poster', Mao ordered it to be broadcast over the radio and published nationally.

The ageing American writer Anna Louise Strong, uncritically sympathetic to the Red Guards, described Nie as a 'slender, friendly woman who . . . showed no pretension to power . . . she was approachable and intelligent, the qualities of a teacher'. Yue Daiyun, watching Nie carried on Red Guard shoulders at the first chaotic meetings, had the opposite impression. '"Chairman Mao has said that I am the first red banner," she would cry, "so anyone who opposes me opposes Chairman Mao himself!" How arrogant she is, I thought; how curious that sometimes history pushes to the forefront someone so completely undistinguished.' Yue guessed that Nie had become friendly with Kang Sheng's wife through her own husband, who served with her on the Central Disciplinary Commission.

Red Guards and Communes

Throughout the revolution, the students had never been more than an auxiliary force. In the Cultural Revolution of 1966–8 (the broader definition extending it to 1976 was only made retrospectively) they became the vanguard force. Already concerned to create a new generation of 'revolutionary successors' which would steer China away from the revisionist trap into which the Soviet Union had fallen, Mao pinned his faith upon its youth. The Red Guards were loose groupings of college and secondary school students, formed initially to 'struggle' against teachers and cadres in their own institutions but soon encouraged to act as the catalyst of a wider movement. Red Guards could be as young as 12 or as old as 30, but the majority were in their teens. Red Guard representatives attended the Eleventh Plenum of the Central Committee in August 1966, which adopted a sixteen-point directive on the Cultural Revolution. A million Red Guards had already reached Beijing in time to welcome the sixteen points at Mao's first mass rally on 18 August. At least another million passed through the capital during the autumn. Red Guard activists from the provinces reported to the new Cultural Revolutionary Group appointed at the Plenum and were sent back to initiate new 'struggles' against local Party leaders. In most cases the targets compounded their presumed crime as 'capitalist-roaders' by seeking to muzzle or 'suppress' their youthful persecutors. 'All those who have tried to repress the student movement in China have ended up badly', Mao warned his colleagues.

Red Guards, mostly from the secondary schools, led the movement to criticize the 'Four olds' which involved house-to-house searches for books, money, documents, art treasures, and so on, which were considered decadent or counter-revolutionary. Red Guards from the colleges were dispatched to stir up rebellion against the Party bureaucracy among the urban workforce in the main cities and towns. Less systematically, Red Guards conducted propaganda for the Cultural Revolution as they passed through the rural areas, often hiking or hitching rides on their travels to 'exchange revolutionary experiences' throughout China—a mission which served many as the excuse for tourism. Early in 1967, a *Red Flag* editorial coined an extraordinary generalization in the students' favour:

All cultural revolution movements in contemporary Chinese history have begun with student movements and [have] led to the worker and peasant movements, to the integration of revolutionary intellectuals with the worker–peasant masses. This is an objective law . . . In 1967, China's great proletarian cultural revolution will continue to develop in line with this objective law.

This sequence of development was, according to a later

statement by Mao, supposed to result in the emergence of the workers and peasants as the main force, after which the students would 'fall back into a subsidiary place'. In the event, a large number of urban workers became active but the movement had only limited impact upon the countryside. This was due in part to nervousness at the centre about the effect of the Cultural Revolution upon the economy. Red Guards were ordered not to 'exchange experiences' or 'engage in debates' with rural officials, while the peasants' own campaign against the 'Four olds' should be carried out only 'in the slack season'. The countryside remained quiet, but discontented interest groups in the urban workforce—lower-paid employees and ex-peasants on limited contracts without job security, in particular— began to join the movement as 'Red Rebels'. The armed forces were explicitly exempted from Red Guard activity, and within a few months were called on by Mao to intervene to maintain essential communications and to police the factional struggles of the Red Guards and Rebels.

In the first months of the Cultural Revolution, when officials in one Chinese city and province after another were denounced and hounded out of office by young teenagers, it seemed to some observers that Mao's ultimate aim was to replace the Party itself. Mao had described Nie Yuanzi's Beida poster as 'the Manifesto of the Beijing People's Commune of the 1960s'. His remark was later interpreted (1 Feb. 1967) by *Red Flag* as a prediction that 'our state organs would take on completely new forms'. In the end Mao himself backed away from such a radical step, but the implied challenge to Party hegemony would not be forgotten.

The August 1966 sixteen-point Decision on the Cultural Revolution had called for the 'struggle and overthrow of those in authority taking the capitalist road', a formula usually reduced to the single word *dou*, 'struggle' and linked to *pi*, 'criticize' (bourgeois academics and ideology) and *gai*, 'transform' (the world of literature and education and wherever else necessary in the superstructure of culture and politics). But it was not clear how comprehensively the struggle was to be carried out. Was it just a question of removing a few 'capitalist-roaders', or would it require restructuring the party machine which supported them? The new Cultural Revolutionary Groups set up after August 1966 were defined as 'organs of power', but their jurisdiction was confined to the Cultural Revolution itself 'under the leadership of the Communist Party'. However, the sixteen-point Decision also specified that the Cultural Revolution would take 'a very, very long time', and that in this sense the new mass groups would be 'permanent and not temporary'. All the evidence pointed not just to a compromise reflecting the current balance of political forces (Liu Shaoqi, though demoted in status, still held his Party offices, and Zhou Enlai had worked to insert moderating phrases into the Decision) but to a sense of improvisation on Mao's part similar to his hesitancy in the early stages of the Great Leap Forward.

'You must pay attention to affairs of state and carry through the revolution to the end!', Mao had told one of the Red Guard rallies in Tiananmen Square. But which affairs of state? The sixteen Points did contain a hint which chimed with the inchoate urge of the Red Guards to challenge all authority. The new Cultural Revolutionary Groups, it stated, should be established by 'a system of general elections, like that of the Paris Commune . . .'. Once elected, members could be criticized at any time and recalled if they proved incompetent. Earlier in 1966 a long *Red Flag* article, probably written by its editor Chen Boda, had suggested the relevance of the Paris Commune to current events in China in the same terms. 'The masses were the real masters in the Paris Commune', it argued. They supervised the work of their elected officials, and ensured that they should be not the masters but the servants of society.

When, in January 1967, groups of revolutionary activists— discontented workers and dissident cadres as well as students— began to 'seize power' from the Party bureaucracy, they appropriated the name of the Commune and claimed to embody its principles. The most famous was the 'Shanghai People's Commune', briefly proclaimed early in February. Others were announced in Beijing, Taiyuan, and Harbin, but neither Shanghai nor these were given national publicity. The new name implied a new organizational form which for a moment seemed to threaten the very existence of the Party. *Red Flag* again had hinted in this direction. Through the 'wisdom of the masses', it said, 'a completely new organizational form of political power better suited to the socialist economic base will be created'. The lesson of the Paris Commune, as Marx had pointed out, was that the existing state machinery must not only be taken over but thoroughly smashed. 'It is absolutely impermissible to merely take over power while letting things remain the same and operating according to old rules.'

Zhou Enlai was quick to observe, however, that the new 'communes' had been set up in a fever of factional struggle, and without the mass participation on which the analogy with Paris in 1871 depended. The Shanghai Commune, far from having been 'elected', had excluded one of the two most important rebel groups in the city, which now took its grievance to Beijing. Mao himself had to adjudicate on two questions: was the name right, and should the new organization supplant the Party? Mao's answer to the first question (which attracted most attention) was that a self-styled 'commune' which failed to live up to its name would ultimately undermine the enthusiasm of the people of Shanghai and elsewhere. The commune's advocates in the national leadership, Zhang Chunqiao and Yao Wenyuan, returned to Shanghai with instructions that the Shanghai People's Commune should become the Shanghai Revolutionary Committee. On the second question, which had also been raised by the few surviving moderates (particularly Tan Zhenlin) in the central leadership, Mao's answer was unequivocal. Shanghai could not be governed by students and workers alone, Zhang told a rally in the city on his return from consulting Mao. To keep the city functioning needed the co-operation of senior army leaders and cadres. The number of top officials required, he said precisely, was six thousand. He conveyed orally Mao's comments, which characteristically ranged from a diplomatic quibble about the name to a firm affirmation of principle.

If the entire nation established People's Communes, should the name of the People's Republic of China be changed? If it is changed to the 'People's Commune of China' will we be recognized by everyone? The USSR may not recognize us while the British and French may recognize us. After the name is changed, what happens to our embassies in the various countries? Have you considered these and other questions? . . .

I believe that we need it because we need a hard core, a bronze matrix, to strengthen us on the road we still have to travel. You can call it what you please, Communist Party or Socialist Party, but we must have a Party. This must not be forgotten.

Whither China?

By the autumn of 1967 the central authorities had made some progress in throttling back the Red Guard movement, although this would not be finally achieved until late summer of 1968. The People's Liberation Army (PLA) had been licensed to intervene when public order broke down, and was beginning to do so with more confidence. The provincial 'revolutionary committees' which Mao preferred to the embryonic 'people's communes' were based on a 'three-way alliance' between army, cadres, and 'revolutionary masses' in which, as time went on, the rebel forces played an increasingly junior role. In Beijing, after the shocking events of the summer when ultra-left leaders of the Cultural Revolution Group (CRG) encouraged attacks on the PLA—notably the 'Wuhan incident' in August—the most outspoken had been purged (including the sponsors of 'madman' Chen Lining). Jiang Qing herself had felt compelled to warn the Red Guards to leave the army alone.

The *Shengwulian* (Hunan Proletarian Committee) was an alliance of some twenty Hunanese groups, mostly student bodies from secondary schools but including at least one civil service organization and numbering two former PLA officers in its own leadership. Set up in October 1967, it published three documents in the winter which were rapidly denounced by the CRG in Beijing. Jiang Qing described it as 'a hotchpotch of rubbish from the old society' and much was made of the fact that the father of one of its student leaders was a former Secretary-General of the provincial committee. But as K. S. Karol has noted, the *Shengwulian* could claim that they were merely remaining faithful to the ideas of Mao and his team from the first phase of the Cultural Revolution. They even quoted a directive from Lin Biao stating that 'Hunan is the vanguard area of revolutionary struggle of the whole country.'

The *Shengwulian's* famous essay 'Whither China?' began by evoking the spirit of the 'People's Commune of China', which Mao had 'brilliantly foreseen' at the start of 1967. It accepted reluctantly that Mao was right to oppose the establishment of the Shanghai Commune—although this was something that 'the revolutionary people find hard to understand'—because what was being established was only a 'sham commune'. But it insisted that the committees must be regarded as only a 'transitional form' to prepare the way for the ultimate product of the Cultural Revolution: the genuine commune. The struggle had to continue within the Revolutionary Committees, which were dominated by the army and Party cadres and simply amounted to 'another kind of bourgeois rule of bourgeois bureaucrats'.

... the Cultural Revolution is not a revolution to dismiss officials from their office or a 'dragging out' movement, nor is it a purely cultural revolution, but it is 'a revolution in which one class overthrows another'. Seen from the facts of the storm of the January [1967] revolution, the class to be overthrown is none other than the *class of bureaucrats formed in China over the past 17 years.* ... The programme of the first Great Proletarian Cultural Revolution was put forward in editorials in an embryonic, not very concrete state in the final stages of the storm of January. [It included] the decaying class that should be overthrown, the old state machinery that should be smashed, and even social problems on which people formerly had not dared to express a dissident view [my italics].

If the Cultural Revolution was directed against 'capitalist-roaders', argued the *Shengwulian*, then one must ask how such people had emerged since 1949. The answer was that China had inherited a state machinery, particularly the army, police, and judiciary, almost unchanged from the past (here they found an apt quotation from Lenin). The majority of cadres who operated this apparatus, they claimed, had embarked upon the capitalist road unknowingly. But those who did so deliberately now formed a 'privileged stratum' which was the real target of the Cultural Revolution. The relations of production, to the extent that they were controlled by this privileged layer of cadres, had degenerated, and now lagged far behind the economic base which was capable of supporting a more genuine socialism. Only through the Cultural Revolution could a 'true beginning' be made in the socialist revolution.

The *Shengwulian* avoided the usual eulogies for the PLA, which was by now supposed to be the 'Great Wall' and bastion of the Cultural Revolution. It would be foolish to believe, it argued, that the PLA could be immune from the revival of bourgeois values in political life since 1949. Before Liberation the relationship between army and people was indeed like that between fish and water. But 'as soon as Chairman Mao issued the order for the armed forces to live in their barracks [to become a garrison rather than a revolutionary army] they became separated from the masses'. Why then had Mao ordered the PLA to 'support the Left' if it did not genuinely do so? The *Shengwulian* provided a subtle explanation. It was the Chairman's 'ingenious means' for extending the Cultural Revolution into the armed forces by involving it at second-hand.

The text for the *Shengwulian*'s brave new China was Mao's Directive of 7 May 1966, which was the first, and by far the most Utopian, of his Cultural Revolutionary pronouncements. It was interpreted to mean that there should be no specialization or exclusivity in fields of work. Soldiers, to whom the message was primarily addressed, should learn to take part in politics, run factories, and engage in agriculture, as well as how to fight. Workers, peasants, and students should similarly diversify their activities. Of course the workers should still work, the peasants should still farm, and the students should still study. That was their 'primary task'. But by adopting secondary tasks outside their own field, they would break down the barriers between town and country and between intellectuals and workers. Everyone should be developed in 'an all-round way' to become 'a new communist person with proletarian political consciousness'. While Mao's colleagues attempted to ignore this embarrassing Utopian vision, the Hunanese rebels said frankly that it was the only way forward. 'People in general rejected the sketch [of China's future] as an idealistic "communist Utopia" ... Only some intellectual youths still keep reciting it ... because they realize that only the new society sketched in the May Seventh Directive ... is the society in which they may have liberation.' But, they claimed, the January 'seizure of power' had already shown that the idea was workable.

People suddenly found that without the bureaucrats they not only could go on living but could also live better and develop more quickly and with greater freedom. The bureaucrats had tried to intimidate the workers before the [January] revolution, saying: 'Without us, production will collapse and the whole of society will be in chaos' ... But after the Ministry of Coal collapsed, production of coal went on as usual. The Ministry of Railways collapsed, but transportation was carried on as usual. ... For the first time the workers felt that 'it was not the state that managed them, but they who managed the state'. For the first time they felt that they were producing for themselves.

This was far from the reality of packed trains running on abandoned timetables, and factories where production slumped by half, which even the left leaders in Beijing had to agree justified the return of the cadres and intervention of the PLA. But the *Shengwulian* was accused not of naïvety but of counter-revolution. By spelling out to a logical conclusion the ultra-left argument opportunistically used by the clique around Mao, they brought too visibly into the open its underlying challenge to Premier Zhou Enlai and the army leadership. In an episode which is unique for the Cultural Revolution, central leaders were compelled to argue their case against an alternative before a meeting of Hunanese delegates, even though they did so tendentiously. Kang Sheng claimed that the Hunan group had distorted their quotation from Lenin—and besides, it was an obscure one which no student could have known, which pointed to the *Shengwulian*'s programme being written by some member of Liu Shaoqi's counter-revolutionary black gang! But his real rage was directed against the alleged existence of a 'privileged stratum' which, said Kang, 'vilified the socialist revolution'. Jiang Qing's criticism of the group was briefer and more guarded, drawing a distinction between its 'backstage bosses' and the rank and file who had been 'hoodwinked'.

This radical challenge from the grass roots was soon submerged in the wider tide of disorder which, a year later, led to the intervention of the People's Liberation Army on Mao's instructions to restore public services, reopen the schools, and send large numbers of students to the countryside. With life in China now restored to something approaching normality, the Cultural Revolution put on its best face to the outside world. But the *Shengwulian* stands in a classic line of revolutionary challenge which extends from Mao's own early pronouncements through the Beida protests of the Hundred Flowers to the post-Mao democracy movement.

CHAPTER FIVE

Second Cultural Revolution

THE ABORTIVE GREAT DEBATE

Just one month after Zhou Enlai had outlined the policy of the Four Modernizations at the 1975 National People's Congress, a great debate broke out among working-class students at the Shenyang College of Mechanical and Electrical Engineering over the relationship between technical skill and political morality.

Modernization, said one group of students, taking their cue from Zhou, required what Chairman Mao himself had called a 'huge contingent' of 'technical cadres' in order to build socialism. Why should those who sought to become proficient at their jobs be accused of 'just wanting to be a famous expert?' It was true that college students should not behave like 'intellectual aristocrats', but neither should they be deterred by criticism from making the best use of their training so as to become 'leaders of the working masses' after graduation. Otherwise how would China ever advance its national economy to the front ranks of the world?

The opposing view was also published as a wall poster. Like the first, it came from a group of 'worker-peasant-soldier' students who were the product of the Revolution in Education, but took a more rigorously leftist line. They began with an assertive echo of Red Guard rhetoric: 'We should criticize revisionism and uphold Marxism ... We think we should be nothing but ordinary workers, the more ordinary the better!' Those students who thought otherwise were merely repeating the old idea that 'he who excels in learning can be an official' and that 'the highest are the wise and the lowest are stupid'.

A proletarian intellectual is nothing but a member of the worker ranks. Moreover, to train such a vast contingent we do not primarily rely on the university. The forefront of the three great revolutionary *movements is more important than ten, a hundred, or even one thousand universities. If the new-type socialist universities train nothing but plain, ordinary workers, then we can proudly say that they have completely destroyed the ladder for climbing to higher positions.*

The two opposing views were published in the Liaoning Daily *with an invitation to the reader to 'discuss and truly understand'. It was a rare example of real debate without editorial pre-judgement in the Chinese press. China did face genuine alternatives in the mid-1970s, and the Cultural Revolution had encouraged new forces in society capable of taking part in such a debate. But it had also generated factionalism and a warped political culture which debased most arguments into a distorted polemic. While the Liaoning students were arguing in public, secret discussions in the Party Politburo in Beijing were being conducted in a very different spirit which would lead to the final Deng Xiaoping–Gang of Four showdown a year later.*

The Maoist vision

There were two Cultural Revolutions. The first ended in July 1968 when Mao's reluctance to discipline the 'little generals' was finally overcome. Mao summoned the main Red Guard leaders in Beijing and reproached them for their lack of unity. A year's fighting was quite enough, and factionalism was creating 'tens of thousands of centres' throughout China.

Now, I am issuing a nation-wide notice. If anyone continues to oppose and fight the Liberation Army, destroy means of transportation, kill people, or set fires, he is committing a crime. Those few who turn a deaf ear to persuasion and persist in their behaviour are bandits, or Guomindang elements, subject to capture. If they continue to resist, they will be annihilated.

In Guangxi province, Lin Biao added, a thousand houses had been burnt down and no one was allowed to quench the flames—the same tactic used many years ago by the Guomindang generals whom he fought during the revolution. (So many people had been killed in Guangxi—many of them innocent victims of factional violence—that bodies floated down the Pearl River to emerge, bound and bloated, in Hong Kong harbour. Mao still spoke with a touch of indulgence towards the

Red Guards. Young people were entitled to make mistakes, and they reminded him of his own youth. But the people were tired of 'civil wars' between the factions. It was time now to send in the armed forces and the workers to restore order in the schools. These would be reopened under military supervision, accepting new students, while those Red Guards who should by now have graduated were to be sent to the countryside. Society, said Mao, was the biggest university.

In theory, power had now been 'seized' from the capitalist-roaders in the Party apparatus, and the new Revolutionary Committees, established at every level from factory or commune up to the province, had opened up management and government to popular participation. The bureaucrats had been chastened by criticism and by attendance at cadre schools in the countryside. Young people, the generation of revolutionary successors, were in the vanguard of social change, bridging the gap between town and village by going 'down to the countryside' to 'join the team and settle in a new household'. In reality a substantial transfer of authority had indeed taken place, and there was a genuine new spirit of involvement, but with certain important qualifications. First was the continuing struggle in the highest ranks of the leadership between the ultra-left and centre-left, which made ideology a battleground rather than a field for new ideas. This struggle was also diffused at lower levels, where policies were distorted into dogmas and political success usually depended upon their unquestioning implementation. Second was the dominance of the People's Liberation Army, which controlled more than one-third of the new Central Committee chosen at the Ninth Party Congress in 1969. Members of Revolutionary Committees, for example, visibly deferred to the army representative sitting democratically in their midst. Third was the continuing victimization of many of those detained in the first stage of the Cultural Revolution, often merely on the basis of past family or work connections or because they had been targets of the 1957 anti-rightist campaign.

Nevertheless, China now entered a second phase of Cultural Revolution in which an attempt was made to translate the Maoist egalitarian vision of the mid-1960s into an approximate social reality. Visitors to China saw an idealized but not wholly untruthful version of this. No tour was complete without a conversation with college students drawn from the ranks of 'worker-peasant-soldiers', another with students who had been 'sent down' to the countryside, a visit to a school-farm for city cadres (May Seventh Cadre School), a performance of a 'revolutionary opera', an inspection of a rural clinic run by 'barefoot doctors', and a session with a Revolutionary Committee in commune or factory. These were the *xinsheng shiwu*, the 'new (socialist) achievements', of the Cultural Revolution, and those taking part were the *shehuizhuyi de xinren*, the 'new socialist people'. Although the collective structure of the people's communes antedated the Cultural Revolution, its practical approach to organizing peasant labour through the year had been integrated with a coherent theory on how to move to a higher socialist level in the medium to long term. Many visitors were greatly impressed, finding evidence of what the British sociologist Peter Worsley described after his own visit as an 'alternative reality' which posed 'a moral challenge ... both to capitalism and to existing forms of Communist culture [in Eastern Europe]'. K. S. Karol, author of the most serious western attempt to grapple with the ideology of the Cultural Revolution, observed that 'Mao's words struck home to them [the Chinese students], as to their counterparts in Berlin, Rome, and Paris.' After my own first visit in 1971, I reported in the *Guardian* that I had observed 'a collective way of life ... which provides the moral imperatives for the youth of China'.

The possibility that this second Cultural Revolution offered any sort of desirable social goal or effective weapon against bureaucracy has been denied repeatedly by the post-Mao leadership. The 1981 Communist Party resolution summing up Chinese history since 1949 insisted that the Cultural Revolution 'did not in fact constitute a revolution or social progress in any sense, nor could it possibly have done so. It was we and not the enemy at all who were thrown into disorder by the "cultural revolution" ... It decidedly could not come up with any constructive programme, but could only bring grave disorder, damage, and retrogression in its train.' Examples of principled behaviour and self-sacrifice are either caricatured as a ritual response to political requirements of the time, or attributed to the efforts of good people to mitigate the worst evils. In this view, Mao's scathing comment on the public ethics of the Soviet Union under Stalin—

'there was supposed to be "selfless labour", but no one did an hour's more work and everyone thought about himself first'—could be paraphrased to apply to his own China. Common sense suggests that this is an excessive denial. Although enthusiasm faded, and in retrospect is often labelled by those personally involved as misconceived, it was a genuine factor in the great social movements of the time which cannot be accounted for solely by political coercion. One Red Guard recalls:

When I went to university in 1973, we former Red Guards met to exchange our experiences. We agreed that our stay with the people in the country had taught us the value of things—and of life itself.

Looking back dispassionately, whatever motivated Mao to launch the Cultural Revolution, some of the ideas which emerged from it are still valuable. The 'barefoot doctor' and 'barefoot teacher' system is certainly good for a country like China ... Basic things like how to read, write, and calculate can be taught very cheaply if they are organized by the local people themselves.

At the beginning of the Cultural Revolution I feel the ordinary people were exhilarated by their new right to criticize and even to attack their bosses. The suppressed humiliation that one suffers at the hands of a faceless bureaucracy builds up a resentment that is like the surging tide blocked by a dam.

Socialist new man might not be actually tilling the fields, but he could be perceived far-off on the horizon. The peasant leader of the model Dazhai brigade, Chen Yonggui, an honest man who would later become totally out of his depth in national politics, summed up what seemed a reasonable ideal: 'A man's ability may be great or small, but if he works heart and soul for the public, he is respected and ensured a secure life even if he has limited labour power.' The Great Leap goal of narrowing the 'three great differences' (between industry and agriculture, town and country, and manual and mental labour) was reasserted. Both at the material and spiritual level, many from outside China found much to admire. 'Visitors to China consistently report', wrote an agricultural specialist in *Scientific American* (June 1975), 'that the population appears to be healthy and adequately nourished.' The economist John Gurley observed correctly that China's pavements and streets were not covered with multitudes of sleeping, begging, hungry, and illiterate human beings'—one of the earliest achievements of commun-

ist rule after 1949—but went on to draw a sweeping conclusion:

Maoists believe that while a principal aim of nations should be to raise
the level of material welfare of the population, this should be done only
within the context of the development of human beings, encouraging
them to realize fully their manifold creative powers. And it should be
done only on an egalitarian basis—that is, on the basis that development is not worth much unless everyone rises together; no one is to be
left behind, either economically or culturally ... Development as a
trickle-down process is therefore rejected by Maoists.

Worrying signs of factional feuding in the Chinese leadership
were relegated to a subordinate place by those looking to China
for solutions to more general Third World problems. It was
assumed that the 'production in first place' mentality ascribed to
Liu Shaoqi had been liquidated for all time, and that, especially
after the 1975 National People's Congress, a broad consensus
had been forged under Zhou Enlai. 'What should not be in
doubt', wrote one commentator, 'is the shared commitment [in
the Chinese leadership] to completing the task of the "transition
to socialism", in spite of these controversies over the means and
the place of implementation, nor should this be blotted out by
the echoes of factional struggle too often magnified beyond their
proper volume by Western China-Watching techniques.' (I was
the author of this optimistic judgement.)

Revolution in education

The Revolution in Education, which between 1968 and 1976
sent over twelve million students to the countryside, and brought
some of them back to attend college along with a smaller
number of genuinely rural students, was the most visible 'new
achievement'. Mao had already sharply criticized the educational system in 1964–5. His remarks echoed themes already
discussed during the Great Leap Forward, and were meant to
provoke discussion rather than to prescribe alternatives. Examinations, he said, were a method of 'surprise attack' on the
students which should be changed completely—he suggested
publishing examination questions in advance so students could
learn through preparation. Too many teachers 'rambled on and
on', he said, and students were entitled to doze off when they did

so. The syllabuses were lifeless, the time spent studying was too long, and students were divorced from real life. 'We shouldn't read too many books', Mao told his startled colleagues (who nevertheless agreed hastily). 'We should read Marxist books, but not too many of them either. It will be enough to read a dozen or so.' After all, Gorky only had two years of primary education, and Franklin 'was originally a newspaper seller, yet he discovered electricity'. The Red Guards, not surprisingly, would welcome Mao's ideas. In September 1966 the Beijing No. 1 Girls' Middle School wrote a letter urging Mao to abolish college entrance exams:

> Quite a number of students have been indoctrinated with such gravely reactionary ideas of the exploiting classes as that 'book learning stands above all else', of 'achieving fame', 'becoming experts', 'making one's own way', 'taking the road of becoming bourgeois specialists', and so on. The present examination system encourages these ideas . . .
>
> We think that at a time when their world outlook is being formed, young people of 17 or 18 years old . . . should first of all get 'ideological diplomas' from the working class and the poor and lower-middle peasants. The Party will select the best . . . and send them on to higher schools.

At the start of the Cultural Revolution, Mao also revived the notion of 'all-round people' first put forward by Chen Boda in 1958. In the May Seventh Directive he instructed Lin Biao to ensure that the armed forces should study 'politics, industry and agriculture' as well as practising their military skills. Workers and peasants should also diversify, although their main tasks were still in industry and agriculture. The same held good for students: 'They should in addition to their studies learn other things, that is, industrial work, farming, and military affairs.' This did not constitute an alternative educational theory (and no one else dared to construct one except some foreign sympathizers who did so on China's behalf), yet it did suggest a very different spirit from the mixture of Confucian and Soviet pedagogy which the Chinese system had inherited.

When the schools and colleges reopened in the early 1970s, they possessed new features which to Western educationalists were recognizably 'progressive'. Schoolchildren took part in regular manual work—up to two months a year at secondary level (this had been done on a smaller scale before the Cultural Revolution). Local workers and residents served on school management committees, and taught useful skills in class. Tuition was still fairly formal, but there were few or no examinations. The 'key schools' were no longer supposed to practise selective admission of the most able or privileged. College education was completely transformed, with all curricula reduced to a maximum length of three years. All applicants were required to have three qualifications: (*a*) two to three years practical experience in factory, countryside, or armed forces; (*b*) the recommendation of their fellow-workers; (*c*) at least three years of secondary education (rather than the full five previously required). Students who could claim a 'worker-peasant-soldier' (*gongnongbing*) background were preferred. Practical work was stressed during university courses. Architecture students would work on building sites; language students would serve as waiters in hotels for foreigners; art students spent time on the factory floor before painting industrial themes. The underlying approach was known as 'open door schooling', which also involved a large number of short and part-time courses run by colleges for the community. Another directive by Mao (22 July 1968) had urged the setting-up of vocational colleges at the place of work. 'Students should be selected from among workers and peasants with practical experience, and they should return to production after a few years' study.' By 1973 there were twenty-three factory-run 'universities' in Shanghai, and Beijing's prestigious Qinghua University had twenty part-time lecturers from local factories. Universities also ran correspondence courses for peasants, and established 'branch schools' in the countryside.

The problem with the Revolution in Education lay not in its philosophy but in the highly charged political atmosphere which surrounded it. Mao had instructed that 'teaching material should have local character. Some material on the locality and the villages should be included.' But all textbooks were tightly controlled by the provincial or national authorities, and scrutinized so closely for 'incorrect' material that no one ventured to innovate. Recommendation 'by the masses' for a college place usually meant selection by the Party committee—sometimes of the offspring of influential cadres, at other times to get rid of trouble-makers. Teachers were reluctant to criticize students for fear of being criticized themselves. (A 12-year-old girl named Huang Shuai in Beijing became nationally famous for denouncing her teacher.) Many of the best university teachers were still condemned to menial tasks while their places were taken by the ambitious and the ill-qualified. 'Open door schooling' was often organized merely to satisfy the requirement for a fixed number of days spent away from college, with little educational value. It was not surprising that education became the new battleground in the mid-1970s between the leftists and the modernizers, or that, when they gained victory after Mao's death, the latter should condemn the whole period as 'ten wasted years'.

The ultra-left fostered its own model of 'going against the tide' in the dubious case of Zhang Tiesheng, the student who filed a 'blank exam paper' with a letter addressed to the authorities on the reverse. Zhang was sitting a college entrance test in 1973 after five years in the Liaoning countryside. Unable to complete it (critics later pointed out that he had not actually left it 'blank'), he protested against the new requirement for a written exam:

> To tell the truth, I have no respect for the bookworms who for many years have been taking it easy and have done nothing useful. I dislike them intensely. During the busy summer hoeing time, I just could not abandon my production task and hide myself in a small room to study. That would have been very selfish . . . I would have been condemned by my own revolutionary conscience.
>
> I have one consolation. I have not slowed the work of the collective because of the examination . . . The few hours of the examination may disqualify me from college and I have nothing further to say.

But he had, spoiling the effect by going on to claim that given a couple of days' study he could have passed the test. He was then successful in a second 'supplementary test', arranged specially for him by the authorities. His letter was published in the provincial newspaper and then nationally, and Zhang was rewarded with a place in college. He later published an embroidered account of the famous exam: he had dozed off in the lunchtime break and had to climb into the examination room through the window. He could more or less have answered the questions, but felt that they were not a proper test of real ability.

Revolution in health

The Revolution in Public Health, another 'newly born achievement' which attracted favourable attention abroad, showed similar strengths and weaknesses. It too was based on a pre-

Cultural Revolution directive from Mao (26 June 1985) criticizing the Ministry of Health for its bureaucratic ways, and stating that the centre of gravity for medical work should shift to the rural areas. ('The Ministry of Health', Mao said, 'is not a Ministry for the people, so why not change its name to ... the Ministry of Urban Gentlemen's Health?') Training periods were shortened to three years for doctors and between six months and a year for 'barefoot doctors' (paramedics). Many urban doctors were sent to improve rural health services, and research was directed away from complex areas to 'the prevention and improved treatment of common diseases ... the masses' greatest needs'. New rural clinics were opened, and others which had been closed since the Great Leap were reopened. The most visible reform was the nation-wide introduction of a rural co-operative medical scheme by 1968, organized at the brigade or commune level. A similar scheme during the Great Leap had failed because peasant incomes were too low to subsidize it effectively. Although the co-operative system was open to abuse by local cadres who claimed preferential treatment, its positive role has not been seriously challenged by post-Mao reformers. But it became a casualty of the reaction against collective organization and a return to individual peasant 'responsibility' for the land in the early 1980s.

Health also became a political battlefield. In 1976 *Spring Shoots*, a feature film in praise of barefoot doctors, was widely promoted by the ultra-left propaganda apparatus as a work which 'reflects the maturing of barefoot doctors and new socialist sprouts in the thick of the struggle between the proletariat and the bourgeoisie'. It told the story of Chun-miao, a young woman peasant who seeks to become a barefoot doctor after seeing a baby wrongly treated by a local witch-doctor and then allowed to die by the commune hospital. Eventually she is allowed to study at the hospital, but her efforts to learn are 'obstructed by the bourgeoisie'. 'Using an injection needle is not the same as wielding a hoe', she is told. 'Filled with indignation', she returns to the village, gathers herbs, and makes the round with a medical kit. Eventually a plot to frame her by administering a toxic injection to a peasant for whom she is caring (a poor peasant naturally) is exposed. The villains are denounced, and the hospital returns to the hands of the people.

A year later the same film was being condemned in anti-Gang of Four propaganda as a big poisonous weed which slandered the leadership of the Communist Party (responsible for running the hospital) and, worse still, 'advocates spontaneous mass movements' for medical reform! Between these two extremes there was little room for serious discussion of the uses and limitations of barefoot doctors. (A new play, *Loyal Hearts*, staged in 1978, gave a very different picture of the Revolution in Health. It told the story of how an old doctor was accused of being a 'bourgeois specialist' and prevented from conducting research into heart disease. 'I simply wanted to do some medical research in order to cure more patients!', he cries. 'Is this a crime?') In 1980 the Minister of Public Health Qian Xinzhong said that 'under the slogan of putting the stress on the rural areas, medical and health work in cities, factories, and mines was weakened'. Certainly there was a shift of resources to the countryside at the expense of the urban system, although some basic-level urban services were extended in compensation.

Rural revolution

From outside it was the collective structure of the people's communes which most often impressed those with experience of rural dislocation and urban immigration elsewhere in the Third World, or of the errors of Soviet collectivization in the 1930s. By the early 1970s, a coherent theory seemed to have emerged on how this post-Great Leap structure would in time evolve towards a higher level of socialism. China appeared to have struck a rational balance between individual and collective interest within a socialist framework which linked the further socialization of production and distribution to material as well as political factors. Accounts were kept and the proceeds of work were distributed mostly at the basic 'team' (village) level. But larger enterprises which would benefit the community—irrigation dams, roads, rural industry, secondary schools, and so on were handled by the higher-level commune. The intermediate-level brigade would frequently run smaller enterprises, primary schools and often a co-operative medical scheme. The individual peasant in the team could still increase his or her income by working harder and earning more work-points, which would be converted into cash in the annual 'share-out'. But the value of these was aggregated at the village level, so that the industrious to some extent supported those who were less strong or able. (The system also benefited the more lazy, as post-Mao critics complained but few remarked at the time.) The lesson of the Great Leap Forward had apparently been learnt. There would be no 'leaping ahead' to a higher stage of socialist collectivization regardless of local circumstances. Progress to a higher stage— transferring the accounting level from teams to the brigade and eventually to the commune—was to wait until sufficient material progress had been made for all those participating to benefit more or less equally from pooling their resources. Precise figures were set. Transfer of land ownership back to the commune from the villages would only be allowed when:

(*a*) the economy of the commune as a whole has developed so far that the cash income per inhabitant exceeds 400–500 *yuan* . . .

(*b*) the commune-owned sector has attained absolute preponderance [more than 50 per cent] within the economy of the commune as a whole.

(*c*) the income of the poorest teams has caught up with that of the more prosperous; and

(*d*) mechanization has reached at least the half-way point.

The transition from collective to state ownership was even further away. But in the meantime each team contributed 'cheap' labour, especially in the slack season, for the construction of collective projects which would provide the material basis for this gradual progression. The strategy of incremental advance towards the point where the collective unit could be expanded was explained in Mao's own province of Hunan as:

To actively develop the commune and brigade enterprises, expand the accumulation of the commune and brigade, purchase large farm machinery which the production teams have no means to purchase themselves, build farmland and water conservancy projects which they also cannot manage by themselves, and help the poorer production teams to develop production . . . Speaking in the long term, ownership in the people's communes always advances from ownership by the small collective to ownership by the big collective and then to ownership by the whole people.

The hidden weaknesses of the system and the existence of large areas where rural poverty remained extreme were not easily visible (see Chapter 7). It still remains unclear how widespread was the pressure to advance the transition, contrary to the guidelines quoted above, 'ahead of time', as has since been alleged. Even Zhang Chunqiao's 1975 polemic on the need to limit 'bourgeois rights' had insisted that 'the wind of "communization" ... shall never be allowed to rise again', and that changes would only occur 'over a fairly long time'.

Revolution in leadership

Another 'achievement' of the early 1970s was the Revolutionary Committee which replaced local government organs up to the provincial level and also provided a collective substitute for the administration or management in factories, schools, and all other standard units into which China is divided. At the government level, the Committee was a device to harmonize the different interest groups which emerged during the first Cultural Revolution, typically, the 'rebel' radicals, the Party cadres, and the armed forces. Painfully, between January 1967 and September 1968 the twenty-nine provinces, autonomous regions, and major cities set up their Committees (the earlier ones had a more radical complexion than those at the end, which were dominated by the army). In the enterprises the magic three-thirds formula was varied: workers, cadres, and technicians in the factory; teachers, parents, and students in the school. Sometimes it was expressed in terms of 'old' (cadres), 'middle-aged' (technicians), and 'young' (workers). Meaningless in some cases, in others the formula did reduce conflict and incorporate new voices into the political system, but before long the post-1971 search for unity rehabilitated many cadres and reduced the radical influence.

In 1974 a new round of wall-posters appeared on the walls of Beijing for the first time since the Red Guard movement. Their authors had evidently taken heart from the Tenth Party Congress (1973), which wrote into the Party constitution a new clause saying that it was 'absolutely impermissible to suppress criticism and retaliate' against those who exercised their right to complain to the authorities. They were also encouraged by the new Party Vice-Chairman, Wang Hongwen, presented as the proletarian ideal of new China, who told the Congress that 'we must ... constantly use the weapons of arousing the masses to air their views

freely, write big-character posters, and hold great debates ...'
Yet the 1974 posters had a spontaneous character, although their
authors took advantage of the license granted by Wang to 'go
against the tide' and criticize authority. In Beijing six writers
describing themselves as 'worker rebels' put up a poster of
complaint in June 1984:

We worker rebels joined the Beijing Revolutionary Committee during
the great Cultural Revolution in a Great Alliance with the peasants,
students, and Red Guards, but no one took any notice of us! The
authorities said 'The Rebels can fight but they should not sit down.'
They repressed the Red Guards and told the Rebels to go back to work.
The result is that out of 24 workers on the Committee only one
remains, which is just four per cent of the total. Many of the Rebels
have been dubbed as counter-revolutionary elements. They have been
arrested, struggled with, reassigned, dismissed, and suspended.

Other posters revealed a call for more industrial democracy by
factory workers who took seriously the 'Two Participations'
(cadres taking part in work and workers taking part in management—another 'new achievement'). There were claims that
protesting workers had been laid off, that posters were banned
upon factory premises, and that factory revolutionary committees failed to meet. The official press published reports of posters
which criticized factory managers for attempting to reintroduce
bonuses and for stifling 'the revolutionary enthusiasm of the
masses', but there were also less orthodox, unreported expres-
sions of workers' dissent, including strikes (which were to be
legalized in the new 1975 state constitution). Matters came to a
head in the summer of 1975 in Hangzhou, where industrial unrest
spread to twenty-five factories and required army intervention to
settle. It is said that Wang Hongwen, who in theory championed
the workers' right to strike, was first sent by Deng Xiaoping to
handle the situation and totally failed. The strike was settled by
improvements in collective welfare for the workers and by
arranging for cadres to 'participate in labour' as they were
supposed to. But Hangzhou's real significance was the emergence of an assertive workforce, partly radicalized by the Cultural Revolution, whose demands were unpalatable to all leadership factions in Beijing. Even the behaviour of the Shanghai
workers who denounced the restoration of quotas (under the
slogan 'Let's be masters of the wharf, not the slaves of tonnage'),

though acceptable for propaganda purposes to the ultra-left, implied a rejection of 'unreasonable' Party control. While condemning managerial 'economism', the workers' argument was ultimately based on sound materialist grounds: the work would be achieved more successfully and under better working conditions if they were not obliged to pursue rigid targets. (One shift of dockers, for example, could more usefully prepare the ground for a second shift to unload cargo than attack the task itself by merely unloading the most accessible items.)

The final struggle

In January 1975, at the long-delayed Fourth National People's Congress, Zhou Enlai made his last public appearance outside hospital to deliver the crucial 'Report on the work of the government' which set the policy guidelines for the whole country. Zhou revived a target date originally set by Mao himself for substantial economic development by the end of the century—the 'Year 2000', by which time China should have become a strong socialist industrial country capable of making 'a bigger contribution to mankind' (Mao, November 1956). Zhou now presented a two-stage economic plan. The first, which in theory had been operating since 1965, would build a 'relatively comprehensive' industrial and economic system by 1980. The second, which would run from 1980 to 2000, was to achieve 'the comprehensive modernization in agriculture, industry, defence, and science and technology'. Thus the Four Modernizations appeared on the political agenda. Zhou sought to validate them by reminding his audience that he had mentioned them, with Mao's approval, at the last Congress in 1964.

The NPC convened in an apparent spirit of compromise. It elected a strong team of Vice-Premiers spanning the political spectrum. After Deng Xiaoping and Zhang Chunqiao came former finance minister Li Xiannian. The 'new left' of the Cultural Revolution had three places, including Chen Yonggui, the peasant leader of the model Dazhai Brigade. They were matched by three ministers with experience in economic planning and construction, including Yu Qiuli who had almost single-handedly written China's interim one-year plans since the Cultural Revolution began. Control of the armed forces was balanced between Deng Xiaoping as chief of staff and Zhang Chunqiao as head of the political department. The appointment of this new team with an emphasis on economic expertise also seemed to indicate a political consensus for the new strategy. Deng, in charge of the team, now effectively ran Zhou's state apparatus as the Premier returned to spend the last year of his life in hospital.

But behind the scenes a bitter factional struggle had already broken out in which Mao played an ambiguous role. It came after months of indirect sniping at Zhou Enlai and Deng Xiaoping by the ultra-left. They had taken control of a propaganda campaign originally authorized by Mao, to 'Criticize Lin Biao and Confucius', publishing barely disguised attacks on Zhou Enlai as the Duke of Zhou (founder of the Zhou dynasty and traditionally the source of the Way which Confucius developed). At the heart of the new dispute were legitimate questions of economic strategy, particularly concerning how far China should seek foreign imports of new technology and how they should be paid for. The reopening of relations with the US in 1971 had led to a shopping spree in which thirty complete industrial plants were purchased from the West in 1973–4 alone, worth some US $2,000 million. A second round concentrating on the energy sector was now proposed. But this debate was intertwined with a struggle for the post-Zhou and post-Mao succession, which falsified any attempt at serious argument. The struggle had begun with the 'Fengqing' affair and would not end until Mao's death nearly two years later. Its intense and intricate nature is revealed by the record of the first few weeks:

4 October 1974. Mao proposes that Deng should be elected First Vice-Premier of the State Council at the NPC.

17 October. At a meeting of the Politburo, Deng has a row with Jiang Qing over the Chinese-built freighter 'Fengqing'. The ship, though hailed in the media as the first 10,000 ton ship built in China, has a poor performance which for Deng indicates the futility of a narrow policy of 'self-reliance'. Deng walks out of the meeting, and the Politburo is unable to reconvene for more than a month.

18 October Jiang Qing sends Wang Hongwen to Changsha where Mao is resting, to sow doubt in his mind about the relationship between Zhou and Deng. He is to insinuate that 'although the Premier is hospitalized, he is busy summoning people for talks far into the night', and that 'the atmosphere in Beijing is now very much like that of the Lushan meeting [in July 1959]'. Wang is rebuffed by Mao, and told (according to the later version) not to 'gang up' with Jiang Qing.

On the same day, Mao's two interpreters, Wang Hairong (his niece) and Tang Wensheng, due to take some foreign guests to meet him in Changsha, are summoned to the Diaoyutai Guesthouse. Jiang Qing asks them to make a report to Mao about the 'Fengqing' incident. Zhang Chunqiao tells them that some 'leading members of the State Council [are] worshipping everything foreign and spending too much on imports, thus causing state deficits'. Wang and Tang rush to tell Premier Zhou what they have been asked to do. Zhou explains that Deng Xiaoping has been baited many times at Politburo meetings, and has restrained himself till now.

20 October. After Mao has seen the foreign guests, Wang and Tang pass on the story (as interpreted by Zhou, they later claim, not by Jiang Qing). Mao is very angry, dismissing the freighter row as a trifle which has already been settled. He sends them back to Beijing with an 'instruction': The Premier should remain in charge. Matters relating to the National People's Congress and new appointments should be 'handled jointly' by Zhou and Wang Hongwen. Deng should be appointed First Vice-Premier, a Vice-Chairman of the Party, and Vice-Chairman of the Party Military Committee.

But Mao would change his mind again, failing to attend the Congress or even send it an opening message. The *People's Daily* on 9 February quoted a new 'instruction' from him warning that 'lack of clarity' on the need to 'exercise dictatorship over the bourgeoisie' would 'lead to revisionism'. The editorial clearly labelled Deng Xiaoping's group as 'sham Marxists' and reproached the mainstream Maoists—leaders such as Chen Yonggui—with having 'muddled ideas of one kind or another . . .' This was soon followed by two polemical articles by Zhang Chunqiao and Yao Wenyuan which plunged the country into a new campaign to 'study the theory of the dictatorship of the proletariat'.

The flawed debate

The articles by Yao and Zhang, backed up in the official press, presented an ambiguous mixture of serious theoretical argument and vicious polemic. Their starting-point, already endorsed by Mao and capable of being supported by carefully chosen quotes from Marx and Lenin, was the persistence of inequality under socialism and of the conditions in which a 'new bourgeoisie' could re-form. Mao provided the authority with an 'instruction' which reflected that, although China's system of ownership had changed, it still possessed an 'unequal' wage-system and a commodity economy which was not so different from that under capitalism. It would be quite easy, he reflected moodily, 'for people like Lin Biao to push the capitalist system, if they came to power'.

A group of theoretical workers in Shanghai, under Zhang Chunqiao's guidance, had been preparing since 1971 a new textbook on the political economy of socialism. Their work (no doubt nudged in the desired direction by Zhang) strongly emphasized the 'incomplete' aspects of socialist society which provided the material basis for the possibility of the emergence of a new bourgeoisie and the restoration of capitalism. Echoing Mao, they argued that 'many cultural revolutions' would be required to prevent this happening, until the surviving capitalist factors in the 'relations of production' (ownership, distribution, and management) had all been eliminated. Only when this had been done would the material basis for a new 'privileged class' have been eliminated.

The political cutting edge of this theory of 'capitalist restoration' (which had originated in Mao's view that such a restoration had already occurred in the Soviet Union) lay in the assertion by Yao and Zhang that a new bourgeois class could be formed *within the ranks of the Communist Party itself*, and indeed that in some areas this 'new bourgeoisie' was already in place. The ideological form of such a restoration, it was argued, would be a new 'theory of productive forces'. Thus the target was pinpointed as Zhou and Deng, the champions of the Four Modernizations. The argument also underlined the necessity of maintaining forward progress in the development of new 'socialist achievements' and in the struggle to substitute the new for the old. The Cultural Revolution, it implied, must be resumed. One ultra-left polemicist wrote:

Socialist new things may look somewhat weak and not deep-rooted at the start, but they are full of revolutionary vigour. Compared to the old things which seem strong and deep-rooted but reek of decay, they have a fine future for development... The development of new things always proceeds from superficial to deep, from weak to strong, and from a low to a higher level. A big revolutionary movement, like the turbulent Yangtze rushing down from the gorges on the upper reaches to swell at the mouth, must pass through a process involving a beginning, a climax, and a deepening stage.

This call for a new revolutionary tide—Yao liked to say that 'the tide of history is just like a river'—was given a precise political target by Zhang. One-half of his article was a rational discussion of the 'incomplete' nature of socialist ownership in China. He pointed out that state ownership in industry accounted for nearly all the fixed assets but only 63 per cent of the industrial population, while agriculture was almost entirely still in collective hands, and hence that the issue of ownership had 'not yet been entirely settled'. The persistence of the 'capitalist factors' discussed above meant necessarily that 'new bourgeois elements would be engendered'. Then abruptly shifting style and mood, Zhang attacked his real target:

There are undeniably some comrades among us who have joined the Communist Party organizationally but not ideologically. In their world outlook they have not yet overstepped the bounds of small production and of the bourgeoisie. They do approve of the dictatorship of the proletariat at a certain stage and within a certain sphere and are pleased with certain victories of the proletariat, because these will bring them some gains; once they have secured their gains, they feel it's time to settle down and feather their cosy nests. As for exercising all-round dictatorship over the bourgeoisie, as for going on after the first step on the 10,000 *li* march, sorry, let others do the job; here is my stop and I must get off the bus. We would like to offer a piece of advice to these comrades: it's dangerous to stop half-way! The bourgeoisie is beckoning to you. Catch up with the ranks and continue to advance!

Deng regarded these documents correctly as a declaration of war, and decided to take on his enemies while Mao was still alive and all around him hesitated. In the summer of 1975 Deng launched a counter-attack on the ultra-left. He called them 'sham Marxist political swindlers' and announced his intention of purging them from the Party. 'These anti-Marxist class enemies', it was said in the first important document (the

General Programme of Work) which Deng inspired in his role as deputy for Zhou Enlai, 'have stepped into the shoes of Lin Biao. They take over our revolutionary slogans all the time, distort them, twist them, and appropriate them for their own use, mix up black and white, confound right and wrong.' Judging correctly that the ultra-left would overreach itself and that accounts would be settled after Mao's death, Deng challenged them on their own ground, orchestrating a critique of leftist policies in education, led by the Minister of Education Zhou Rongxin. Other documents inspired by Deng in 1975–6 dealt with problems of industrial development and science and technology, where he argued that China had fallen dangerously behind. He rephrased his provocative view that the colour of the cat did not matter so long as it could catch the mice. The best scientists, he said, should be 'red and expert', but those who were 'white and expert' could also serve China. They were a much greater asset than 'those who just lie idle, cause factional fighting, and hold up everything'. With a touch of Mao's scatological style, Deng denounced the Gang and their followers as the sort of people who would 'sit on the lavatory and not do a shit'.

The argument on foreign trade and economic strategy also continued. An anti-Jiang Qing cartoon published after the Gang's arrest would show her shouting 'Foreign slave! Compradore' at an unseen Deng Xiaoping, while wearing a wig made in France and false teeth made in Japan. Total two-way trade had already increased significantly from some US $3.9 billion in 1969 to 14 billion in 1975. Trade deficits were incurred in 1974–5 for the first time, and China had begun to purchase complete plant from the West on deferred terms, although still refusing to accept foreign loans. Deng proposed to modernize the Chinese coal and oil industry through the import of new technology, to be paid back out of future production. More generally, he argued that for China to 'catch up' with the advanced world, it must study foreign technology with an open mind and import it where required. Technology was international, argued Deng. 'Dismantle any imported product and you will find that many of its parts are from yet other countries.' Raw materials should also be imported if the alternative was idle production lines. Oil customers should be sought in Europe as well as Japan in return for 'fine technical equipment'. The ultra-left seized on the target presented by Deng, but countered it in chauvinistic terms:

We absolutely cannot place our hopes for realizing the four modernizations on imports. If we do not rely mainly on our own efforts but, as Deng Xiaoping advocated, rely solely on importing foreign techniques, copying foreign designs and technological processes and patterning our equipment on foreign models, we will forever trail behind foreigners and our country's development of technology and even its entire national economy will fall under the control of foreign monopoly capital ... China would be reduced step by step to a raw materials supplying base for imperialism and social-imperialism, a market for their commodities, and an outlet for their investments.

The educational debate was resumed in an atmosphere of tragicomedy. Zhang Tiesheng, the student with the 'blank paper', now toured the country as a spokesman for the ultra-left attacking Minister Zhou Rongxin. Zhou complained that 'culture' and even 'socialist conscience' had become forbidden words. He did not object to students being selected from the working-class, but asked why after graduation they had to go back to being 'simple workers' instead of using their talents as technicians and cadres. Zhang Tiesheng challenged Zhou to a debate, which was widely believed to have precipitated a heart attack from which Zhou died soon afterwards. After the Gang's fall Zhang was denounced in the press as 'not worth a horse's fart' (he had trained as a veterinary student), and was later gaoled as a counter-revolutionary. A young man who found himself totally out of his depth, Zhang Tiesheng illustrates how the potential material for serious discussion, based on the ideals of the Cultural Revolution, was turned so easily into farce by its warped political culture.

Confrontation

At noon on 5 April 1976, with Mao Zedong just five months from death, China's supreme leaders—several of them barely on speaking terms—gathered in the Great Hall of the People to watch an amazing event outside. On the previous day thousands of Beijing citizens had come to Tiananmen Square with wreaths to mourn the recent death of Premier Zhou Enlai. (The Gang of Four had tried, unsuccessfully, to ban the sale of crepe paper in the mourning colour of white.) Slogans, letters, poems, and cartoons had been held aloft, pasted to the marble sides of the Martyrs' Memorial, or chalked on the polished stone pavement. One or two were written in blood and read out by their authors. A banner saying 'We mourn the Premier' was launched, suspended from a bunch of balloons. During the night, all the wreaths were removed from the square by pro-Gang militia. The demonstrators returned on the morning of the 5th, and furious quarrels broke out with militia and policemen on the steps of the Great Hall. Soon after noon, the first car was set on fire. Later on, a police station was also set alight. The square was eventually cleared by force as darkness fell.

All of this was watched by the leadership from inside the Hall, through binoculars which aides had hastily provided to help them read the slogans and follow the action on the other side of the square. No one had any doubt that by demonstrating *for* the late Premier, the crowd was also demonstrating *against* the ultra-left leadership. The question to be asked—and ten years later it had still not been satisfactorily answered—was whether it was spontaneous or had been stirred up. Zhang Chunqiao had no doubt. Laying down his binoculars, he turned to Deng Xiaoping and accused him of having organized the demonstration. Zhang 'scolded Deng face to face', according to the account given four years later at the trial of the Gang of Four, and called him 'an ugly traitor'. Within days, Mao had been persuaded to dismiss Deng from all his Party offices, and Zhang, the number two in the ultra-left leadership, wrote triumphantly to his son that the struggle for the succession had been decided. But he was wrong.

CHAPTER SIX

Economics in Command

THE MODERNIZATION OF CHINA

'It is not a question of whether we achieve the Four Modernizations', said the cadre at the banquet table in the headquarters of Shengli (Victory) Oilfield. 'It is only a question of how soon we achieve the targets ahead of time.' Shengli is planted on the eastern coast in Shandong province, on low-lying, poor, and alkaline land. In the village next door to the oilfield headquarters, the peasants could be seen defecating into open cesspits, whipped by the cold wind blowing across the salt marshes from the Yellow River.

The oilfield cadre was not concerned with the local people—they were the responsibility of the county government. Shengli's workers had all come from outside, mobilized into a General Battle Headquarters under the Ministry of Petroleum. At first they lived in mud hovels with straw stacked a foot high on the roofs like those of the peasants. Now they had cinemas, schools, and new apartment blocks.

The time was September 1978 and oil was China's Magic Weapon. With the profits from expanding oil production, said the cadre, China would fund the foreign imports for Chairman Hua Guofeng's Four Modernizations of Agriculture, Industry, Science and Technology, and National Defence. In northern Hebei province, in the South China Sea, oil had been found so sweet and so sulphur-free that the Japanese would gorge themselves on it.

The Four Modernizations was a Magnificent Plan, Chairman Hua had said, to build China by the Year 2000 into a Powerful Socialist Country so that its economy would rank as among the Most Advanced in the World. The current Ten Year Plan had started two years late, but it did not matter.

The state plans to build or complete [by 1985] 120 large-scale projects, including ten iron and steel complexes, nine non-ferrous metal complexes, eight coal mines, ten oil and gas fields, thirty power stations, six new trunk railways, and five key harbours. [This] ... will provide China with fourteen fairly strong and fairly rationally located industrial bases and will be decisive in changing the backward state of our basic industries.

Outside the Shengli headquarters a roadside poster promoted the Four Modernizations. Against the background of the figure '2000', pierced by a speeding rocket, stood a worker, peasant, and soldier, looking resolutely ahead over a landscape of oil derricks, factory complexes, and satellite dishes. The peasants' carts, piled high with winter fodder, shambled past the hoarding, their drivers wrapped in sacking against the cold.

(Visit to Shengli Oilfield, Nov. 1978)

The economic plateau

By the 1970s China had reached an economic plateau at which the Maoist policy of 'hard struggle and self-reliance', though admired by many abroad as a superior model of development for the Third World, offered diminishing returns to the Chinese people. A healthier, better educated, better organized population lived, still mostly in rural areas, on land which had been considerably improved through the massive application of labour-intensive inputs. Grain production had at least kept pace with the rapid increase in population, and higher yields were achieved on the same or even smaller sown areas. Industrial development had tripled steel production, laid the foundation for a significant petroleum industry, created a machine-building industry virtually from scratch, and provided the base for China to become a nuclear power. Light industry provided a reasonable flow of consumer goods by comparison with, for example, the Soviet Union, although still a long way below potential demand. In spite of political disruptions, China held together as a coherent economic entity with nation-wide communications and functioning mechanisms for shifting surpluses to areas of need. The first World Bank report on China concluded that Chinese development had been impressive: GNP per capita had grown at between 2 and 2.5 per cent per annum during 1957–77 in spite of a 2 per cent per annum population growth rate. This compared with an average growth rate of only 1.6 per cent for other low-income countries. Net output of industry grew at an annual average of 10.2 per cent during 1957–79, well above the average for other low-income countries of 5.4 per cent. The World Bank report 'regard[ed] China's most remarkable achievement over three decades as making its low-income groups far better off in terms of basic needs compared with their counterparts in most other poor countries'.

Yet for a variety of reasons China could no longer continue on this path. A high psychological price had been paid by which self-reliance led to self-destructive isolation during the Cultural Revolution. This further reduced the motivation, difficult to sustain at best of times, for the Chinese population to work harder indefinitely for the sake of far-off rewards. The abandonment of the policy of 'containment' by the United States offered China choices in economic strategy which had not been available before and were immediately seized. In 1971–3 China signed contracts for US $1.8 billion worth of imports of machinery and equipment. It was also becoming apparent that the Maoist model was not so different from the Soviet model of centralized planning with excessive emphasis upon heavy industry, which it had set out to avoid. China suffered from most of the defects of the Soviet and other planned socialist economies. Incomes rose much more slowly than GNP; hardly at all in the rural areas. Far too high a proportion of the national income was 'accumulated' by the state for investment rather than passed back to the producer to stimulate 'consumption'. (The rate was an average of 33 per cent in the first half of the 1970s.) Industrial growth was based on huge investment spurred by the high rate of accumulation, but output per unit of fixed capital actually declined. In spite of the policy of putting agriculture first, the peasants continued to be starved on investment funds and were poorly rewarded for their produce. Urban incomes were twice as high as those in the countryside, where inequalities between rich and poor areas persisted. The system of centralized 'command planning' encouraged wasteful use and duplication of resources in industry. The domination of planning by the Party also discouraged innovation and experiment which might lead those responsible to be criticized. The decentralization of industry to the interior of the country for defence reasons also duplicated scarce resources. Meanwhile, shortages in consumer goods, with privileged access to goods in short supply by Party and government cadres, further reduced popular commitment to what was sometimes referred to as 'socialism which we cannot eat'.

The reforms take off

Previous attempts at reform of the systems of planning and production had been contained within a framework of socialist thinking which always put 'politics first'. Material incentives, autonomy for enterprises, the encouragement of competition, pricing goods according to the real cost of production, and similar proposals were judged on political as well as economic grounds. The decade of reform which began in the late 1970s saw a steady loosening of these constraints, as socialism was first redefined and later more or less put to one side. The scene by 1989, with agriculture effectively privatized and the profit motive now accepted as the dominant force throughout the economy, was unimaginable at the start of the decade. 'Having mounted the saddle', Trotsky had written of the unknown art of organizing a socialist economy, 'the rider is obliged to guide the horse in peril of breaking his neck.' In China the horse was soon galloping in a very different direction.

At first, when new priorities were asserted after Mao's death, it was done in a hyperbolic style which owed much to the recent past. The rhetoric of round-number targets and millenarian goals was deployed by cadres who effortlessly switched slogans from those of the Cultural Revolution. The 'magnificent plan' of the Four Modernizations, proclaimed by Hua Guofeng (appointed Party chairman after Mao's death at the Eleventh Party Congress in August 1977), legitimized the shift to economic objectives by claiming continuity with Mao's own concern to 'catch up and surpass' advanced world levels of production and technology 'at an early date'. Hua's grandiose plans, requiring continued high levels of accumulation and investment at the expense of consumption and living standards, helped to make the initial turn from Politics to Economics in Command more acceptable, but soon proved unrealistic.

The economic 'readjustment' of 1979–80 (later extended to 1982–3), which strengthened the hand of Deng Xiaoping's reformers, scaled down Hua's targets and sought to remedy the imbalances in the Chinese economy, boosting consumption instead of accumulation, raising farm prices at the expense of industry, and focusing on infrastructural needs—transport, energy, and communications—while reining back the grandiose goals of heavy industry (particularly where they involved expensive imports of foreign technology). It also began to tackle the over-concentration of authority in economic management and recognized a growing problem of urban unemployment. But it was anchored by the admission—unthinkable only two or three years before—that the Chinese people were still mostly poorly fed and badly housed, and unimpressed with a socialism that could not remedy either condition. Deng Xiaoping's veteran colleague and critic of the Great Leap Forward, Chen Yun, later to be a critic of Deng's reforms too as they began to break orthodox boundaries, warned of the consequences of continued popular hardship in a memorable speech. There are four main reasons, he said in the spring of 1979, why people criticized the Hua Guofeng leadership in spite of its achievements in liquidating the Gang of Four:

(1) They understand things that were not understood before. For example, they point out that workers abroad have a higher standard of living than workers here ...

(2) They are not willing to swallow the same old line. For example, the slogan that the situation is good—and yet you need a ration coupon to eat. You have to stand in line to buy commodities. In this situation you can mouth slogans all day without filling your stomach.

(3) They want to be reapers of the harvest, not offerings to adorn a tomb. They want to live well in this present life. Since Communism is a kind of heaven, they are willing to leave it for the next generation to enjoy.

(4) They are impatient and tired of waiting. They feel they have been waiting thirty years and now have to wait another thirty years ... They say: You cadres have already been rewarded for your suffering. Why must we the people go on suffering without end?

The route to communism did not lie through enforced accumulation of state funds to invest in industry and public works while material conditions failed to improve. The Hua leadership was criticized for allowing the national income percentage of accumulation to rise from 30.9 per cent in 1976 to 36.5 per cent in 1978, a rate exceeded only during the Great Leap. Such a rate, said the critics, occurred at a time when the Chinese population had increased by more than two hundred million in the past fifteen years, while living standards had not improved, average incomes had hardly risen, and problems in welfare, housing, education, and health had in many areas actually worsened. As Deng was to explain:

During the 'Cultural Revolution' there was a view that poor communism was preferable to rich capitalism. After I resumed office in the central leadership in 1974 and 1975, I criticized that view. Because I refuted that view, I was brought down again.... The main task of socialism is to develop the productive forces, steadily improve the life of the people, and keep increasing the material wealth of the society. Therefore, there can be no communism with pauperism, or socialism with pauperism. So to get rich is no sin (2 Sept. 1986).

As the reforms developed and deepened, theory struggled to catch up with practice and to explain it in politically acceptable terms. The Hua Guofeng leadership had reasserted economic against political priorities but still maintained that Chinese socialism was well advanced and capable of attaining high targets. After Hua it was conceded that China had progressed very little distance along the transition to socialism. This now legitimized a widening range of incentives and the encouragement of market forces. The planned economy remained supreme in theory but increasingly the reforms led into areas which challenged its domination and undermined the parallel supremacy of state ownership. The wider targets of reform may be summarized as follows:

(i) the need for enterprise autonomy involving a system of profit retention. This would only stimulate production effectively if decision making power was devolved to the enterprise management and not to the local government or Party hitherto responsible for the enterprise. Real autonomy would also require provisions for hiring and firing labour (abolishing the 'iron rice bowl' or unconditional guarantee of jobs to those already in employment) and a bankruptcy law as the ultimate sanction for inefficiency.

(ii) the need for price reform which would eliminate hidden subsidies to both producer and consumer, and ensure that resources and products were not over-ordered or over-produced or stockpiled and allowed to go to waste. This would involve the shedding by the state of responsibility for fixing prices for all except a very small number of essential goods and services.

(iii) the need for a market not just in goods and services but in labour (the selling of skills and job mobility), housing and land (to replenish the ageing stock of urban housing and discourage wasteful use of 'free' land by enterprises), and capital (enabling enterprises and entrepreneurs to raise funds for expansion either by more readily available loans or from stocks or bonds).

Deng Xiaoping sought to channel these new ideas into an acceptable package labelled 'Socialism with Chinese characteristics'. But by 1984 he had begun to part company from Chen Yun and other conservatives for whom reform meant returning to the ideas—mostly their ideas—of the mid-1950s, which they had labelled the 'economic laws of socialism'. Most younger reformers no longer accepted such laws, and believed that China was now engaged on an exploration of new territory. Not far below the surface lurked the thought that if 'skipping the capitalist stage of development' had weakened China's ability to enter into socialism, perhaps some of the features of that stage should be restored.

The rapid progression of economic theory to keep pace with the escalation of reform is well illustrated by the writing of the leading economist Xue Muqiao. Xue was a liberal associated with the Chen Yun group who since the middle 1950s had, whenever possible, argued against the high level of accumulation and in favour of relaxing the planning structure, but he also (like most of his colleagues) clung to some elements of Maoist orthodoxy. Xue was only able to resume work on his research into socialist economics after the Cultural Revolution, bringing out a standard textbook in 1979. His first edition stated as 'economic laws of socialism' a set of propositions which Mao himself would have accepted in the early 1960s. The aim was 'to secure the maximum satisfaction of the constantly rising material and cultural requirements of the whole of society', by the 'planned, proportionate development of the national economy'. Collective and state forms of ownership still existed side by side, together with 'some remnants of private ownership', but would eventually merge into a higher form. But two years later

Xue published an 'addendum' to cover the new reforms already under way: his book, he said, had left much to be desired in clarifying the 'Left' mistakes of economic policy within the Party. Xue now criticized the tendency of 'blindly going after a higher level of public ownership' and the domination of state planning. It was time to reconsider whether moving from smaller to larger collective units in the countryside was invariably the best form of progress. Xue also wrote more positively of 'the existence of a small number of other forms of ownership, for example, private ownership'. He attached more importance too to the role of the market, with which state planning should be 'kept in line'. Price controls should be loosened, and the state-owned monopoly of commerce should be supplemented by 'large numbers of collective retail stores and some private ones'.

Five years later, Xue's ideas had progressed further, though he still lagged behind his more adventurous colleagues. He now wrote that China had 'blundered' after 1949 in trying to substitute 'planned production and distribution' for the market, and in imposing restrictions on the 'commmodity–money relationship'. A planned and centralized economic system belonged to communism, not socialism. Xue criticized Marx for taking an 'abstract' view of socialist society and predicting the complete public ownership of the means of production. He envisaged instead a system of 'free competition between the state, collective, and private sectors' under the guidance of broadly written— 'macro-economic'—state plans. The state sector was still dominant, wrote Xue, so why should one fear private enterprise? Finally, after the 1987 Party Congress, Xue argued openly that certain 'capitalist factors' would continue to exist in China in 'co-operation' with socialism, just as in the world as a whole there was collaboration as well as competition between the socialist and capitalist countries. Capitalism need not become 'extinct' during the initial stage of socialism—which the congress had agreed would last for a hundred years.

Bonuses in command

'More work more pay' is the straightforward Chinese way of referring to the Marxist principle of 'From each according to his ability, to each according to his work.' No one has ever denied that reward for labour cannot be wholly equal during the socialist transition. Only once communism has been achieved will the conditions for 'distribution according to need' have been satisfied, when (a) there will be more than enough to satisfy everyone, and (b) people will have sufficient 'communist spirit' to accept an egalitarian ethic. But from the time of the Great Leap onwards, the conventional wisdom was that wage differentials should be narrowed and increasing use should be made of moral rather than material incentives to stimulate labour productivity. During the Cultural Revolution bonuses at work were progressively abolished. Piecework rates were also condemned, although some factories quietly kept them in operation. All workers were paid a monthly wage according to the national eight-grade scale. Only the lower rates were increased during the 1960s, and promotion was by age rather than ability. The result, said many Chinese after the Cultural Revolution, was a situation of 'more work less pay'. Even worse, the conscientious worker subsidized the lazy worker who enjoyed the luxury of 'less work for more pay'. Similar complaints were heard in the countryside, at least from the younger and more able, or those with larger families possessing more work-power who could now benefit from higher reward for individual effort. This writer recorded dozens of scornful jingles about the past in autumn 1978 as the bonus movement gathered pace:

'Work or skive, we all got five', one is told contemptuously by a commune leader with reference to the work-point system where allegedly everyone had been credited with the same total regardless of achievement. 'Work, slack, or game, it was all just the same', was the corresponding jingle at a grain warehouse in Beijing which during the Cultural Revolution adopted a time rate system and abolished bonuses with disastrous results, it is claimed, on productivity. Phrases like these, which sound particularly effective in monosyllabic Chinese, are not just incidental to the argument . . . 'No reward for the workers: no punishment for the shirkers.' It often seems as if the very neatness of the phrase is supposed to convince one of the soundness of the argument.

Meanwhile wages in real terms had declined in purchasing power in the past two decades, rising by only 10 per cent while inflation for the urban worker had increased by over 16 per cent.

Bonuses and piece-work rates were restored cautiously at first. The rule was that only heavy manual workers should be paid by results rather than by the day, and that bonuses should not exceed 10–12 per cent of standard wages. In many places bonuses were only awarded after 'discussion by the masses', rather than automatically in response to above-average performance. The new policy was to 'combine material rewards with moral encouragement', which took the form of public praise for advanced workers, the award of banners and flags to 'advanced units', recording 'merits' in personal dossiers, and awarding the title of advanced worker. However, the limits were soon relaxed. Many factories adopted a mixture of time and piece-rates, and a fully fledged system of bonuses linked to the retention of a proportion of above-the-plan profits became a concealed supplement to wages. By 1980 the bonus boom had become alarming as Deng Xiaoping told a Central Committee meeting on 16 January:

Some [workers and factories] have gone so far as to ignore the interests of the country as a whole and to flout discipline. For example, because we were somewhat negligent in our work last year, bonuses were issued indiscriminately to the tune of over five billion yuan. While many such bonuses were distributed legitimately, a considerable proportion of the total, amounting to a sizeable sum, was not. Bonuses were issued even by some units which failed to fulfil their quotas of production and profit. Indiscriminate price rises for some commodities were often directly related to the pursuit of bonuses by certain enterprises. In many places, workers' real income was doubled as a result of excessive bonuses.

After many years of depressed wages, the pent-up demand was bound to lead to inflationary rises. This was only encouraged by the official explanation (which later had to be denied) that China needed to emulate the developed world by moving from 'low wages and low consumption' to 'high wages and high consumption'. The problem, it was soon realized, was that as long as factories were not responsible for their profits and losses, bonuses could become concealed pay rises at the expense of the state. The existing wage scale was also far too complicated to administer efficiently. The eight-grade scale had led to 'bunching', with most workers clustered in the medium grades regardless of their job or aptitude. Each branch of industry had its own rates of pay, based not on performance but on its presumed value to the nation, with heavy industry the most highly rewarded.

Reforms in the early 1980s made bonuses in theory dependent upon profits, while enterprises were required to pay taxes to the state. But by 1985 many factories were paying bonuses equivalent to one-third of annual wages. The problem was exacerbated by distortions in the pricing system: factories which produced goods which were over-valued came into large windfall sums through the profit retention scheme, arousing considerable envy among workers whose products were under-valued. The habit of equal distribution of extra rewards which had been part of the old system also helped to undermine the economic rationality of the new system. 'Many enterprises issue bonuses equally, thus turning them into disguised extra wages', wrote Liu Guoguang in 1987, attributing this to 'the long historical background and broad social basis of egalitarianism in China'. Egalitarianism had long since become a term of abuse. The Gang of Four were censured within two years of their fall for trying to 'limit' the necessary inequalities of the distribution system, thus causing 'great ideological confusion and economic loss'—and as they were conspirators whose only ambition was to seize power in the ensuing chaos, this had been their purpose, it was argued, all along!

Demoting the plan

Higher wages and bonuses would not lead to greater efficiency, it was already realized by the Chinese reformers, unless accompanied by substantial changes in economic management and in the running of industry and commerce. This required an assault upon what up until then were regarded as the two prime indicators of progress towards socialism—the domination of the plan and state ownership—opening the door for the growth of a substantial market sector and the expansion of collective and private ownership. After thirty years of communist rule, the planning network had enmeshed more than 90 per cent of the economy. This was equally true whether the plan was supervised from the 'centre' (Beijing) or by the local authorities. In these three decades, planning had shifted several times between the centre and the provinces, devolving in theory at times (as in the Great Leap) to even lower levels. But the planners in every case were administrative cadres working in Party or government

2. 'Another day begins.' Rural poverty before Liberation, 1948.

1. 'By the well.' Urban poverty before Liberation, 1948.

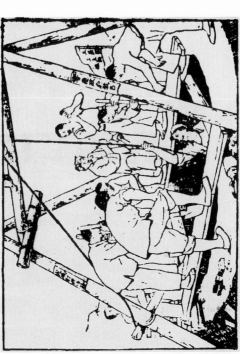

3. 'Secretary Wang serves the people' (see Ch. 2, sketch). A village cadre listens to the poor peasants, and helps them dig a well, 1952.

4. 'Here comes the tractor!' The joys of mechanization in a rural co-operative, 1954.

5. 'Honour to the army-men's families.' Village youth present the wives of serving soldiers with honorific titles, 1954.

6. 'Let's celebrate the great wheat harvest!' Peasants light firecrackers in Great Leap euphoria, 1958.

7 'Taming the Yellow River.' Mass construction team building a dam during the Great Leap, 1959

9. 'I must be a good student of Chairman Mao.'
Young Red Guard at work, c.1967.

8. 'Youth.' Themes of study and modernization are revived
after the Great Leap, 1961.

11. 'Socialist new woman.' A student sent to the

10. 'The three constantly read articles.' Worker, peasant,

12. 'Before leaving the garage.' A bus driver cleans her windscreen, with a copy of *Red Flag* on the seat, 1974.

13. 'Building the culvert and making the field.' Peasants change the landscape of Dazhai Model Brigade, 1975.

14 (*above*). 'In my grief I hear demons shriek.' Wang Lishan reads his subversive poem at the Tiananmen demonstration, 5 April 1976 (see Ch. 8); woodcut, 1978.

15 (*right*). 'The ladder of ambition.' Zhang Chunqiao, with Yao Wenyuan (lower left) and Wang Hongwen (lower right), climb Jiang Qing's ladder to power, 1977.

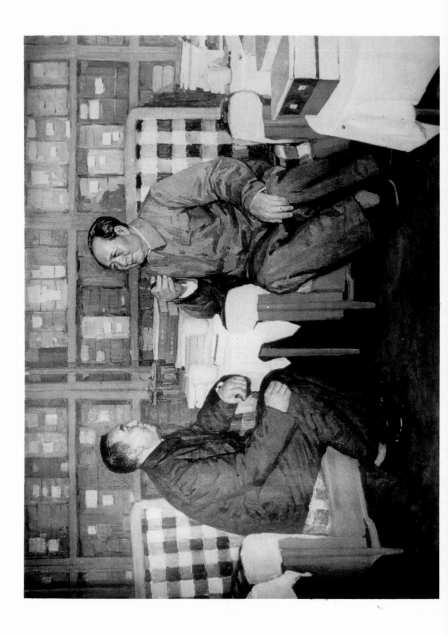

17. 'The Four Modernizations.' Roadside poster shows Chinese youth speeding ahead to the Year 2000. Shengli oilfield (see Ch. 6), 1978.

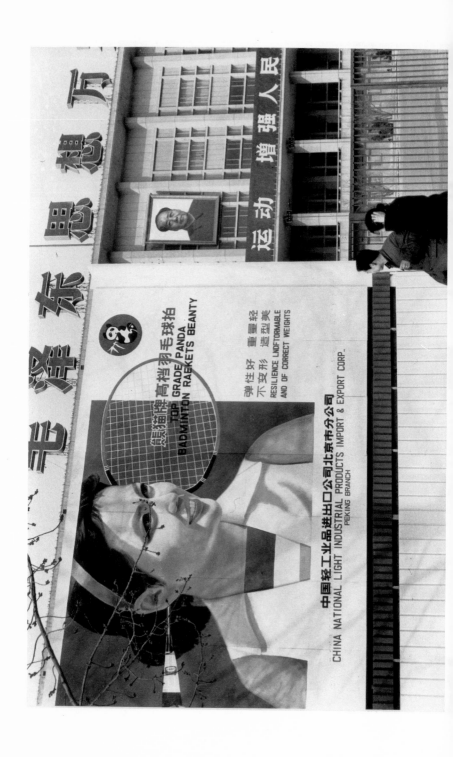

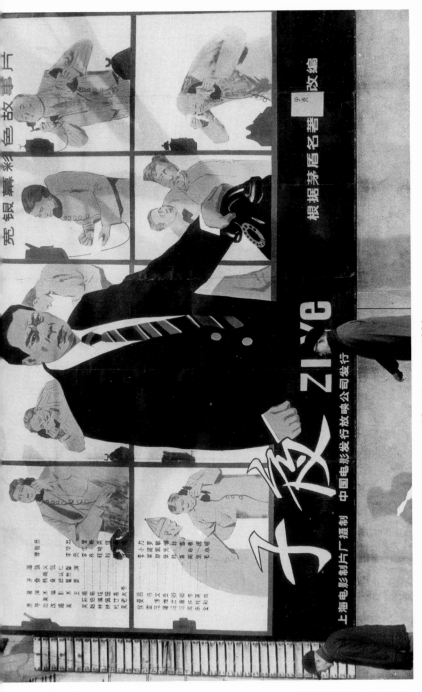

19. 'Midnight.' Film advertisement for 1930s novel by Mao Dun, 1982.

offices, not the factory or enterprise managers. There was more decentralization in Mao's last years, but with 'politics in command' even less attention was paid to such criteria as real costs of production, the need to secure a return on investment, the fixing of proper prices, and other 'market' factors. Local cadres were often more tempted than central planners to downgrade the satisfaction of ordinary consumer demands, investing instead in prestigious 'capital construction' for industry and public works.

Critics of planning orthodoxy had to proceed 'bashfully', as one of them later recalled. The 1981 resolution on Party history defined Chinese post-Mao economic strategy in cautious terms: 'We must carry out the planned economy on the basis of a system of public ownership, while at the same time developing the subsidiary role of market adjustments.' This amounted to a return to the mid-1950s and the policy associated now as then with Chen Yun. In March 1979 Chen stressed that, though the market was indispensable, it was 'supplementary and secondary in nature'. The conservative reformers warned that 'we cannot waver in the policy of taking the planned economy as the key, nor can we abandon directive planning, centralization, and unification of administrative methods'. If the plan and the market were put on an equal footing (argued *Red Flag*, No. 8, 1982), this would lead to a return to capitalism. The plan should still dominate the heights of economic production—iron, steel, grain, cement, fertilizer, and so on—which would be both produced and sold by the state. The market should be confined to the circulation of 'local products' and other less essential items. Chen argued in his memorable 'birdcage' analogy that the planning framework should not be loosened too far:

While reviving the economy, we must guard against the tendency to diverge from the state plan. Revitalization should be under the guidance of the plan; it should not depart from the plan. This can be compared with the relationship between a bird and its cage. A bird cannot be held tightly in one's hand because that would kill it; it must be allowed to fly. But it can only fly within the cage; without the cage it will escape. If the bird represents economic revitalization, then the cage represents state planning.

But a more formidable critique was developing against the plan, with implications for political as well as economic reform, and influenced by experiences in Eastern Europe which were

beginning to be studied seriously. Critics argued that the planning process had led to the fixing of grandiose targets and
excessive accumulation of funds at the expense of living standards. By setting targets in terms of quantitative output and
value it had encouraged stockpiling of raw materials and the
production of poor-quality goods to meet the norm. Because the
state was responsible for profit and loss, there was no incentive
to innovate or to improve product quality. The complexity of
a vast society also meant that no planning mechanism could
accurately carry out the thousands of statistical operations
necessary to measure consumption and demand. Examples were
numerous: planners in one city had arrranged for production of
1.4 million pocket-knives which would take thirty years to sell.
Factories imported coke from hundreds of miles away instead
of buying it from local mines which belonged to a different
ministry. Locating raw materials and spare parts was so difficult
that on any one day up to three million people were travelling
around China on purchasing missions.

By the late 1980s, economic theory had progressed from
regarding the plan as primary and the market as secondary to the
unification of the two concepts. The goal was a 'planned
commodity economy' in which the 'law of value' operated
throughout the system, and there was an 'organic unity of
planning and the market'. This also meant that those products
which were produced and disposed of on the basis of the plan
were no longer regarded as immune from market forces. Liu
Guoguang wrote, 'It had long been held that in a socialist
economy only consumer goods are commodities. Commodities
were limited to those items obtained without ration coupons,
and only these commodities were actually regulated by the
market.' But now the 'means of production'—industrial products, technology, finance, land, and labour itself—were all to
be regarded as commodities which could be priced, bought, and
sold. The plan no longer had a special 'socialist' character.
Planning and the market mechanism were merely 'methods' by
which production and consumption could be regulated, and they
were both used in capitalist as well as socialist societies, argued
another leading reformer, Gao Shangquan.

As the 'market' lost its 'subsidiary' relationship to the plan, so
collective and private enterprise began to assume a more equal

relationship with the state-owned sector. The number of workers employed in the collective sector grew by 32 per cent between 1978 and 1986, against 23 per cent growth in the state sector. The collective units were becoming larger and more productive, and their total share of industrial output rose in the same period from 19 to 29 per cent. No longer regarded as a necessary legacy of 'bourgeois right'—as Zhang Chunqiao had argued in his famous 1975 polemic—they were now seen as an often more productive alternative to the comparable state-owned enterprise. In the retail and service trade, the increase in privately owned small shops and trades was even more striking. The number of private owners or employees grew from 4 per cent in 1978 to just under 50 per cent in 1986, accounting for more than one-sixth of total business. Everyday urban life had been transformed by the return of private restaurants, cobblers, bicycle repair shops, small food and clothes shops, and peddlers. By the end of this period, it was agreed not only that the private sector could coexist with the state sector, but that it provided healthy competition and could create new jobs more cheaply than if funded by the state. Some economists wrote of a 'multi-ownership system' in which private and public enterprise learnt from each other—for example, state shops were forced to provide better customer service to compete with the private sector, while private businesses copied the state sector's provision of labour insurance for their employees. Attempts were made to define an acceptable proportion of state to collective to private enterprise in the retail industry—the ratio of 5:3:2 was suggested.

The new entrepreneurs

By the mid-1980s, economic thinking had reached the point where for the first time a distinction could be made between 'ownership' and 'management', borrowing from the capitalist system where the two are usually separated. The great error of the past, said the Central Committee in October 1984, had been to equate the concept of 'ownership by the whole people' with 'management by the state institutions'. Reform in the countryside had already handed over management of the land to the peasant while reserving the title of the land to the collective.

Why should a government department—a ministry or provincial bureau—run a factory as well as own it? Real ownership 'by the whole people' meant letting them manage affairs at their own workplaces (or at least find a capable managerial team to do so for them), the 1984 resolution argued.

The well-spring of vitality of the enterprise lies in the initiative, wisdom, and creativeness of its workers by hand and brain. These can only be brought into play when the status of the working people as masters of their own enterprise is guaranteed by its rules and regulations and when their labour is closely linked with their own material benefits. This has been vividly and convincingly proved by our experience in rural reform. In restructuring the urban economy, it is imperative to handle correctly the relationship of the workers and staff to their enterprise so that they are its real masters and can work as such at their jobs.

The most important and controversial reform to flow from this decision was the attempt to give the factory director full responsibility for management, while the Party and state, whether represented by the factory committee or by local government organs, ceased to 'interfere'. In theory this would leave their hands free to concentrate on larger questions of economic policies, principles, and plans. In practice the reform could easily offend vested interests in the bureaucracy.

This 'separation of ownership from management power' was called a breakthrough in traditional economic theory. Adapting the responsibility system from agriculture, it was proposed that managers should sign contracts with the state with their incomes pegged to the profitability of their enterprise. They would no longer 'eat in the state canteen'. The new policy required several provisos. Managers must reinvest part of their profits rather than distribute them entirely as income. It was also necessary 'to avoid indiscriminate price increases, shoddy building, scrimping on materials, or any other illicit means of increasing income'. The managers sometimes found that, in spite of the new policy, underlying relationships of power had hardly changed. Some complained that they had to accept over-staffing and incompetent performance while taking the blame for its economic consequences. It was quite usual to find whole families at work in the same factory—work allocation in the past was often based on family connections—who formed powerful 'clans'. Managers resented their responsibility for social welfare, traditionally based upon the place of work. 'When you're a factory manager', said one, 'you have to take care of everything: what the workers eat, where they live, their medical care, birth, ageing, sickness, and death. . . . How much energy can you have left for production and business?'

But management reform in spite of these difficulties was regarded as essential for the more than 800 large and medium enterprises which account for over 40 per cent of total industrial production. The first priority of the Seventh Five Year Plan (1985–9), said Premier Zhao Ziyang, was 'to make socialist producers and managers wholly and truly independent, self-managing, and solely responsible for their own profits and losses'. The reform was carried further for smaller factories and many shops which could now be leased outright to their managers, thus reducing what the *Economic Daily* called 'the "government run" feeling that businesses of this kind often have' (26 June 1987). Critics still claimed that this was opening the door to capitalism. A woman manager in Benxi in the north-east became the subject of national debate in 1987, after leasing a total of eight food stores in the space of two years. She employed 1,000 workers and soon dominated food sales in the town, paying herself an income equivalent to twenty times the average worker's wages. The arguments were deployed for and against:

Against: Guan Guangmei may work hard, but who does not? The manager of any business or factory is as busy every day, doing his best for his enterprises, his workers, and the state. But their salaries are only two or three times that of their workers. Why should she earn so much?

For: It should be remembered that she took over the business on contract, with six guarantors . . . and assumes full financial liability. If her profit falls below the level stipulated in the lease agreement she has to pay the difference herself, so she takes a high risk. Anyone who cannot accept the fact of her high income should tender for the business himself and make his fortune! (*Economic Daily*, 16 June 1987)

Mrs Guan was an 'entrepreneur', a term previously unknown in Chinese socialist economics but now increasingly valued. Directors and managers before, said the *People's Daily*, had been 'simply government officials with no freedom to make management decisions independently'. Now they had the opportunity to become entrepreneurs 'through competition, taking risks and demonstrating ability'. Studies were made of the role of the entrepreneurial manager in the West, from his nineteenth-century origins when ownership first became separated from management to today. The entrepreneurial manager played the key role, it was said, both in small risk-taking enterprises which were in the vanguard of scientific research, and in the multinationals which were 'the most advanced form of production'. Modern entrepreneurs were 'a group of brilliant people', and a country with foresight should 'go all out to develop the enterprise economy' (*People's Daily*, 30 May 1985).

By 1985–6 the reform of ownership was hovering on the brink of restoration of shareholding and the stock-market—potent political symbols of economic collapse 'before the Liberation', and easily represented by critics today as 'restoring capitalism'. Experiments were launched in Shenyang and Shanghai, and leaders in Beijing gave a warm welcome to the chairman of the New York Stock Exchange. The rationale was that industrial autonomy from the state as ultimate owner would only work if industry was able to raise the bulk of its own funds for investment and improvement. Bank loans and retention of profits would not necessarily suffice. If markets were now allowed in commodities, technology, and labour, why should there not be a 'socialist financial market?' The first experiments involved mostly small companies whose shares were bought for dividend income rather than speculation. Many shareholders— over 90 per cent in Shanghai in the first year—were employees of the company concerned for whom dividends became a concealed form of extra bonus. With such 'dividends' ranging between 30 and 100 per cent of share value, there were schemes to fix maximum levels and to tax the payments. There were also more ambitious plans, 'What is needed', said the *Workers Daily* (16 Oct. 1986), 'is for a large number of well-established, influential state enterprises to enter a large-scale top-level share market. This market should also include stocks and shares issued by State banks.'

The problem of prices

The most immediate point of contact with the economic reforms for most Chinese was not management or share-owning but prices. As elsewhere in the state socialist world, while the reformers regarded price reform as 'the key to the reform of the entire economic structure' (Central Committee Decision, October 1984), the public regarded it more often as a threat to living standards. They were prepared to accept higher wages but not higher prices, complained the reformers: a 1986 survey showed that 56 per cent of the population of working age believed that 'preserving stable, unchanging prices is what gives socialism its superiority'. The percentage was largest among the poorly educated, workers, the elderly, and others with low incomes (*Guangming Daily*, 12 March 1987).

The most puzzling phenomenon is that though many people have benefited from price reform, they still think it is better to return to the old days when neither prices nor wages rose. This poses a new task to reformers: how to educate people to be better psychologically prepared for a more changeable and unstable society (*China Daily*, 7 Sept. 1987).

The purpose of price reform was twofold: to cut down on state subsidies and (more important but less visibly) to stimulate competitive efficiency among manufacturers. The increase in urban wages and in state purchase prices for rural products in the late 1970s had led to a consumption boom which sharply increased the state's burden of subsidies. The cost of keeping down market prices rose 50 per cent from 1980 to 1981. Subsidies of all kinds (including housing and transport) occupied nearly 30 per cent of state budget expenditure. The news of impending price increases led to panic buying not only of daily necessities such as cooking oil and toilet paper but of quality consumer goods, such as TVs and videos, which should not have been affected. Most urban dwellers were given compensatory subsidies to ease the transition, but these could not match the price increases or keep up with the resulting inflation.

The reformers were in a familiar dilemma: 'As soon as they relax, there is chaos,' went a popular comment on the situation, 'and as soon as there is chaos they draw back.' In theoretical terms it could fairly be argued by Xue Muqiao that problems were to be expected in a transitional period while the old and new systems, regulated and free-market prices, coexisted. But popular trust in the long-term future was hard to generate: the reality of inflation was compounded by visible evidence of corruption and profiteering. In a message to the first issue of *China Consumer News*, Xue Muqiao recounted a familiar tale:

In one small town, I found that Da Qianmen cigarettes were unavailable in the shops but were offered outside by street sellers at ten cents above the fixed price, on condition that one packet of otherwise unsaleable cigarettes should be bought at the same time. I asked if the sellers all had permits and was assured that they had. I then asked why the [relevant] bureau was not dealing with the matter. The whispered reply—after a few moments of hesitation—was that the vendors were all relatives of cadres in the Bureau and the state-run shops. They were not only not prevented from this practice, but were even informed whenever a new shipment of the cigarettes arrived. The shops could sell off their entire stock immediately at the retail price, increasing turnover and profits so that they even won prizes (*People's Daily*, 10 Oct. 1985).

In August 1987 a drive against speculators was launched in Beijing, spreading rapidly throughout the country, with the 'Mr Fixers' who siphoned state goods to the market via the backdoor as prime targets. Price ceilings were also reimposed on some produce. The result was a fall in prices—and in supplies. Many farmers feared that they would be labelled as speculators, while the lower prices offered little reward. Cucumbers, eggplants, tomatoes, and chillies disappeared overnight from the Beijing markets. The price ceilings had to be scrapped within a month.

Land and housing was another sensitive area affected by price reform. In the villages, where the peasants had mostly owned their own houses throughout the political changes of the 1960s, the agricultural boom caused a rash of new building which aroused the envy of town dwellers. Municipal housing authorities now looked for schemes to raise more funds. Town dwellers might live in poor accommodation, they argued, but they paid next to nothing and improvements must be geared to outright sales or higher rents. In 1987 the State Council's housing research office called for the sale of all new housing and market-price rents for the older stock. As incomes rose, average rents had fallen from the already low figure of 2.6 per cent of family income in 1964 to just over 1 per cent twenty years later. A Tianjin newspaper described some of the problems:

Who wants to buy when you can get a home virtually free from the state and there is the fear of losing a private home in another political campaign? For a long time, people have developed an attitude they don't want to change: Under socialism, you do not spend money on buying a home. On people's shopping lists are a colour television, a refrigerator, a set of furniture—but not a home.

The well-off city of Yantai in Shandong province served as the model for a new scheme in which rents were raised sharply and those least able to pay were given temporary subsidies. But cadres who had benefited most under the old system—since they were allocated more living space than others at the subsidized rates—lobbied to exempt their own dwellings from the reforms. Another scheme for land sales (technically speaking, the sale of 'the right to use' land) to industry was pioneered in the Special Economic Zone of Shenzhen adjoining the Hong Kong border.

The real battle over prices took place not in the market or housing bureau but in industry, where most goods previously allocated by the state at fixed prices were now bought and sold under looser or no controls. The 1984 decision had been described as establishing 'a new system which can reflect more sensitively the supply and demand of the market, changes in labour productivity, and which can satisfy better the needs of economic development' (*Outlook*, 3 Feb. 1986). A dual system of prices developed for raw materials, which might be supplied at a controlled price for production falling within the state plan but were otherwise allowed to find their market level. The new entrepreneurial managers were supposed to make rational decisions on investment and output, based upon real costs of production and materials. They should respond to higher prices of raw materials and wages not by turning to the state for subsidies, but by 'reducing costs through technological innovation and selling goods at competitive prices' (*China Daily*, 15 Oct. 1987). Here, too, the 'transition' proved painful. In practice the state still underwrote most industrial and manufacturing operations, although increasingly at local rather than national level. Instead of competition among enterprises, there was competition among local authorities for control of raw materials and markets. 'Enterprises don't take responsibility for increased costs of production', said the economist Dong Fureng (*Washington Post*, 12 March 1987). 'They just ask for an increase in the price of the products they sell.' Planners now favoured more sophisticated forms of price liberalization. These included 'floating' prices with upper and lower limits fixed by the state, and 'authorized' prices where the producer submitted a cost-plus-profit price for approval. Paradoxically, such a system required more subtle state intervention at a time when the role of the state was supposed to be weakened and was already less effective.

The triumph of 'reform'

At the Thirteenth Party Congress in October 1987, the various strands of economic reform of the 1980s were drawn together to form a strong new 'line' of what was still claimed to be a socialist strategy. Reform was not just a mechanism for making socialism work. It was what socialism was about at this early stage in its history. This 'primary stage of China's socialism', which would last until the middle of the twenty-first century, was dominated by the transformation of China from

an agricultural country, where farming is based on manual labour and where people engaged in agriculture constitute the majority of the population . . . into a modern industrial country where non-agricultural workers constitute the majority. . . . The fundamental task of a socialist society is to expand the productive forces. During this primary stage we must shake off poverty and backwardness, and it is therefore especially necessary for us to put the expansion of the productive forces at the centre of all our work. Helping to expand the productive forces should become the point of departure in our consideration of all problems [Zhao Ziyang, *Report to Congress*].

The new approaches to ownership and planning worked out in the past few years were now elaborated in more systematic theory. Zhao was praised in the media for having for the first time given a clear definition of the 'private sector': a sector which involves wage labour and is a useful supplement to the public sector. This sector should be encouraged to expand, along with various forms of co-operative ownership and management. Industrial output value of the private sector only accounted for a mere 0.6 per cent of the national total, and this was not enough (*Xinhua News Agency*, 29 Oct. 1987.) The economists were urged by Zhao to explore further in an area where, he admitted, not much was yet known about its contradictions and laws.

Discussion was also encouraged on the nature of the private sector, although the Xinhua agency report explained somewhat naïvely that this was 'rarely covered by the media to avoid confusion in people's ideology'.

The preferred phrase for state planning was now state 'regulation', using indirect means which were based upon the real value of production and proper reward for good management. In a new formula, it was said that 'the state regulates the market, and the market guides enterprises'. Less than 50 per cent of industrial output was now subject to state planning, said Zhao, and before long this would be much further reduced. Zhao also elaborated upon the various ways in which management could be separated from formal state ownership: entering into contracts between enterprises and/or managers and the state, giving them a financial stake in success to encourage 'entrepreneurship', involving workers and staff in management, selling shares in enterprises, and so on. As one government official told foreign bankers at a conference just after the congress, ways must be found to 'build up a mechanism by which [management] responsibility, power, and profits are closely knit' (*China Daily* on Business Leaders Symposium, 10 Nov. 1987).

For the first time since the break with the Soviet Union, the Chinese again saw themselves as part of an international phenomenon: that of the socialist countries which were in differing degrees breaking away from 'leftist centralized planning' and embarking upon a 'new economic policy'. China, they said, had started with a double handicap. It had to tackle not only the familiar problems of all socialist countries—bureaucracy, low efficiency, and dogmatism—but also those of all developing countries, such as lack of skilled administrators, low educational level, rapidly growing population, and shortage of funds and materials. Yet, argued the economic reformers to whom Zhao Ziyang's report gave a new and brighter green light, this double handicap was a unique challenge. If poor and backward China could succeed, would this not be an even more glorious proof of 'the superiority of socialism' over capitalism than the reformation of the other socialist countries which had started from a higher level of development? (*Beijing Review*, 16 Nov. 1987). Statements of this kind, carrying a powerful echo of Mao's belief in the virtue of being 'poor and blank', indicated a continuing need to present new policies in an optimistic millenarian framework not so very different from the one offered by the Hua Guofeng leadership when it relaunched the 'Four Modernizations'.

More often the word 'socialism' was ignored altogether, particularly in discussions of the relationship between China and the world economy (see Chapter 11). In the countryside, where changes in economic policy offended fewer bureaucratic interests and could proceed with less direct supervision from central Party authorities, the post-Mao reforms had already come close to demolishing the entire structure of what were previously regarded as the 'socialist relations of production'.

CHAPTER SEVEN

Peasant China Transformed

THE RISE OF RURAL ENTERPRISE

The old village houses are built in rows with packed mud walls, tamped mud floor, and a thick thatched roof now dripping in the spring rain. Small children peer out of front doors, buffalo and oxen huddle close to the back doors. A few chickens scurry in the liquid mud. We pick our way carefully to the higher ground, where there is the beginnings of a new housing estate. Mr Yang, the richest man in the village, has built a two storey stone-walled house with a tiled roof and balcony. Mr Yang makes so much money from 'sideline production'—selling pigs, tobacco, and vegetables over and above his grain quota—that the villagers call him 'Mr Five Dollars Everytime He Opens the Door'. There is a couplet outside his door, written on red paper and pasted on both sides in the traditional style for Chinese New Year:

> *Better live among men than in paradise dream,*
> *Better farm my own patch than work in a Team.*

Mr Yang is the head of a Ten Thousand Yuan household in one of the villages of Fengyang County, Anhui province. Once notorious for its beggars who roamed as far as the streets of Shanghai, Fengyang has benefited from the new Agricultural Responsibility System. This allocates the land to individual families and allows them to work it as they choose, after paying taxes and fulfilling a quota of grain to the state. Mr Yang has just returned from a congratulatory conference for Advanced Peasants at the provincial capital, where he was also given a free bicycle. We splosh through the mud to another stone house, with a wall around for privacy, which Mr Yang has built for his eldest daughter and new husband. The couplet outside it reads:

> *My new tiled house is bright and clean,*
> *Here comes the cart with our sewing machine!*

Inside there is an amazing sight. Eight young women and eight sewing machines are crammed into one room, receiving instruction from Mr Yang's daughter. The idea is to establish a small work-shop for making clothes. Sewing machines are eagerly sought after by peasants just beginning to acquire the money to become more conscious of clothes. Officials in the county town are discussing how to import dressmaking and hair-cutting expertise from the big city. It is 1982: the People's Commune of Kaocheng in Fengyang county is being abolished 'experimentally'. Every other province has been instructed to set up a similar experiment, and the whole of China will follow within little more than a year.

(From a visit in Feb. 1982)

The fading of the communes

China's second rural revolution began cautiously within three years of Mao's death, but by 1983 had demolished the essential structure of the people's communes and had largely reversed the philosophy of collective labour and reward on which they were based. At first, attempts were made to reconcile the new 'Agricultural Responsibility System' and its associated reforms with the spirit of the past; later that spirit was sweepingly rejected. Both were political overstatements. The truth was that the people's communes in their modified form after the disasters of the Great Leap did provide a basis for rural development which was slow but consistent with the socialist goals of the time. The post-1980 system, which at first returned to the more cautious co-operative policies of the mid-1950s but soon led to the effective privatization of the land, encouraged much faster rural growth, but its negative effect upon social cohesion was beginning to be assessed by the late 1980s. Whether the communes, if properly managed, could have provided a smoother path, is now an unrealistic question. In rural as in industrial policy, the state and its cadres had proved unable to provide the sophisticated leadership required for a unified system of management. The Great Leap and Cultural Revolution bias against free markets and sideline production meant that at best most peasants had enough to eat but were always short of money. In some areas, as the Chinese sociologist Fei Xiaotong has observed, the situation had begun to improve by the early 1970s with the development of commune and rural-run industry. But it was too late. Most Chinese peasants were no longer willing to be mobilized for 'hard struggle' without more immediate returns, and had been alienated by dogmatic policies restricting initiative and flouting rural common sense. Fei writes of a relatively well-to-do area in the Yangtze valley which he had studied since the 1930s:

Peasant incentives for economic production were drastically reduced by the combined effects of several policies: first, the policy of promoting grain production at the expense of sideline occupations and rural industries; second, the increased power of higher level cadres unacquainted with local conditions, leading to arbitrary bureaucratic command from the top; and third, the leftist emphasis on the doctrine of absolute egalitarianism. As a consequence, the rate of increase in grain production declined from the 8.25 per cent figure of 1966 to 3.95 per cent by 1976. Even these small increases were cancelled out by increases in the population. The average income in 1976 thus lingered around 114 yuan, with no increase from the 1966 level.

China is a cereal-based culture where 'eating food' is synonymous with 'eating grain', and where it is a mark of real dedication to duty to 'let one's bowl of rice grow cold'. No matter what improvements are made in health, education, and the provision of consumer goods, progress still has to be measured by the yardstick of grain output. The average annual increase from 1952 to 1957 was 3.5 per cent, and during the next two decades fell to only 2 per cent (46.8 per cent overall). Even these gains were nullified by the increase in population. The Chinese nation grew from 646 million in 1957 to 958 million in 1978, a rise of over 48 per cent, which meant that grain consumption remained unchanged over the long term. Other necessities showed a similar pattern. Consumption of cloth rose by 76 per cent in the first period, but actually declined by 8 per cent in the next two decades, even though output increased by 32 per cent. This slow progress must be set in the context of improving life expectation (from 57 years in 1957 to 68 in 1978) and a decline in infant mortality from 139 per 1,000 in 1954 to 20 per 1,000 in 1980. Yet even this figure cannot be recorded without also observing that the Great Leap Forward led, according to the best calculations, to 19 million 'excess deaths'—that is, those who died ahead of expectation as a result of severely reduced diet and occasionally outright famine.

In some parts of China life had hardly improved overall since Liberation. A survey in 1977 showed that the level of production in 200 out of some 2,000 counties was not far from that of the early 1950s. Most were located in the backward north-west and south-west. At the other end of the scale, the most advanced production brigades, with an average per capita income in 1979 of over 300 yuan (£60) occupied less than 2.5 per cent of the total number of brigades. Over half of these were located on the outskirts of cities, and one-quarter were located on the periphery of Shanghai alone. Over these detailed statistics hung the largest one of all: agriculture had to sustain four-fifths of the Chinese population, and yet since 1949 it had created only one-third of the total value of industrial and agricultural output. A labour force of 400 million people, plus the aged and the young, were crowded on to a limited area of arable land (10.4 per cent of the total national territory) which had actually declined in the past decade.

In 1979–80 the traveller in China began to encounter two sights which had been rarities for over a decade. The rural fair was no longer infrequent and tightly controlled by local authorities, zealous to 'cut off the capitalist tails' of any peasants too keen to make a profit. Chinese officials were no longer embarrassed if the foreigner witnessed the scene. (The Italian film-maker Antonioni had been denounced in 1973 for filming a rare roadside market. He also filmed, the *People's Daily* complained, 'a tiresome succession of laboured shots of small plots, lonely old people, exhausted draught animals, and dilapidated houses'.) Most localities now reverted to the regular market dates based upon the old rural ten-day week (markets would be held on, say, the 3rd, 13th, and 23rd of each month). The other sight was the urban free market where peasants sold their produce— eggs, chickens, peanuts, and vegetables—grown mostly on private plots. It provided welcome variety to the diet of urban dwellers and was sufficiently profitable for peasants to travel up to 50 miles from the countryside, sleeping overnight on their carts before the market opened in the early morning.

Restoration of the rural and urban markets, coupled with expansion of the size of private plots which thus generated the surpluses for sale, was one of the main decisions taken by the Central Committee's Third Plenum in December 1978 which opened up the new course of reform under Deng Xiaoping's leadership. The Plenum also announced that the state would increase the grain purchase price by 20 per cent, with an additional 50 per cent for grain purchased above the quota, and would raise prices for another sixteen staple items. There would be a shift away from the 'one-sided emphasis on grain production' which had been fostered during the Cultural Revolution when peasants were expected to 'Take Grain as the Key Link', and diversification into cash crops and 'sideline' products would be encouraged. New regulations also prohibited local officials from commandeering peasant labour and funds without proper payment, and provided for democratic management of the communes and for public accounting. All these reforms went no further than to correct some of the excesses brought about by the Cultural Revolution and to restore the more flexible policies of the early 1960s. Official belief in the superiority of the 'Large and Public' organization of agricultural production was still widespread. As recently as November 1977, it had been decided to prepare about 10 per cent of the nation's production brigades for 'unified accounting' (that is, to abolish the financial autonomy of the smaller production teams and handle the accounts at the brigade level). The Plenum countered this tendency by reasserting that the 'system of three levels of ownership with the production team as the basic accounting unit . . . should remain unchanged'.

Within four years the new rural revolution would effectively lower the 'level' of accounting for most productive activity to the household, would divide up the land on a long-term basis, and would remove most administrative powers of the commune, brigade, and team. None of this was even hinted at in the Plenum's decision. 'In a series of changes which gathered pace after 1978', writes the British economist Peter Nolan, 'the rural institutional structure was transformed in as profound a fashion as occurred in the mid-fifties in the "Socialist High Tide". The difference is that this time the Party was *responding to* rather than *leading* the peasant masses.' This voluntarist interpretation of what occurred is essentially true. The new 'rural responsibility system' was at first introduced in a limited form, and was only intended to apply to a minority of areas. Instead, its more radical version spread to 90 per cent of the peasant population. Yet it seems likely that for a small number of leaders and their advisers this was the original intention all along, and their initial silence was necessary to avoid conservative criticism.

In 1979 the Central Committee circulated a document on the 'responsibility system' which emphasized that 'different forms of management should be allowed to coexist in the light of local conditions'. The word 'management' was technically correct. All the 'means of production'—land, and at this stage all machinery, tools, and animals—still belonged to the collective team which continued to 'manage' agricultural production by assigning work to team members. The difference was that production tasks now began to be assigned to smaller groups of peasants, and that their reward was based largely upon performance of those tasks. As one of the early accounts explained:

The general practice is to reduce the size of the labour groups in the production team, which is currently the basic accounting unit in the countryside and which is in charge of twenty to thirty households. A group formed voluntarily by several peasant households or individual peasants' households, or single peasants regularly makes a contract to undertake a certain production task with the production team. According to the terms of the contract, the contractor has certain rights and responsibilities. He is paid for his actual work and will be awarded for overfulfilling production targets and will compensate for reduced production, so as to ensure more pay for more work.

In its least radical form, the contract was made with a group of households for a precisely defined quota of a particular crop, with all the necessary tools, fertilizer, and so on supplied by the collective. This was called 'fixing output quotas based on the group' (*bao chan dao zu*). The other extreme was not just to make the contract with a single household (*bao chan dao hu*), but to extend its scope. The household only needed to supply a relatively small proportion of produce to the collective, which could be regarded as a form of tax. It was still supposed to grow only those crops specified in the contract, but it bought or hired all the necessary inputs for itself, and made its own arrangements for selling the surplus produce. This system was called 'fixing work based on the household' (*bao gan dao hu*).

At first these measures were in theory applied on a sliding

scale, with the most radical forms of assigning production responsibility reserved for those areas which were judged to be least advanced. In spring and summer of 1980 Party leaders toured rural China to investigate the changes. In October a Central Committee directive acknowledged that 'all forms of responsibility system can be adopted including the household contract'. But the assignment of *work* to the household (*bao gan dao hu*) was judged to be only suitable 'in the poor and backward areas' which accounted for less than 20 per cent of rural China, and was not needed 'where the development of production is normal'. At the end of 1981 the Central Committee was still insisting that 'allotting work to individual labourers, households, or production groups . . . is suitable only in places where scattered operations or management are most needed'. Orthodoxy was preserved by insisting on the 'superiority' of collective management at a higher level wherever the conditions were already 'ripe'.

By 1983 this assumption had been abandoned. Household contracts had replaced team contracts among 97 per cent of the rural population, and nine out of ten adopted the most radical form of full contracted responsibility (*bao gan*). This was not all: peasants were now able to buy their own 'means of production'—tractors, and so on—directly from the manufacturer. They could also buy or hire them from the collective. The prohibition on the hire of labour had also been lifted. A 1982 regulation cautiously allowed peasants to hire 'five labourers and two apprentices', but even this restriction was later relaxed. A revolution in rural government was also under way. The people's communes lost their administrative powers and became units of economic management alone. They were replaced by 'township' governments, reverting to the situation before the people's communes, in a process completed by March 1985.

The Fengyang experiment

Two provinces had taken the lead from 1979 onwards, going far beyond the cautious approval from Beijing for their experiments in rural reform. They were chosen for their extremes: populous and fertile Sichuan was guided by its first Party Secretary Zhao Ziyang—shortly to move to the centre as Premier; Anhui, where large pockets of poverty had persisted into the 1970s, was run by another ally of Deng Xiaoping, Wan Li (later Vice-Premier). Their successes gave rise to a peasant jingle: 'If you want some *liang* (grain) ask for Ziyang; if you want to have *mi* (rice) look for Wan Li.'

One of the first models to emerge publicly was Fengyang county in central Anhui, an area of traditional hardship which had generated a much older rhyme:

> Who has not heard of Fengyang's fame,
> From where the first Ming emperor came?
> His folk took all the land, and then
> Fengyang had famine, nine years in ten.

In the year before Liberation, half the population of Fengyang went outside the county begging or looking for work. Local statistics show a rapid improvement after land reform, with grain production rising from 99 million to 260 million *jin* (catty or half-kilo) in 1955. But the People's Communes, local peasants now recall, caused complete confusion. At first the peasants were not allowed to keep a single catty of grain at home, and free food for everyone was handed out from the apparently overflowing public granary. The grain soon ran out, and before long people were eating dog to survive. In the years 1959–61, out of a population of 380,000, more than 60,000 died 'in an irregular manner'—the usual euphemism for starvation. Local officials issued travel permits to let peasants go outside the county to beg for food (as late as 1978, Fengyang beggars still knocked on doors in Shanghai). Grain output recovered slowly, reaching a high of 360 million *jin* in 1977 but falling back to 295 million *jin* in the drought year of 1978. Looking back, Fengyang people concede that collective labour for construction work did lead to improved fertility: three reservoirs were constructed to irrigate two-thirds of the land. But they describe the collective organization of production as inefficient and wasteful. 'We went out to work like a lazy dragon [in a long shuffling dragon's "tail"] but we came back from work like a gust of wind!' While they were in the fields, the peasants now recall, 'we did our jobs all raggle-taggle, just as if we were working for a foreign boss' (slowing down the moment the cadres were not looking).

The system of reward for work is also severely criticized: How could local cadres organize anything between 60 and 120 peasants to work efficiently, record the results, and then assign work-points which distinguished adequately between those who made more and less effort? One exasperated team cadre recalls the difficulties:

I have tried the system of assigning work-points to quotas. I spent a lot of energy making different rules for how many work-points there should be if one does this kind or that kind of work and if one performs a certain amount of work. In the case of ploughing, for instance, the rules for work-points differed depending on whether one used a strong or weak buffalo, or one of average strength. Even for the same kind of buffalo, there were also different kinds of land, and for the same type of land, the case was also different if it had rained or if the soil was dry . . . With so many rules, it was almost endless. If they were printed into a book, it would be quite a thick edition. They were so elaborate the peasants were not interested at all.

Difficulties of this kind had been cited occasionally during the Cultural Revolution as further reason for adopting the 'Dazhai system' of work-points. (At the model Dazhai Brigade in Shanxi province, the only task distinction was between heavy and light work. Work-points were 'self-assessed' and recorded no more frequently than every three days—sometimes only every five or ten, visitors were told in 1971.) Even if this really happened, everyone admitted that it required 'a high level of political consciousness' which had not yet been achieved in most parts of the countryside. In Fengyang and many other places, realistic assessment of work-points caused too much strife, so cadres were tempted to narrow the differentials. The hard worker might get ten points but the lazy would still get seven or eight. Favouritism was also shown towards relatives and friends, and cadres were suspected of exploiting their control of resources. (In one commune the peasants stood around while a grain-processing plant burnt down, saying 'Good! Our cadres' wine-cups have turned to ashes!') The high number of bonus work-points allocated to full-time cadres who did no productive work is also recalled. A production team leader earned 7,000 points worth 700 yuan at a time when the average annual cash income was only 70 yuan.

By the Chinese New Year in 1982 the new responsibility system had been installed throughout Anhui province in its most radical *bao gan* form, with the land parcelled out to individual households. Allocation was made according to the size of a household or the number of adult 'labour power' or a combination of both. It was usually divided into several patches providing a mixture of more and less fertile land located nearer to or further from the village. Title remained with the collective team and a 'readjustment' was promised within five years to account for changes in family size. Every household possessed its *hetong shu* or 'contract book', sitting on the mantelpiece in a shiny red plastic cover. It recorded the area of allocated land, expected yield, sown acreage and prescribed quotas of the main crop, as well as deductions including payment to collective welfare and accumulation funds. Average disposable income had risen from 70 yuan in 1978 to 197 yuan in 1981. (One-third of the increase was attributed to the rise in state purchase prices, the rest to the reforms.) Five per cent of the rural households were estimated to be still in difficulty because of age or sickness, and received welfare aid.

The first trial 'separation of powers' was also under way in Kaocheng commune within Fengyang county. In a vivid phrase, the previous system combining administrative, economic, and political power was described as 'one man wearing three pairs of trousers'. The commune was now turned into a marketing and production company to manage the various collective rural factories and other enterprises. Administration was in the hands of a reconstituted *xiang* ('township') government. The intermediate-level 'brigades' had been abolished. The village 'teams' survived to administer the responsibility system, although with reduced powers. The Party branch was now supposed to stick to education and propaganda, leaving policy to the *xiang* government and production to the peasant. People spoke frankly about the basic problem: under the new system, explained one supporter, 'the bureaucracy from which we have suffered so much may still exist. But if it is separated from production, then it cannot harm the peasants so much.' The cadres themselves admitted they had been reluctant at first to see their political power reduced, but they were now free from 'aggravation' and had more time to 'make money'. In Fengyang and elsewhere it was noticeable that many cadres belonged to the most successful entrepreneurial families. (According to a 1984 survey in Shanxi province, 43 per cent of affluent peasants were either current or former cadres.)

The privatization of land

The abolition of the people's communes as the basic administrative unit in the countryside was part of a second surge of reform which meant that the Chinese peasant now owned his land in practice and controlled the major means of production, legally owning some of them as well. The purpose was not simply to liberate peasant initiative but to stimulate market forces in the countryside and pave the way for a commercialized agriculture. The original 'responsibility system', even when extended beyond the poorest minority for which it was at first intended, had still stressed the role of the collective in allocating land and equipment and of the state in setting quotas. Both principles were sensationally undermined in successive years by the Party Central Committee's 'Document No. 1' on agriculture, by custom the first directive to appear every New Year. Document No. 1 for 1984, it was explained, was drawn up in the face of 'remnants of Leftist influence' with the explicit aim of 'doing everything to make the peasants rich'. To this end it stipulated: (a) that peasants should be allowed to hold contracted land for a period of at least fifteen years; and (b) that contracted land might be transferred from one household to another. The longer lease of contracted land was intended to encourage peasant lessees to invest more labour and capital to develop its productivity rather than to milk the soil dry of fertility for the sake of short-term gains (and for fear that the land might be taken away from the lessee again after five years or less). But it also reinforced the assumption that the land was now individually owned, even though title still belonged in theory to the 'team'. The term was further extended for hilly land, which in 1983 began to be parcelled out to peasant households on a 'from generation to generation' basis. They could not be expected, it was said, to plant timber on the hillsides unless they could be sure that their descendants would enjoy its benefit.

The provision for transfer of land holdings was intended to encourage the concentration of land in the hands of those most able to farm it efficiently, while other peasants would give up cultivation altogether and work in the expanding sector of rural industry and commerce. The transaction was supposed to be handled by the collective, but money would still change hands. Transfer would be accompanied by the payment of 'proper compensation' on the basis of the original land price 'appraised according to its grade'.

A year later the Central Committee issued another directive which was described as 'setting free the rural economy'. The new policy shifted the emphasis from state planning to market demand, in particular by abolishing all purchasing quotas except for grain and cotton. Prices of other agricultural goods were also to be allowed to float on the free market. An increasing number of peasant producers were now becoming 'specialized house-holds', concentrating their effort upon the marketing of a particular crop or product. Some were 'contracted' to produce for the collective, producing cash crops or livestock which previously would have been directly managed by the team or brigade. Specialized households grew fruit trees, flowers, and medicinal herbs; cultivated tea and raised pigs, chicken, and fish; leased agricultural machinery from the collective to process farm produce. An increasing number were known as 'self-managing'. They had no contractual obligation to the collective except to pay taxes, and they purchased their own equipment and other means of production. By the end of 1983, there were nearly 25 million specialized households in China, accounting for 13.6 per cent of all rural households.

By the mid-1980s, the dividing line between specialized households which were still loosely within the collective sector and private businesses outside it was becoming blurred. The 1985 document now encouraged the sale of state-owned vehicles and boats which were lying idle to the specialized households. Allowing peasants to own such means of production had been official policy since mid-1983 after a much-publicized case where local officials in Hunan province confiscated trucks and tractors bought privately, on the grounds that it was 'encouraging capitalism'. Such ownership was now described as forming part of 'the private sector of the national economy which is supple-mentary to the socialist economy'. As this sector expanded, the restrictions on it were relaxed. Reformers now accepted the 'capitalist' label placed on it by critics, admitting that 'when hiring of labour exceeds a certain limit, they become capitalist enterprises'. By the end of 1985 over four-and-a-quarter million rural households came within this sector, owning their own tractors, trucks, and machines. Private and collective ownership now coexisted side by side. The reformers argued that such enterprises would still remain smaller in scale than during the 1950s, when the socialist state was easily able to keep national capitalism 'under control'. Yet the growth of the private sector threatened to undermine the conventional wisdom that new collective forms of production, more genuine and popular than those of the people's communes, would emerge in time spontaneously out of the responsibility system. 'The development of the collective economy', Deng Xiaoping had said in 1980, 'continues to be our general objective.' Local officials in Fujian province in 1983 went further:

Deng Xiaoping has made it clear that the new forms of organization contained in the responsibility system are only satisfactory for the present time. As for the future, we still have to investigate how it can be developed. We have only just made a beginning—it is not clear where we shall go next—but we do know that we cannot return to the old system. We also know that we have to create a new spirit of enthusiasm and a new form of collective.

The Twelfth Party Congress in 1982 had pointed the way: in the not too distant future, it predicted, many forms of peasant co-operatives would appear as 'the main economic formation' in the countryside. It was believed that these new forms would arise organically out of small-scale peasant specialized production, as peasants came to appreciate the advantages of genuine co-operation instead of the enforced collectivization of the past. Such co-operatives did emerge, often replacing operations previously run by the collective (such as orchards and piggeries) and allowing peasant families to invest money as well as—or instead of—their labour, thus creating 'shares'. (This led to charges of capitalism which were answered with the argument that the money invested had accumulated from the peasants' own labour and was not 'capital' from 'capitalists who rely upon exploitation'.) Yet it was increasingly recognized that peasant entrepreneurship could equally well head into the private field, and must be regulated by government control rather than self-regulated by co-operative management. 'China has a long history of agricultural family operation', noted one agricultural journal in 1984, 'which has displayed a surprisingly stubborn vitality.'

The rise of rural industry

By the late 1980s a second rural revolution was underway which went far beyond land cultivation and the reorganization of agricultural production. The great leap forward into rural-based industrialization had at last taken off, a quarter of a century after its over-ambitious beginnings in 1958. By 1985, wrote one observer, 'independent rural enterprises employed seventy million people, 19 per cent of the rural labour force, and generated 19 per cent of China's total industrial output by value. They were responsible for 29 per cent of the country's coal output, half its garment production, 53 per cent of all building materials supplies and earned US $4 billion in exports.' (In 1976 rural industry had only produced 8 per cent of a much smaller gross total of national industrial output.) Some factories were well-equipped with modern machines, including technology bought from abroad. Others used labour-intensive methods to recycle used materials such as old plastic bags and broken glass. Output thus ranged 'from complete sets of equipment to shirt buttons'.

The growth of rural industry had a direct effect on the rise in income levels in the countryside; in the interior provinces where it was less visible, standards of living were also lower. More than a half of all rural industries (usually referred to as 'township enterprises') were located in the eastern half of the country, from Guangdong in the south to Liaoning in the north. Over 30 per cent of the rural workforce in these areas had moved away from crop cultivation. Less than 3 per cent of China's rural industry was found in the underdeveloped north-west, where 85 per cent still worked on the land. Apart from generating more income locally and nationally, rural industry provided employment for China's surplus labour. (The extent of such under-employment had been concealed previously by the all-inclusive provision of work, regardless of efficiency, through the people's communes.) Figures for 1983 now showed that out of the total rural labour force of 350 million only 140 million were needed for agriculture, while another 90 million worked in rural industry and other non-agricultural activities. This left a theoretical labour surplus of over 100 million—in fact these people were nearly all 'under-employed' in agriculture. Projections showed that this labour pool would be increased by a further 100 million by the end of the century.

One of the foremost champions of rural commercialization and industrialization was the well-known Chinese sociologist Fei Xiaotong (quoted at the start of this chapter). It was the only solution, Fei argued, to China's population problem, which as a result of the post-Liberation baby boom had led to an increasing shortage of real jobs in the countryside from the mid-1960s onwards. China's future lay in the development of township enterprises and the growth of small towns, supported by local industry and commerce, with a population of between 20,000 and 50,000 each. In this way China would be able to transfer half of its agricultural labour force to industries and tertiary trades, without the creation of urbanization on the scale familiar elsewhere in the Third World. The small towns would act as population 'reservoirs', helping to prevent a heavy concentration of people in the big cities. But this role could only begin to be played after the Cultural Revolution, when the economic re-forms allowed China's small towns to resume the marketing functions of which they had been largely deprived since the late 1950s. For the past twenty years, collective and individual commerce had been limited and severely criticized while the state's domination of purchasing and marketing meant that only those few small towns which were also administrative centres continued to serve the surrounding rural areas. A revival of this organic commercial relationship between the small town and the rural community around it was only possible after the revival of peasant sideline production and rural industry in the early 1980s. The peasants, wrote Fei, 'figured out new and ingenious ways to make money in addition to farming their small contracted plots. Freed from constraints, the rural labourers developed a flourish-ing industrial base in the small towns across the countryside.' Industrialization in China could now follow an entirely different path from that in the West, where historically modern industry had grown at the expense of the countryside, with farmers driven to bankruptcy and forced to swarm into the cities to become the tools of capitalism:

In contrast, industrialization in socialist China is following an utterly different road. On the basis of a prospering agriculture, the peasants, filled with enthusiasm, run collectively owned township industries. These industries, by assisting, consolidating, and promoting the agricultural economy, bring about the simultaneous development of agriculture, sideline occupations, and industry. The co-ordinated development of all three sectors of the economy has led to a thriving and prospering countryside. This road of industrialization was not planned in advance by theoreticians. Rather, it has been created by the peasants on the basis of their experience in real life. Over the years, millions of peasants have left the land, but not their village, to enter township industrial enterprises.

The costs of reform

In less than a decade the second rural revolution had visibly transformed the face of much of China, but proceeded at a pace which outstripped theory and created new problems of its own. These provided ammunition to more conservative critics whose concern was first given voice by the senior Politburo Standing Committee member Chen Yun at a special Party conference in September 1985. Grain production, after rising by 33 per cent between 1978 and 1984, had fallen back by 7 per cent in 1985. Although bad weather was partly to blame, the abolition of grain quotas in the same year had encouraged a shift to more profitable cash crops by entrepreneurial peasants and a reduction in the size of grain acreage. Chen Yun warned that grain must still be the basis for a healthy rural economy. Feeding and clothing a billion people constituted one of China's major political as well as economic challenges, and grain shortages would lead to social disaster. Controls on grain production were reimposed, but a rise in the price of seed and fertilizers meant that although production picked up again, farmers made little money and often expended more effort on poor land. The answer could have been to allow grain prices to rise proportionately— but the Chinese leadership feared that this would add to concern about inflation and create a 'Polish problem' of urban unrest.

Grain imports were increased in 1986 for the first time in five years.

Chen Yun's criticisms also prompted more open acknowledgement that a significant minority of peasants were still seriously disadvantaged. 'There are regions with around one hundred million people whose problems of keeping warm and not having enough to eat have yet to be solved', commented *Liaowang* (No. 45, 1985), the reformers' popular magazine. More precise figures were later provided by the *Farmers Daily* (8 May 1986): 356 counties, 14 per cent of the total, had average incomes of less than 200 yuan in 1985. Their population totalled nearly 124 million, or 14 per cent of the rural population. Nearly one-third of this group had an average income of less than 150 yuan. (These figures compared with an average rural income nationally of 339 yuan, which included 400 counties—one-fifth of the total—where the figure was in excess of 500 yuan.) Most of the poorer areas had shown at least some improvement since the late 1970s, but a few had made no progress at all. Videos were privately circulated within the Party showing areas where life had not significantly improved since Liberation.

For the majority of peasants whose lives improved, the first priority was to eat more and better food, the second to build a new and better house. While cadres pointed with pride to new building as evidence of successful reform, rural planners voiced increasing concern at the loss of arable land. The housing boom also indirectly caused land deterioration. A village near Fuzhou visited in November 1983 had recently levelled a tangerine orchard while it expanded its local industry, including workshops to produce saws, wooden furniture, plastic rope—and bricks. Tangerine trees grow best on raised mounds of earth: this rich soil from the destroyed orchard provided the raw material for the bricks. A letter in the provincial *Fujian Daily* (25 Nov.) indicated that the problem was widespread. 'The evil trend of digging up the fields to make bricks', said the headline, 'must be stopped.' The writer complained that throughout his county the peasants were helping themselves to good earth for brick-making, in some places baring the soil till they reached bedrock. When reproached they would reply that 'Now the land has been contracted out to us peasants you can mind your own business. What's the harm anyhow in taking a bit of earth to make bricks?'

But more perceptive peasants, according to the letter-writer, understood the problem very well: 'This is killing the chicken to get the eggs', they lamented. 'If it does not stop, we shall be smashing the ricebowl of our children and grandchildren.'

House-building also diverted newly created surpluses away from productive investment which the reforms were supposed to stimulate (although rural investment still increased sharply in the 1980s). In 1986 per capita expenditure on building new houses averaged 51 yuan. Spending for productive purposes in the same year was less than 17 yuan per capita, 10 per cent less than in 1985. Many peasants had gone into debt to build new houses with extravagant features such as porches and balconies. Peasants also tended to regard investment in housing (privately owned in the countryside throughout the political campaigns of the past, including even the Cultural Revolution) as the safest form of family legacy. Not all of the loss went to private housing: it also supplied land for new roads, public buildings, rural factories, and recreation grounds. Figures issued in 1985 showed that in the previous year the amount of arable land had decreased by over 19 million *mu*—an area equivalent to the total of such land in Fujian province. The survey revealed that some land was actually taken back into illegal private ownership, claimed by its original owners as 'ancestral fields' or 'ancestral hills'.

There was also growing concern that the reversion to household farming had weakened the ability of the collective to maintain and improve vital irrigation and drainage facilities. The village or township still had the power to mobilize peasant labour when required. (In Shanxi province, famous for its village opera, there was a saying that 'the collective provides the stage and the peasants sing the opera'.) But the scale of the problem was increasing. China possessed some 68,000 reservoirs and 700,000 kilometres of river dykes, mostly built during the Great Leap or in the Cultural Revolution, and often to low standards. A 1986 survey reported that many had not been properly maintained and were now in 'a dangerous state'. Investment in irrigation and drainage had also decreased—the figure for 1985 was the lowest for twenty-five years—although some argued that it had been much too high and misdirected in the past.

By 1986–7 the new problems generated by the rural reforms

were openly discussed. The journal *Rural Economic Questions* (No. 2, 1986) wrote of a loss of momentum in rural economic reform and the growth of 'a new kind of hesitancy':

The new labour system has on the one hand stimulated economic development and on the other has created challenges for population control ... With the family as a basic economic unit, more children means more work hands. In some places in particular, over the past one or two years there have been large drops in grain and cotton production. As a result, non-agricultural trades have felt the pinch and private individual businesses have withered. ...

In the flurry of encouraging rural development, the problems of collapsing irrigation systems, pests, soil destruction and erosion, and the excessively small scale of farm units have dimly come into view. If rural China underwent a 'quiet revolution' in the 1980s, it is now in a 'silent crisis'.

In broad economic terms, the reformers now concluded that the problem in the countryside was not simply that of institutional reform, which had now been largely completed. The peasant still suffered from the classic 'scissors' of low prices for its produce and high prices for the essential inputs. Because of inflation, a system of indexing to establish price parity between industrial product and farm produce prices was required. The peasant needed more incentive to stay on the land and particularly to grow grain. He also needed assured sources of fertilizer and fuel at guaranteed prices. The experts also argued that agriculture was still under-capitalized. In 1987 agriculture accounted for only 5 per cent of state expenditure against an average of 11 per cent in the previous five Five Year Plans. The state should invest more in the countryside, and persuade peasants to invest more themselves (in agriculture, for local money was being poured into commerce and industry). It was also generally agreed that farm units were far too small, and there was a growing shortage of rural technicians (previously funded by the collective). Early in 1987 a joint investigation by research bodies set up by the State Council and the Communist Party recommended: (1) raising prices to guarantee farmers 'a fair return for their work'; (2) spreading technologies that could give 'high yield for low investment'; (3) curbing use of land for non-agricultural purposes (a building tax was to be levied on the conversion of cultivated land); (4) encouraging large-scale farming by the merger of individual farms; (5) bringing rural workers into the towns to cope with the expected growing labour surplus; and (6) increasing the number of farming technicians by two hundred thousand. In addition, peasants were now assured that the period for which land was contracted to them would be fifty—not fifteen—years, and that children might inherit their rights.

The rural argument

Were twenty years of the people's communes a disaster for China, or was it overall a necessary stage which laid the basis for the higher yield but possibly also higher risk policies of the 1980s? The official view became increasingly critical not only of the Great Leap Forward but the whole ethos of collectivization. In 1980 Deng Xiaoping had cautiously agreed that there was 'some ground' for the view that 'the pace of socialist transformation [in the countryside] had been too rapid'. The result might have been better, he continued, if the transition to higher forms of co-operative organization had 'advanced step by step' (31 May 1980). By 1985 his verdict had become wholly negative: Mao Zedong, he said, had made the grave mistake of neglecting the development of the productive forces, and the people's communes had been established 'in defiance of the laws governing socio-economic development'.

Our experience in the twenty years from 1958 to 1978 teaches us that poverty is not socialism, that socialism means eliminating poverty. Unless you are developing the productive forces and raising living standards, you cannot say that you are building socialism (15 Apr. 1985).

It is evident (although rarely acknowledged today in China) that the specialized farming and rural industry of the 1980s has derived some benefit from the earlier collective efforts of the rural work-force when it was organized into communes, brigades, and teams. An orchard near Fuzhou, visited in 1983, had been planted in 1977 and was just beginning to show a profit which was shared under the new responsibility system. How had the land, previously barren, been cleared in the first place, and when? The answer was that the work had begun in 1972 with the use of volunteer labour to open up the land and plant it with mulberries as a first crop. Yet the suggestion that voluntary labour under the people's communes had played a positive role was greeted with scornful laughter. A more thoughtful response is to admit that current achievements are based upon labour-intensive 'capital construction' investment in land improvement of the 1960s and 1970s, but to argue that under the previous system the investment could never have been fully realized. By emphasizing single-crop (particularly grain) cultivation and by discouraging markets and rural commerce, the advocates of 'Big and Public' production and distribution of agricultural produce made it impossible for the countryside to escape from a low level of self-sufficiency. (Paradoxically, given the lack of a thriving commodity economy in the countryside, a policy concentrating upon grain production did at least guarantee a minimum standard of living—except during the near-starvation which followed the Great Leap.)

Agricultural planners do recognize that the earliest efforts to stimulate rural industry during the Great Leap Forward prepared the way. Many enterprises are the successors to local 'brigade industries'. While the ambitious 'backyard steel furnaces' and other attempts at rapid industrialization collapsed, more modest industrial advances such as farm machinery repair workshops, brick kilns, and simple food-processing plants survived. Great Leap policy has been described as 'misguided, placing excessive stress on manufacturing and assigning no importance to commerce and services'. Policy during the Cultural Revolution was ambivalent towards local industry: on the one hand it was encouraged as a sign of progress towards 'self-sufficiency'; on the other the low level of rural productivity and the discouragement of rural commerce deprived local industry both of funds for expansion and of markets for its goods.

Despite all its defects, the people's communes strategy could hardly be regarded as the neglect of agriculture, and comparisons between Mao and Stalin in this context (heard from disillusioned Chinese economists) are incorrect. Yet Mao's repeated exhortations to decentralize economic decision-making and to shift priorities from industry to agriculture were largely cancelled out by the imposition of inflexible policies from above and the discouragement of the peasant market economy, without which the countryside could never compete against the economic weight of the industrial sector. The irony is that the politics of centralized command and the disapproval of bourgeois-labelled rural commerce also stemmed from Mao. The question remains whether after Mao's death the collective structure could have been made viable by selective reform, or whether it had to be virtually abolished. As has been shown, the original intention had been to adopt the responsibility system only in areas of need, while reviving rural markets and encouraging diversification of crops and the growth of rural industry. But the headlong spread of the responsibility system led the whole of China, within the space of four years, into almost universal private land-use. There was no opportunity to discover whether the reforms in marketing and production could have been effectively linked to a continuation of full-scale collectivization. William Hinton has argued that it is unlikely that if the collectives 'had been given the same autonomy in production and the same freedom to develop markets that private producers now enjoy' they would have lagged behind.

This may be true, but only in the context of the survival of shared collective values which were already severely eroded. The second rural revolution could not be constrained, partly because of the 'all-or-nothing' tendency in the implementation of party policy, but chiefly because most peasants—given a glimpse of something different—quickly tired of a system which had long ago lost the gloss of the first revolution. For the first time since 1949, the Chinese peasant now had the opportunity to enrich himself without being censured. Deng Xiaoping advocated 'getting rich first' on the grounds that 'once a person has become rich, the others will soon follow his example'. Worries about polarization of income were rejected by the evidence that while relative inequalities might increase, in absolute terms the poorer peasants were also better off than before. The *People's Daily* rejected 'the old concepts of egalitarianism' (9 July 1987):

> In the past, we feared prosperity in varying degrees while striving for common prosperity. This resulted in common poverty. Today, we have implemented the policy of allowing some people to become rich before others, and the trend towards common prosperity has appeared ...
> Had we practised egalitarianism as we did in the past, failed to award the diligent and punish the lazy, treated those who do their work properly in the same way as those who do not, we would have only

encouraged people to choose the easiest job, to hold back their efforts in work, and to be satisfied with low efficiency. Many localities would probably still be worried about food and clothing.

But increased opportunities also meant increased risks, even among the 'ten-thousand-yuan households' which had reached this annual income by specializing in farming, crafts, or trade. A 1987 study of 104 such households in a county in Hubei province showed that half of them had 'stopped production, went bankrupt or were in poor condition'. There was a price to be paid for rural entrepreneurship.

CHAPTER EIGHT

The Growth of Dissent

POETS AND DEMOCRACY

The train had slowed down on the Gansu corridor line to the far north-west, pausing at a station so small that there was no platform. Outside there were more people begging for food. 'If they are not landlord elements,' explained a passenger, 'then they must be idlers. Let them starve!' But the 16-year-old Wei Jingsheng, on his way to Exchange Revolutionary Experiences in Xinjiang, felt sorry for a woman wearing rags beneath his window, and leant out to give her some cakes he had bought in Lanzhou. What he then saw would set him on his career as China's most famous dissident.

I twisted my head back and left my hand hanging in mid-air. For what I had just seen was quite beyond imagination and up till then unbelievable. That woman with her hair over her shoulders was a girl of about seventeen or eighteen. Apart from the hair, there was nothing at all to cover her body which could be called clothing. Her whole body was just covered with ashes and mud which from a distance might look like clothes. Since she was among a crowd of little naked beggars, one might miss it altogether.

'There's a lot of them like this around here . . .' explained the passenger, chuckling. 'Some are quite pretty, and if you give them some food then without it costing anything you can. . . .'

Wei spent the rest of the journey pondering how such things could be allowed under socialism. In Xinjiang he met students 'sent down' to the countryside, demobilized soldiers, 'rightists' who had been exiled there for years, all with stories to tell about being cheated or victimized by the Party. He learnt a great deal more serving in the army for four years, then working quietly as an electrician in Beijing. His first wall-poster 'Democracy: The Fifth Modernization', attracted a small group of readers at Democracy Wall in December 1978. Their 'unofficial magazine'

Exploration *was the most outspoken, criticizing even Deng Xiaoping. In October 1979 Wei defended himself against charges of betraying secrets and counter-revolution. 'The fate of Marxism,' he told the court, 'is like many religions in history: after the second and third generations its revolutionary essence is abstracted and its theoretical ideals are used to deceive the people.' Wei was sentenced to fifteen years in jail.*

(From Wei's account of his Red Guard experiences in 1966.)

The Red Guard legacy

The Cultural Revolution took an entire generation of young students or slightly older 'educated youth' and gave them an unintended education into how the Chinese political system worked. They learned through experience, one ex-Red Guard recalled, that 'the new authorities were a hundred times harsher than the old, that "eleven years [1966–76] are not as good as seventeen [1949–66]", and that the revival of feudalism is a much more real danger in China than the rebirth of capitalism'. (The Cultural Revolution leaders had argued that the first seventeen years had been mostly wasted until they discovered the correct revolutionary path.) New perspectives were opened up by allowing large numbers of young people to travel freely around the country to 'exchange experiences' and by their subsequent immersion in factional fighting. 'One might say that the first two weeks of March [1967] marked my political coming of age', recalled a Red Guard from Canton. 'It was the first time that I ever really sat down and independently questioned politics in China.' Personal suffering also prompted unfamiliar questions. 'Why should two good people like my parents be forced to divorce each other?' asked the Hunanese student Liang Heng after enduring a long interrogation. 'Why did the peasants fear the cadres so terribly if they were representatives of our great Communist Party?' More profound politicization followed the 'sending down' to the countryside of twelve million young Chinese. The reality of hard rural life and the experience at first hand of oppressive and ignorant cadres led to disillusion with the Party and often with Mao himself, mixed in retrospect with a certain pride at having survived. A poem written (in English) in 1984 by a language student at Xiamen University conveys something of the reality of being a 'worker, peasant or soldier'.

Poem: The Past

I dreamed my yesterday last night,
It made me toss about in bed.
The past I've undergone in the border areas
Was fully ten years long.
Could you imagine that
My family was sent into exile,
From the capital city to the centre
Of Taklamakan Desert?!

A boy soldier only fifteen had to risk
His life in numerous dangers.
He left bloodstains in anti-atom tunnels in the depths
Of Tianshan Mountains.
He dripped sweat in large crop fields in the hinterlands
Of the Gobi Desert.
He indulged in fantasy that he might contract a serious disease
And was sent to hospital to take a rest.
Oh, what a poor thing!

I rejoice that the past at last has passed,
Our country and people have been reliberated.
I prize my yesterday,
It tested and taught me a lot.
People say that 'When the bitter is finished,
Then comes the sweet'.
I believe that to prevent
The reappearance of yesterday's nightmare,
Forever we must keep sober and work hard.

Dissenting arguments were expressed sometimes obliquely through the medium of the 'great democracy'—wall-posters and manifestos—of the Cultural Revolution itself, but more often were circulated clandestinely. To write anything at all was regarded as dangerous. The poet Bei Dao recalls how he took advantage of his employment as a photographer, recording progress on a building site, to lock himself in a hut which he designated as a darkroom to work on his first novel, *Waves*. Later he borrowed a room in the suburbs but was spotted writing by the local neighbourhood committee through the window, fled, and never dared return. The Tiananmen demonstrations of 1976 (the 'April Fifth Movement') brought together many young activists for the first time, who formed friendships and began to discuss politics in private. Those who survived persecution or in some cases escaped execution formed the core two-and-a-half years later of the Democracy Movement.

Poets who do not believe

Poems which had been written in private notebooks and passed from hand to hand in the early years of the Cultural Revolution were read out in Tiananmen Square in April 1976, chalked on the pavement, and inscribed over mourning wreaths to Zhou Enlai. The authors of the most famous verses were pursued wrathfully by the ultra-left authorities. The immediate post-Mao leadership under Hua Guofeng not only failed to rehabilitate those who had suffered after Tiananmen but allowed the arrest of many more activists. Prison established new links between individual protesters who had previously been isolated, while underground literary journals began to circulate outside. Many of the poems had been copied and secretly preserved—in 'flower-pots, hollowed-out candles, the linings of coal stoves, or [by] burying them in the countryside'. The issue of whether or not to 'reverse the verdict' on Tiananmen was taken up by Deng Xiaoping's economic reformers as a way of discrediting the centre-left Maoists led by Hua who had acquiesced at the time. Sixteen teachers at the Second Foreign Languages Institute in Beijing pasted up on the college wall a collection of poems on the first anniversary of Zhou's death. Later they published, unofficially but evidently with covert official support, several volumes totalling more than 1,500 poems and prose pieces written in April 1976. Finally, on 15 November 1978, the original verdict was 'reversed' by the Beijing Party Committee, which declared it to be 'a completely revolutionary event'. On the day of the announcement, a bus from the Foreign Languages Institute parked in Tiananmen Square to sell the unofficial poetry books. Hua Guofeng hastily yielded ground and wrote an inscription for an authorized edition of one of the volumes—to the anger of its original compilers. Hua had been Minister of

Public Security at the time of the Tiananmen demonstration and was therefore responsible for its suppression.

The poetry of this period was heroically defiant, asserting the ultimate triumph of revolutionary values which, many young participants in the Cultural Revolution still believed, had been subverted by a coalition of left- and right-wing 'feudal bureaucrats'. They condemned the feudalism of the first emperor of China, with whom Mao in his final years liked to compare himself:

The premier's spirit lives for ever,
Children and grandchildren will lift the Red Flag.
China is no longer the China of the past;
The people are not completely stupid.
The feudal society of Qin Shihuang is gone never to return
And we believe in Marxism-Leninism.
Those Outstanding Scholars who have emasculated Marxism-
    Leninism
Can go to hell!

A four-line poem with a total of twenty Chinese characters by Wang Lishan, a young factory worker from Shaanxi province, was judged by the ultra-left leaders to be the most 'counter-revolutionary of all'. To add to their fury, its text was quoted in full by the official account—supposedly hostile to the demonstrators—of the Tiananmen incident. (Yao Wenyuan, in charge of the ultra-left's propaganda, suspected this inclusion was itself a 'counter-revolutionary' act.)

> In my grief I hear demons shriek;
> I weep while wolves and jackals laugh.
> Though tears I shed to mourn a hero,
> With head raised high, I unsheathe my sword.

Wang was pursued in a national police hunt but evaded arrest. In December 1978 he joined the Communist Party, thus symbolizing the reversal of verdicts on Tiananmen. Soon after he published a challenging article in the unofficial Democracy Movement journal *Beijing Spring* (No. 5), which must have pushed Party tolerance to its limits: Wang argued that in the revised constitution then under discussion, the clause on freedom of speech should include the freedom to make counter-revolutionary statements, including those which were 'against the Party'. His own experience showed that what was counter-revolutionary at one time could be applauded at another. He also argued that the Party was not the state but a private body whose discipline should only extend to its own membership.

The defiant optimism of this transitional period was shared by other less evidently political poets. 'Trust the future!' by Guo Lusheng had been written in 1970–1 and became widely known as it circulated illegally among Chinese youth. Guo was one of the very first Red Guards, belonging to the United Action group which was condemned at the time as 'conservative' but had itself attacked Lin Biao, at that time Chairman Mao's 'chosen successor', as a conspirator against the Cultural Revolution. *Beijing Spring* now published a sequel to 'Trust the future', with the title 'Trust in life' (the first and last verses are reproduced here).

> When I was imprisoned in the black cage
> I could still endure the pain after punishment
> By struggling to my feet, biting my finger
> And writing in blood on the wall: Trust in life . . .
>
> .   .   .   .   .
>
> As long as the earth continues to revolve,
> So long as history advances,
> So long as my successors do not come to an end
> Then I will—trust the future, trust in life.

An early poem by Bei Dao, 'The Answer', written in 1972 but revised at the time of Tiananmen, was reprinted from the first issue of the unofficial journal *Today*, which he jointly edited, and published in the official *Poetry Journal*.

> I come into this world
> Bringing only paper, rope, a shadow,
> To proclaim before the judgement
> The voices of the judged.
>
> Let me tell you, world,
> *I do not believe!*
> If a thousand challengers lie beneath your feet,
> Count me as number one thousand and one.
>
> I don't believe the sky is blue;
> I don't believe in the sound of thunder;
> I don't believe that dreams are false;
> I don't believe that death has no revenge.

Publication of this poem marked the start of what became known by its critics as the 'poetry of shadows', upsetting older poets by its loose structure, unusual imagery, and lack of a clearly positive message. Poetry groups were formed to discuss and recite shadows poetry and a national conference was organized in April 1980, while numerous examples were published in provincial and local poetry journals. Bei Dao himself was attacked by the distinguished elder poet Ai Qing, who had in his youth urged Chinese poets to follow the revolutionary rhythms of Whitman and Mayakovsky. Ai mocked a 'poem' of one word supposedly published by Bei Dao for being shorter than its two-word title. (In fact this was a misunderstanding: the 'poem' was only a stanza, with subtitle, from his 'Notes from the City of the Sun'.) Ai had been the target of a bitter campaign during the 1957 'anti-rightist' movement and remained silent for twenty-one years, spending much of the time in labour camps. Like other rehabilitated intellectuals who now sought to regain confidence in the system which allowed them a second chance, Ai was disturbed by the subversive implications of the new 'obscure' poetry. He celebrated his return to writing with a more positive affirmation:

> Red fire,
> Red blood,
> Red the wild lilies,
> Red the azalea blooms, a red flood,
> Red the pomegranate in May,
> Red is the sun at the birth of day.
>
> But most beautiful of them all,
>   the red flags on forward march!

Martyrs of the Cultural Revolution

The Party also rehabilitated posthumously some of the dissenting voices of the Cultural Revolution who had paid for defiance with their lives. But its nervousness is illustrated by the contrasting treatment of the three most famous 'martyrs' of this period, Yu Luoke, Zhang Zhixin, and Wang Shenyou.

'So the Chinese ping-pong team has won thanks to keeping Mao's Thoughts in Command', wrote China's earliest young dissident in his diary in May 1966. 'But people are asking, didn't the basketball team also study the Chairman's Works ... and how come they were beaten by the Russians?' Yu Luoke, then aged 24, had already written an article criticizing the ultra-left propagandist Yao Wenyuan, part of which was published in a Shanghai newspaper—but as 'negative material' inviting criticism by the 'revolutionary masses'. Later, in the first year of the Cultural Revolution, Yu wrote an essay, soon to become famous, 'On Class Background', in which he demolished the so-called 'blood lineage theory' (*xuetonglun*) that only the sons and daughters of revolutionaries could be good revolutionaries. Bands of Red Guards with the correct class pedigree were searching out and murdering whole families who came from the 'five black categories' of class enemies. They chanted a jingle: 'Heroes breed heroic sons; baddies all hatch rotten ones.' The Red Guard magazine in which Yu's essay appeared became a valued item on the unofficial market for swapping Cultural Revolutionary materials, worth many prized Mao badges. Yu argued at length that the influence of the family was outweighed by that of society, and that to condemn future generations to wear the same black political label was the product of feudalism and not socialism. Soon put under secret police surveillance, Yu was arrested in January 1968 and executed in March 1970. He had been offered a chance to recant but, so the story goes, contemptuously rejected it, telling his gaolers instead: 'I've thought things over. My toothpaste has run out. Could you ask my family to send me another tube?'

Post-Mao leaders of the Chinese Communist Party have adopted a cautious approach towards those who, unlike most of them, boldly challenged the ultra-leftists (and sometimes Mao himself) during the Cultural Revolution. Yu was formally rehabilitated in 1980, but has been rarely mentioned in the official press. Unofficially he is the foremost folk-hero of Cultural Revolutionary dissent, the subject of many poems and eulogies by activists of the Democracy Wall period. His reputation has also been spread through his sister Yu Luojin, whose autobiographical novel *A Winter's Tale* is dedicated to him and circles obsessively around her guilt at having failed to conceal his diary from the authorities—desperate for a hiding place, she left it in a public lavatory where it was discovered and used in evidence against him. Luojin herself became a controversial figure in 1981 by denouncing conventional sexual morality—she fell out of love with her second husband and was granted a divorce. In 1986 she left China and sought political asylum in West Germany.

The authorities felt easier with the story of another dissenter, Zhang Zhixin, a young Party member in Liaoning province who was executed after having her throat cut so that she could not profess continued loyalty to the Party with her last breath. Zhang had defied the provincial leadership, headed during the Cultural Revolution by Mao's nephew and 'Gang of Four' supporter Mao Yuanxin, refusing to accept that the previous leadership consisted of 'capitalist-roaders'. Similarly she defended the reputation of Peng Dehuai and Liu Shaoqi at the national level and criticized Lin Biao's ultra-leftism. She was sentenced to indefinite imprisonment in August 1970. In 1975 the new ultra-left campaign to 'exercise all-round dictatorship against the bourgeoisie' led to a call by Mao Yuanxin for exemplary death sentences on those deemed to have deserted the revolutionary cause for the bourgeois camp. 'Every day she lives longer she becomes more counter-revolutionary. Let's kill her and have done with it', Mao Yuanxin is alleged to have said. Her windpipe was severed without anaesthetic at six o'clock one evening. The next morning, with her throat heavily bandaged, she was paraded before the other prison inmates for a formal sentencing, then taken to the execution ground and shot.

In March 1979 the case of Zhang Zhixin was finally reversed. Her tale offered safer ground for post-Mao beatification than that of the principled Red Guard Yu Luoke. The particularly horrible circumstances of her death, combined with her firm support for the (in retrospect) 'correct' leadership of the Party, provided an apt morality tale for the late 1970s when the Cultural Revolution was being officially blamed solely on a small handful of 'anti-Party' criminals. Two songs which she had written in prison (she came from a music teacher's family) called 'Whose Crime?' and 'Seeing the New Year In' were published. Even so, the fact that her dissenting views began with criticism of Mao himself, for having gone too far to the 'left' from the Great Leap onwards, did not feature in the official hagiography. Zhang Zhixin's defiant essay, 'My Views Remain Unchanged', said of Mao that after the Great Leap 'his scientific attitude grew weak, his sense of modesty diminished, and his democratic style of work also weakened'. The ultra-left's argu-

ment that new bourgeois elements could 'emerge' under socialism also originated with Mao. The Party's uneasiness even while
rehabilitating her is reflected in a speech by Ren Zhongyi,
successor to Mao Yuanxin in Liaoning province, which sought
to explain why no one protested at her death at the time:

First, when the Gang of Four were on the rampage doing all they could
within the Party to stifle the atmosphere of 'seeking truth from facts', it
was impossible for the case of Zhang Zhixin to be brought up in detail
and freely discussed at meetings. Secondly, because of the evil
influence of the Gang of Four's ultra-left ideas, some of our comrades
failed to recognize the correctness of Zhang's views and did not
consider her innocent. Thirdly, lack of political courage in face of the
despotic rule of [Mao Yuanxin] in Liaoning led some people to remain
silent before the abuses and depredations of the Gang and their
henchmen; a few persons even followed the Gang servilely.

It was left to the unofficial magazines to publish her argument in
full, and to complain that many of those involved in the case
(including the prison doctor who cut her vocal chords) still
remained at large. The doctor is alleged to have cut the
windpipes of more than sixty prisoners before their execution—
Zhang was the forty-third.

Wang Shenyou, a third pioneer dissenting voice from mainstream Maoism, had still not been officially rehabilitated ten
years after his death. What made his case particularly unmentionable was the date of his execution, 21 April 1977, *after* the
overthrow of the Gang of Four. The son of a working-class cadre
family, Wang discovered Marxism for himself during the
Cultural Revolution, but believed that it had been corrupted
into a rigid dogma, compounded in China's case by the non-
proletarian composition of the Communist Party. In an article
seeking to rehabilitate Wang, the Shanghai dissident Fu Shenqi
wrote:

He felt that the dogmas that Mao proposed in his old age were simply a
cover for feudalism. Since China lacked a mature working class, the
Communist Party developed as a peasant party led by revolutionary
intellectuals, and the revolution it carried out was not proletarian-
socialist but peasant, with a strong feudal tinge. After the revolution
Chinese society therefore gradually evolved into a new form of oriental
despotism. Once Wang said, 'Mao is just a peasant with a military
cap'.

Wang also supported the post-Stalinization reforms in the Soviet Union as a sign that 'scientific socialism' was gaining ground. Wang was arrested immediately after Mao's death, when Shanghai was still under ultra-left control, but was sentenced after the change of regime. 'It would be disloyal to Chairman Mao not to kill this person', the Shanghai authorities are supposed to have said. The crusading journalist Liu Binyan has cited Wang's case as an example of the still unmentionable 'hidden corners' of recent history. Wang was 'a much better thinker than Zhang Zhixin', a 'real hero deserving our admiration'. Liu told a conference in Shanghai in November 1986 that there were as many as eighty similar cases of such people who struggled against the Gang of Four and were executed by their successors. Naming those high officials who had signed Wang's death warrant, he asked why no writer had yet tackled the story. (Two months later Liu himself was expelled from the Communist Party, accused of 'making trouble' by his investigations: see pp. 217–18.)

The search for genuine Marxism

One of the most remarkable features of the Cultural Revolution was the speed with which young rebels graduated from mechanical repetition of the dogmatic slogans of the Mao-cult to a search for 'genuine Marxism-Leninism', especially after disillusion set in with the Lin Biao affair and the 'educated youth' were consigned to the countryside. 'This search for a yardstick against which Mao could be measured', notes Anita Chan in her survey of ex-Red Guards, 'brought most of my interviewees to read Marxist classics for the first time.' The ex-Red Guard Liu Guokai has described the effect of the 1968 'Whither China' critique by the Shengwulian group (see pp. 78–81) upon an emerging political consciousness:

The Cultural Revolution widened people's horizons. They learnt so many things hitherto unknown to them. They began to think and analyse. After the onslaughts of the Cultural Revolution, the existing regime lost its former holy lustre. Cadres were unmasked and lost their former prestige, which was built upon deceit, whitewash, and administrative order....

The outcry of 'Whither China' struck a responsive chord in the hearts of many people. It made people think, and had a profound and far-reaching influence. Although such ultra-left thinking made only a brief appearance in society, the ideas were spread far and wide ... Those who read it told others about it in secret. Quite a few students and educated young workers accepted ideas in the article and developed them further. They lost interest in factional struggles and turned their attention to the bigger issues of the existing system.

In Guangdong a group of young ex-Red Guards studied the Marxist classics so well that Jiang Qing, while condemning the result of their work, conceded that 'the right-wing seems to study Marx and Lenin better than the left!' In the more relaxed political atmosphere of the south, the group displayed its first draft of 'On socialist democracy and legality' in September 1973, written under the collective pseudonym Li Yizhe, with a revised version in November 1974 timed to coincide with the eve of the long-delayed Fourth National People's Congress. Condemned as a 'reactionary document', the essay became the target of a compulsory criticism campaign. In Guangzhou alone, 7,600 'Criticize Li Yizhe' groups were formed within four months. Worse followed *after* the fall of the Gang of Four, when the authors were perversely accused of being followers of the Gang and sent to labour camps. Writers on the 1978 Democracy Wall in Beijing called for their release, which was achieved in February 1979, but the most active member of the group thereafter, Wang Xizhe, was rearrested two years later.

The Li Yizhe document argued that many of the characteristics of the political system established by Lin Biao persisted after his death. The main danger to the socialist system was a 'feudal social-fascist dictatorship' which appeared ultra-left on the surface but in reality belonged to the extreme right. No intelligent reader would fail to grasp that Li Yizhe's description of the Lin Biao 'system' still largely applied; indeed, the document openly argued that it was a fundamental part of the political practice of the Communist Party. 'China went straight into socialism from being a semi-feudal, semi-colonial society', they wrote. 'The evil habit of feudal autocratic tyranny is buried deep in the minds of the masses and of nearly all members of the Communist Party.' Their targets were easily identifiable as stock-in-trade dogmas of current ultra-leftism:

- the theory that 'a "genius" appears once every several hundred or thousand years, that a "genius" deserves unbounded

adulation and absolute loyalty...and that anyone who
opposes a "genius" should be overthrown'. (The 'genius
theory of history', commented Li Yizhe acidly, 'simply abo-
lishes eight hundred million brains'.)

- the emergence of a 'highly privileged stratum' in the leadership, which constituted a 'new form of bourgeois ownership
[whose essence] is the private takeover of public property
when the means of production are socially owned'. (The ultra-
left leadership, who themselves privately enjoyed many
'socially owned' privileges, later appropriated this argument to
criticize Deng Xiaoping for allegedly representing the 'new
bourgeoisie' in the Party.)

- the wholesale condemnation of loyal Party cadres, nominally
blamed on Lin Biao but (as everyone knew) the result of much
more widespread ultra-left intrigue. 'Why should the
thousands of unjust verdicts at national and local levels not
be set right? . . . Should such comrades as Deng Xiaoping
and Zhao Ziyang never be readmitted to the Central
Committee?'

- the undermining of enthusiasm for work by 'the craze for
common ownership which did so much damage to the basic
interests of the workers and peasant masses'. This was a
particularly daring criticism which anticipated the post-Mao
virtual abolition of the people's communes.

- the favourable comparisons made between the first Chinese
emperor Qin Shihuang and Mao which helped to legitimize
the semi-feudal system now in operation. If one said that
feudalism had been progressive in its time, asked Li Yizhe,
should one not say the same about bourgeois democracy? 'As
we are such merciless critics of the bourgeoisie from Cromwell
to Robespierre . . . why do we find the landlord regime of Qin
Shihuang so splendid?'

The Li Yizhe group still believed, as did many young Chinese
in the mid-1970s, in the forms of mass democracy which had
been popularized early in the Cultural Revolution. They welcomed a circular by Mao in 1974 which approved of the display
of handwritten posters. They approved the idea of young
revolutionaries 'going against the tide' which was promoted by
Wang Hongwen at the 1973 Tenth Party Congress. Yet they
commented that such exhortations were meaningless as long as

'fetters, manacles, bars, and bullets still awaited those who spoke out fearlessly without the backing of important people at the Party's centre'. Li Yizhe also mocked the famous 'blank exam paper' which was supposed to have 'boldly challenged the revisionist line in education' (see above, p. 90):

In August [1973] someone called Zhang Tiesheng emerged to 'go against the tide'. But the result was not that his head was cut off, nor that he was sent to jail; nor, apparently, did he have a wife to divorce him. Instead he soared right up to the top. It is said that he retired to some palace of learning to invent the profound mystery of 'going against the tide'. But as for many of the revolutionaries who really fought against the Lin Biao system, many were beheaded and are still headless, many were sent to gaol and are still inside, while those who lost their jobs are still jobless.

Copies of the Li Yizhe manifesto circulated clandestinely among groups of educated youth, just as the 'Whither China' document had done previously, and both documents in turn provided a theoretical basis on which other Marxist—and to some extent neo-Maoist—enquirers would build. Perhaps the most remarkable of these was Chen Erjin. Chen, who worked as a teacher and statistician in a coal mine for most of the Cultural Revolution, is known to us only through the text of his essay 'On Proletarian-Democratic Revolution', written in the early 1970s but published in an unofficial Beijing magazine during the 1979 democracy movement. (Later active in the National Association for Democratic Journals formed by dissidents after the suppression of Democracy Wall, Chen was sentenced in 1982 to ten years' imprisonment for counter-revolution and specifically for 'trying to organize a political party'.) Chen, in the words of his English commentator Robin Munro, produced a synthesis of key aspects both of anti-bureaucratic Cultural Revolutionary theory and the post-Mao movement for democratization: 'On the one hand, revolutionary transformation, class struggle, erosion of the division of labour, direct mass action, and the building of genuine organs of workers' power; on the other, constitutional integration, stability and social harmony, economic rationality, individual freedom, and institutionalized democracy and legality.'

Chen described the emergence of an embryonic new ruling class in post-revolutionary China which was based on the possession not on capital, as under capitalism, but on power. The Party asserted a unified dominance over the twin powers of political leadership and economic control. Further adapting Marxism, Chen argued that classes in this new society were determined not, as in the past, by the 'division of labour' in the process of production, but by the 'divison of labour' in the exercise of power. China now found itself at the crossroads between further degeneration into a 'social-fascist dictatorship by the new ruling class', and the emergence of a true 'proletarian-democratic' system. This would be based on a system of people's conferences possessing real legislative power—here Chen's stress on the separation of powers anticipated official Party policy of the mid-1980s. Chen went further still by arguing for a two-party system in which a second party, also communist, would have a membership and run candidates in free elections against the existing Party. This would provide a 'rational form' for the conduct of internal Party argument which had hitherto been conducted out of the public eye and by conspiratorial 'inner-Party struggle'. Chen's scheme also included detailed proposals for grass-roots democracy in the factory, countryside, and even in the armed forces. Officers up to regimental level would be elected by the rank and file, although higher appointments were prudently reserved for the Minister of Defence! All of this, Chen insisted, was not 'pie in the sky' but arose inevitably from the growing resistance of the Chinese people themselves to being oppressed by the Party's monopolization of privilege, which amounted to a new form of private ownership:

Privilege-ownership involves the stripping from the working people as a whole of all human rights, as the bureaucrat class strives with might and main to reduce these to such 'rights' as are commonly enjoyed only by beasts of burden. Such a reduction of rights is utterly intolerable! Gradually, steadily, there is arising within the proletariat and working people as a whole, the most powerful call-to-arms of our time: Give us back democracy! Give us back freedom! Give us back equality! Give us back human rights! We want to live as human beings—we *will not* be beasts of burden!

Democracy Movement and new dissent

The rehabilitation of the 1976 Tiananmen demonstration in

November 1978 gave the green light to a revival of *dazibao* (big-character) posters on the streets of Beijing, which soon escalated into the Democracy Movement. This served a specific political purpose for Deng Xiaoping. It targeted the mainstream Maoist leadership around Hua Guofeng, denouncing them both for complicity in past injustices and for current privileges, and generated a genuine expression of public opinion which helped Deng to isolate this group (though not yet Hua himself) at the important Third Plenum in December 1978 where Deng's reform policy was launched. Thus Mao's former bodyguard Wang Dongxing, whose unit played a critical role in the arrest of the Gang of Four, was now denounced for building a palace (at an alleged and doubtless exaggerated cost of one hundred million pounds!) in the *Zhongnanhai* government area. Yet the posters originated as an outpouring on paper of a wide range of grievances, often brought to Beijing by petitioners with complaints to the central authorities, which gave the Democracy Movement a broader basis, linking for the first time a specific political argument with the demand for social justice. A central theme was that the past could not be blamed just on a handful of wicked leaders: 'Every government unit', said one of the earliest posters, 'still has secret lairs where the minions of the Gang of Four still hide. Unless we dig them out, then their poison will rise again and infect the masses.' New toleration for a degree of exposure to foreign ideas, and the presence of foreign journalists and students, also encouraged a more eclectic range of political thought. One journal, in discussing constitutional reform, quoted in turn from the American Constitution and that of North Korea. Another sent a message of support to 'our Dear Brothers, the Workers of Poland' on behalf of 'the young generation of the working class in China'. Poems and short stories emerged from underground, while young artists, many of whom were seeing their first reproductions of Impressionism, Expressionism, and other modern forms in the liberalized art magazines, experimented with new styles.

Pasting posters on the walls led to the publication of a score of unofficial magazines, including one or two which were believed to have the backing of reform-minded cadres. The young men and women, mostly workers with high school or college education and a Red Guard background, could be contacted through addresses or post box numbers. They soon made contact with other dissenters around the country, and some talked with foreign journalists (just as Deng himself had done in order to send a positive message in December 1978 to Democracy Wall, when the posters were beginning to attack his leftist opponents). Though Deng's tolerance was short-lived, those who were arrested no longer simply disappeared without trace. They could, to a limited extent, assert some rights under the newly emerging system. Many of the arrests led to new protests, generating a complex set of case histories known abroad as well as at home. The social issues to which ideological dissent was now linked soon included the inhumanity of the same prison system under which many dissenters would suffer.

The first to be arrested was Fu Yuehua, a 37-year-old unemployed woman who had petitioned the authorities, accusing a Party cadre of having raped her, and came to know many other petitioners who suffered injustice. Up to 10,000 flocked to Beijing that winter—mostly people from ordinary working families whose complaints against authority dated back many years. Fu was charged with 'disrupting public order' after helping to organize two demonstrations of peasants who carried banners calling for democracy and an end to 'hunger and persecution'. Eventually she was also charged with libel for the rape allegation: this rebounded embarrassingly for the authorities when at a second trial Fu revealed 'certain new questions'. According to one story, a jurist from outside Beijing, invited to join the hand-picked audience at the trial, had recognized the alleged rapist—who complained against the 'libel'—as a man of bad reputation. In another version, Fu had revealed intimate details of his anatomy before the court. After a two-month adjournment, Fu was sentenced to two years' imprisonment on the original charge. The charge of libel was dropped, although the judge still dismissed her claim of rape. 'The rulers have their swords—the people only have their mouths!' protested Fu's supporters.

Wei Jingsheng, China's most famous dissident of this period, who was sentenced to fifteen years' imprisonment on Deng Xiaoping's personal intervention, had been an outspoken agitator on Fu's behalf. His magazine *Exploration* championed the cause of the *shangfang* (literally, those who 'visit upwards' to appeal to the authorities), and published an account of Wei's visit to the police station responsible for Fu's arrest. An article by Wei exposing conditions in the main prison for political prisoners just outside Beijing, 'The Twentieth Century Bastille', was widely circulated in the dissident press. Wei was sentenced in October 1979 for passing 'military secrets' to a foreign journalist and for producing 'counter-revolutionary' writings. The first charge related to his incautious revelation of details about the Chinese action in Vietnam (which had been published in the internal bulletin *Reference News*). The second arose from an article directly criticizing Deng Xiaoping which precipitated his arrest.

Wei was a natural polemicist in a tradition which consciously referred back to the early years of the Republic. 'Those who fear that democracy will lead to disorder', he wrote in his first wall-poster ('Democracy: The Fifth Modernization'), 'are the same as those who said at the time of the 1911 revolution that if China has no emperor there will be lawlessness.' A sequel to the first essay echoes the challenging rhetoric of Mao's early polemics:

Can the Four Modernizations be achieved in a society governed by overlords and worked by professional and amateur slaves? Impossible! The situation in our country presents a tragic reality: not so long ago we were even forbidden to mention the Four Modernizations. The fact that we can talk about them now is put forward as a great dispensation, a favour granted us by those on high. Aren't you overwhelmed with gratitude? If you fail to shed tears of emotion, beware. Someone is likely to take down your number. Not all professional slaves are in uniform.

Wei was arrested within days of publishing an article calling on people to ensure that 'Deng Xiaoping does not degenerate into a dictator'. In response to Deng's recent speech (16 Mar. 1979) which set strict limits on the Democracy Movement, Wei called for a 'genuine general election' as the only way to save the leadership from its chronic afflictions—personal ambition and megalomania. More political rhetoric than programme, Wei's arguments nevertheless touched on a nerve still sensitive eight years later during the 1987 student movement, when Deng would condemn as 'bourgeois liberals' those who called for his release. Deng's colleagues were less sure: Chen Yun refused to get involved, commenting that 'others arrested him [Wei] and others must dispose of him'. Wei was reported to have been placed in isolation because his 'defiant spirit' infected other prisoners, but later there were rumours that his mental health had suffered and that he was being treated for schizophrenia.

The unofficial journal *April 5th Tribune* (No. 9) had taken issue with Wei's last article, arguing that to call Deng a dictator was to follow the Gang of Four's habit of 'capping' people with labels. It would take time to recover from problems whose roots lay deep in a defective system, the editors wrote. The upper levels of government were 'sincere' in wishing to reform it; opposition came from bureaucrats at the 'lower and middle levels'. Yet the journal's co-editor Liu Qing, a machinist and ex-student from Nanjing, obtained a transcript of Wei's trial and attempted to sell it at Democracy Wall. Though Liu escaped arrest in the confusion, he went straight to the police station where his friends were detained and defended his action: Wei's trial was supposed to be public, and the *People's Daily* had talked about it to the whole world. 'What divine law are we breaking? What is there about it that's illegal?' Arrested himself that night, Liu was assigned without trial to three years' 're-education through labour'. On completion of this period he was secretly sentenced to seven years' imprisonment, apparently having provoked the authorities with a nearly 200-page letter (*Notes from Prison*) which was smuggled abroad. Liu described in calm, scientific detail the regime of the re-education camp, most of whose inmates have not been sentenced by a court but are consigned by an administrative police order. A fellow-prisoner at his first gaol in Beijing summarized the system humorously for him:

You haven't done anything? Fine. You haven't broken a single law? Even better. Then we won't sentence you; we'll just send you to a camp for reform through labour ... Even if you haven't done anything wrong, you're capable of it, because you're the type that easily turns to crime ... Please believe me, this is for your own safety and your own good. That's why I am swallowing you up. You won't feel better until you're in my stomach, because there nothing can happen to you.

At the end of 1979 Democracy Wall was moved from the main avenue of Beijing to a small park in the western district where poster-writers had to formally register their names in a prefabricated building specially erected for the purpose. Deng Xiaoping now proposed cancellation of the right to display posters—one of the 'four great freedoms' (speaking out freely, airing views fully, holding great debates, and writing big-character posters) first coined by Mao in 1957 and later included in the Constitution. It was withdrawn at the National People's Congress in September 1980 (one delegate dared to spoil his ballot in protest), and the displaced Democracy Wall was closed down.

The surviving dissidents had enjoyed a breathing space during 1980 although kept under close surveillance. An informal provincial network developed between the various unofficial journals which survived, leading to the formation of the National Association of the People's Press in August 1980. In April 1981 more than twenty of these activists were arrested across the country, many of them charged with organizing or participating in 'counter-revolutionary groups'. Liu Qing's co-editor, Xu Wenli, was sentenced to 15 years' imprisonment on the evidence of a provocateur. Xu's account of his arrest and trial, also smuggled out of prison, is a moving document of courage by a young man who loved his wife and child but could not keep silent. During eight months of interrogation, he kept his spirits up by winning (or imagining) small psychological victories over his questioners. By this time there was some form of legality— Xu praises his defence lawyer—but the verdict was still a foregone conclusion:

I fixed my gaze directly upon [Judge] Ding Fengchun, and the more I looked at him the more panicky he became, until his voice—for he had been affecting a northern accent—went right out of tune; finally, he became utterly discomfited, and as he uttered his last hysterical shout of 'Take below the counter-revolutionary element Xu Wenli', I turned around even before he had finished speaking, let them handcuff me, slightly raised my head, assumed a rather amused expression, and— without looking to either side—walked calmly out of the courtroom, leaving total silence behind for the benefit of Ding Fengchun, who was by then probably in danger of falling out of his judge's throne. I thought to myself: I've recovered my dignity!

Xu and those arrested with him still belonged to the generation which was formed politically during the Cultural Revolution, although neo-Marxist influence from abroad was beginning to filter through (Xu argued in favour of polycentrism and quoted Eurocommunist arguments for a multi-party system). Xu's

generation still believed in the power of selfless action: in his
'Self-defence' he quotes the last words of the Copernican
Giordano Bruno before being burnt at the stake for denying the
myth of the Deluge. The document ends appropriately with Xu's
invocation of the first dissenting martyrs of the Cultural Revolution: Yu Luoke, Zhang Zhixin, and Wang Shenyou. 'In comparison with these great figures, these household names,' he wrote,
'I am merely a minor "counter-revolutionary element"—unin-
formed, and of little learning or scholarship.' But he hoped that
his would be the last generation which needed to join their
struggle. It was certainly the last to engage in a struggle still
grounded ideologically in Marxist thinking and with the declared intention of defending and improving socialism in China.

From dissent to protest

The mass arrests of 1980–1 combined with the enormous
material changes now under way to break the link between the
Cultural Revolutionary dissent and contemporary protest.
Young people in the late 1980s are criticized by the 1970s
activists for being unconcerned with 'social issues' and over-
preoccupied with personal lifestyle, especially sex and material
comfort. They in turn criticize the older activists for being too
'political' and failing to jettison 'all that Cultural Revolutionary
stuff'. The new generation has not been inactive: the student
demonstrations for democracy in December 1986 in Shanghai
were the largest since the Tiananmen demonstration ten years
before, and provided conservative leaders in the Party with the
pretext for forcing the resignation of the reformist Secretary-
General, Hu Yaobang. Yet the character of protest had changed.
Student discontent was less focused and easier for the authorities
to contain temporarily, but at the same time more likely to seize
opportunistically upon a new issue and break out again. Its
political statements, no longer rigorously argued in neo-Maoist
terms, often sounded closer to those of the young Republic in
rejecting traditional doctrine (then 'Confucian', now 'Marxist')
and in looking to foreign example for reform. The messages on
posters and in manifestos were shorter and more emotional,
reminiscent of 4 May 1919.

A campaign in 1980 for participation in local elections marked the transition from ideological argument to single-issue action. The new election law (June 1979) had sought to demonstrate a new spirit of democracy by insisting that contests for local People's Congresses should not be unopposed, and providing that any member of the electorate could stand on the nomination of only three voters. With the closure of Democracy Wall, student activists tested the limits of this new tolerance, particularly in the traditional seat of protest at Beijing University and at the Hunan Teachers' Training College in Changsha, resonant with Mao's memory. The Beijing contest was notable for the lively debates in which seventeen candidates (for two seats) took part, accompanied by election posters, still allowed within institutions though by now banned on the streets. The candidate with the highest number of votes, Hu Ping, had as editor of an unofficial journal in Chengdu at the start of the Cultural Revolution published Yu Luoke's famous article refuting the 'blood lineage theory'. (Five years later Hu would be in exile in the United States, editing the dissident magazine *China Spring*.) Hu was not allowed to take his seat, and the University also refused a run-off to fill the second seat as required by the election law. In Hunan the authorities intervened at an earlier stage, provoking a students' hunger strike which was only settled after mediation from Beijing. One candidate, Liang Heng, had married an American student (after a direct appeal to Deng Xiaoping), through whom the election row became known outside China. A new election was supposed to be held but this never took place. The other leading popular candidate, Tao Sen, was expelled from college a year later and sentenced to three years' labour education. Released early, Tao Sen headed in the opposite direction from Hu Ping, deciding that China's future lay with the economic reforms, and set up a private company to market the works of China's most famous painter (and native of Hunan) Qi Baishi.

The generation of the Cultural Revolution was increasingly dispersed, and the next round of elections in 1984 was uncontested by democracy activists. When student protest reappeared a year later, it had more in common with the single-issue campaigns familiar in the west. In June 1985 more than three hundred former Beijing students, 'sent down' to Shaanxi province during the Cultural Revolution and still unable to return, staged a sit-down demonstration outside the Beijing city hall. (Similar demonstrations in Xinjiang province, where large numbers of Shanghai students had been 'sent down', had taken place in 1980–1.) In September 1985 Beijing students marched to Tiananmen Square to commemorate the Japanese invasion of China, protesting at Japan's new economic 'aggression'. Their slogans included 'Down with Japanese militarism', 'Down with Nakasone', and 'Boycott Japanese goods'. The anti-foreign overtone of these demonstrations was embarrassing to Deng Xiaoping, and there were suspicions that conservative opponents had encouraged it. In fact, some aspects of modernization, particularly the re-equipment of the Chinese police with new technology (including electric batons), were widely unpopular among young people, who complained that the police were 'worse than ever before'. One poster linked the two themes of police oppression and Japanese commerce (which was alleged to have flooded the Chinese market with inferior goods). 'What has all our sacrifice of blood given us?', it asked. 'Police and refrigerators.' Other demonstrations planned for 9 December, the fiftieth anniversary of the 1935 anti-Japanese protest, were deflected after lengthy meetings between students and senior reformist Party leaders. The students' own economic situation, with grants unable to keep pace with inflation, had increased their unhappiness, and one of the proposed slogans for 9 December was 'We have to eat'. The price of books had risen sharply, and students could see young people of their own age earning large sums in street markets and through inflated factory bonuses. Officials made a point of showing their concern, eating in student canteens and inspecting the heating facilities in their dormitories. At the same time police surveillance was stepped up, and activists were warned 'not to start a new cultural revolution'. Any protest meetings in Tiananmen Square would be regarded as a challenge to the Communist Party and subject to punishment.

A new issue now surfaced in the north-west minority region of Xinjiang. More than a thousand students in the capital of Urumqi demonstrated on 12 December 1985 against nuclear tests in the region, and against family planning policies which they claimed had depressed the birth-rate of the Uighur minority. A second demonstration by Uighur students in Beijing compelled a vice-mayor to make an unprecedented explanation to foreign journalists: 'It is necessary for our country to conduct a small number of nuclear tests', he said. 'This is supported by the people of the whole country. These tests were carried out with effective safety measures. Data compiled in the past has shown that these tests brought no ill effects to the inhabitants and surroundings.'

During 1986 the Party reformers, with encouragement from the Hu Yaobang group and (more equivocally) from Deng Xiaoping, pressed their arguments further. Just as in 1979–80, when the Party's Third Plenum reawakened perennial hopes as to Deng's liberalizing intentions, Chinese youth now responded. The student demonstrations of winter 1986/7 were on a larger scale, but more diffuse and less coherent politically than the Democracy Movement, snowballing in the space of less than a month from the relatively isolated provincial capital of Hefei via Shanghai and Tianjin to Beijing. Hefei students in early December 1986 returned to the election issue, complaining that they had no say in the selection of candidates for the local People's Congress. Later, large demonstrations broke out in Shanghai, often turning into rallies which professed support for Deng Xiaoping and the official reform movement but called for speedier democratic change and for greater press freedom. Educational authorities at the time said it was 'understandable' that students should voice their opinions, and there was speculation of behind-the-scenes encouragement, this time from the Party reformers. (A few slogans calling for the overthrow of the Communist Party, however, were probably provoked by conservatives who wished to discredit the movement.) The students' manifestos were passionate rather than closely argued: 'Maybe the police will come and break us up', shouted one leader (in fact the police mostly refrained from intervention), 'but the Chinese people will not be slaves!' They also reflected the same sense of shame at China's backwardness that had informed so many demonstrations of the 1920s:

Between the past and the future lies the present. We cannot rewrite history, but we can change the present and create the future. Faced with the reality of poverty and dictatorship, we can endure it. But we cannot allow our descendants to grow up in the stranglehold of lack of freedom, democracy, and people's rights. We cannot let them stand beside the offspring of foreign countries and feel like poor and ashamed ghosts. Citizens, please understand! Bureaucracy, the policy of looking down on the people, lack of democracy and powerlessness, these are the sources of our backwardness.

Spreading to Beijing, the student demonstrations became a direct challenge to the Party's authority, both by their scale and by their mere presence in the political capital and traditional starting-point for national movements. Conservative forces played on the Party's fears that China might see a revival of 'disorderly' behaviour of the Cultural Revolutionary type, and warned that other issues, such as the students who were still 'sent down', might be raised again. They soon won Deng Xiaoping's support for a crack-down, and the demonstrations turned into a series of confrontations with municipal and police authority. The traditional rhetoric of Beijing University blossomed briefly. One poster echoed an argument used by Hu Ping in the 1980 election campaign:

The Chinese people already have two thousand years of history behind them. Two thousand years! Archimedes said 'Give me a place to stand on and I can lift the world.' Now there is a place to stand on. It is one billion people. Students of Beijing University, why don't you spring into action!

Their optimism was short-lived. New regulations were published banning unauthorized demonstrations, student leaders were arrested, and the rank and file warned that their job prospects would suffer if the action continued. Parents and relatives were mobilized to summon the students home for the Chinese New Year—with rail vouchers thoughtfully provided by the authorities. For the second time in less than a decade, Deng Xiaoping was seen by many to have betrayed his own supporters, although others still believed that he had been either misled or forced to concede ground tactically to the conservatives. Whatever the explanation, the struggle soon subsided. As far as is known no organized activity continued of the type which had kept the Democracy Movement alive for two years after it was officially suppressed. The students of the 1980s were more easily cast into a mood of confused dejection, well illustrated by one of the last posters from Beijing University. Signed anonymously by 'A Very Frightened Person who Loves Life', it lamented:

I thought our superiors were working hard, that they were trying to bring about a better life for the people. I had no idea that in their eyes the people counted for nothing—nothing at all. Their first priority is to protect the *status quo*. They want to hold on to what they've got—and then get more. They use smiles to get it. Their attitude is 'Democracy is something we can give you out of our own generosity' . . . They carry out their 'reforms'. But if you want to participate and if those reforms develop to the point where their interests are in danger, what do they give you?

I'm afraid. I'm not afraid. I'm still afraid. It's really tragic.

CHAPTER NINE

The Party Under Pressure

REFORM AND REACTION

The reform of the Chinese Communist Party is a slow and painful process, which began only haltingly after Mao's death and is still far from complete. For the first three years, a vast oil painting hung in the Beijing railway station above the two escalators in the marble foyer. It showed Hua Guofeng, now Party Chairman (and Premier, and also Chairman of the Military Commission) receiving his mandate from Mao.

The scene is Mao's study; the date 30 April 1976, just weeks after the Tiananmen demonstration. Mao's face is passive, as if barely able to control the effects of Parkinson's Disease from which he now suffered severely. Hua is beaming with warm deference, against the background of traditionally bound Chinese books. Every railway passenger knew that at this meeting Chairman Mao, no longer able to speak intelligibly, had handed a sheet of paper to Hua, bearing the phrase: 'Ni ban shi, wo fang xin'—'With you in charge, I feel at ease.' The same picture was reproduced on propaganda posters available for a few cents at the station bookshop. Others bore slogans including:

Chairman Mao trusted Chairman Hua completely; the people and army warmly endorse him too! *(a picture of vast crowd marching in celebration with portraits of Mao and Hua).*

Chairman Hua, the people of China love you! *(a picture of representatives of all China's nationalities holding banners).*

Chairman Hua leads us in drawing a new map for the future! *(Hua and workers amidst blocks of stone on a hillside).*

Sincerely support our brave outstanding leader Chairman Hua! *(portrait of Hua surrounded by smiling Uighurs and Kazakhs).*

The picture disappeared from Beijing railway station after the December 1978 Third Plenum, but it took over two more years

before Hua was finally replaced by the reform-minded Hu
Yaobang. There were several theories about Hua's 'mandate'
from Mao. Perhaps Mao was merely expressing approval of
Hua's conduct of the 1976 campaign against Deng Xiaoping (in
which case Mao was wrong). Or else the note was simply a
forgery. Was not Mao too ill to write the characters so clearly?
If it was not a forgery, then it lacked his signature and so was
not a proper mandate. Even if it had been signed, was that the
right way for a modern Communist Party to settle the succes-
sion?

The post-Mao transition

At a crucial moment in 1975, the 40-year-old Wang Hongwen,
China's youngest Party leader and Mao's chosen model of a
'revolutionary successor', had taunted Deng Xiaoping with his
age. 'Let's wait and see how things stand in ten years' time', he
threatened. Deng was sufficiently worried to discuss the matter
with some of his old companions. 'I was then already 71',
he later recalled. 'In terms of life expectancy we were no match
for the Gang.' In the ensuing struggle, age triumphed over
youth, with the restoration to power of the generation which
had been pushed aside in the Cultural Revolution, and the re-
establishment of the ideas which they had advocated in the
1950s. The magnitude of this turn-around can hardly be exaggerated. It required not just a change of personnel at the top,
but the reshaping of both Party rank and file and its body of
cadres who themselves had been substantially reshaped in the
previous ten years. This in turn necessitated the rejection of a
complete set of theoretical positions adopted during the Cultural
Revolution, and the search for a comprehensive substitute. Both
in terms of power and principle, Deng in the decade 1977–87
masterminded an arduous campaign involving the demolition of
the old apparatus—a task which was fairly complete by the
Twelfth Party Congress in 1982—and its replacement by the
beginnings of something labelled (from 1986 onwards) 'political
structural reform', which was much more contentious.

The coalition leadership established at the 1975 National
People's Congress had been destroyed by its own internal
contradictions and by Mao's erratic judgement in accepting the

exclusion of Deng Xiaoping after the Tiananmen demonstration. It fissured within a month of Mao's death. The mainstream
Maoists led by Hua Guofeng sought the help of the armed forces
under Ye Jianying to remove the ultra-left from its control of the
Party propaganda apparatus. At their trial four years later, three
of the Gang (but not Jiang Qing) were accused of having
planned an 'armed rebellion' in Shanghai. The actual evidence
shows that the ultra-left had attempted to build up the Shanghai
militia as a defence against any move against them ('What
worries me most', Wang Hongwen had said, 'is that the army is
not in our hands'), but that their followers surrendered without a
shot being fired. The coup which they planned was based not on
military strength but the attempted manipulation of the Party
apparatus. The heart of the charge against them was not the
methods which they used but their effect, which would have
resulted (in the view of the old guard which now regained power)
in the 'destruction of the socialist state'.

The final act which precipitated their arrest was the re-
publication (in the *Guangming Daily*) of one of Mao's last
instructions which had allegedly been tampered with. When
Mao transmitted his ambiguous 'mandate' (see above sketch) to
Hua Guofeng after the Tiananmen affair, he also conveyed two
other instructions. One of these, which Hua promptly read out
to the Politburo (although oddly he did not read out his own
'mandate'), conveyed the message 'Act according to past principles.' The Gang of Four misquoted this to read 'Act according
to the principles laid down.' The significance of the difference
between the two versions is obscure but it had immense political
symbolism. It could perhaps have prepared the way for the
production of a forged 'testament', allegedly 'laid down' by
Mao, appointing Jiang Qing as his successor. Or the 'tampering'
with it may merely have provided Hua and his supporters with
the necessary pretext for joint action against the ultra-left.

It was the anti-Gang coalition which now summoned a secret
Politburo meeting and moved into position the special forces led
by Mao's bodyguard, Wang Dongxing, to arrest all four Gang
members in the night of 6/7 October. When Jiang Qing was
arrested, the story goes, her personal attendants spat upon her,
demonstrating the hatred in which she was held and perhaps also
a healthy instinct for self-preservation. An awkward period now

followed in which the mainstream Maoists led by Hua were obliged to reincorporate Deng Xiaoping's forces while seeking to keep intact as much as possible of the Cultural Revolutionary past. Some Chinese journals published in October inserted correction slips to say that Deng was no longer a 'capitalist-roader' although he had still 'made mistakes'. On May Day 1977 Hua said that China would cling to Mao's 'correct line' and 'continue the revolution'. At the Party Congress two months later he announced that the smashing of the Gang of Four had marked 'the triumphant conclusion of our first Great Proletarian Cultural Revolution'—indicating that there would be more. But his emphasis upon the need to 'grasp the key link of class struggle' was balanced by a new call to 'bring about great order across the land'. Ye Jianying (who had guaranteed military support for the anti-Gang coup) tipped the balance more sharply: centralism was more essential than democracy, and Party discipline must be restored. A new group of five was established with Chairman Hua and the four Party chairmen (again including Deng) as the Standing Committee of the Politburo. In his closing speech to the congress, Deng called for the goal of making China 'a great, powerful, modern socialist country by the end of the century'.

History now briefly repeated itself as farce, with a cult of Hua being developed along lines which comically aped that of Mao. His portrait appeared everywhere beside that of the late Chairman. His hair was grown longer and in a swept-back style to match Mao's more poetic look. His simple calligraphy was appended to books and monuments. Factory workers were exhorted to greater efforts by rhyming jingles: 'The heights to which he does aspire / are what the masses all desire.' Tales were told endlessly of his simplicity and homely style. A 1978 New Year poster showed him making dumplings with peasants at the earthquake site of Tangshan.

Hua's behaviour demonstrates the persistence of a political culture which had become so enveloping that he and his supporters could not see its danger to their own cause. Hua also blundered theoretically, producing a formula not so far removed from the 'fabricated' one which had precipitated the Gang of Four's downfall. This was the famous Two Whatevers: 'We will resolutely uphold whatever policy decisions Chairman Mao

made, and unswervingly follow whatever instructions Chairman
Mao gave.' This statement was intended to deflect efforts to
'reverse the verdict' on the anti-Deng campaign of the previous
year and on the Tiananmen incident. It was countered by Deng
and other veteran leaders, particularly Chen Yun, with the call to
'Seek Truth from Facts' (a phrase once used by Mao which
implied that policies should be based on reality and not on
dogma). At stake was not just a factional quarrel but two
opposing views on the relation of theory to practice. The Two
Whatevers, Deng argued, took statements by Mao out of
context and ignored the fact that he himself had said that some
of them were wrong. Truth could only be tested by practice;
otherwise thinking would turn rigid and everything would be
done disastrously by the book:

The more Party members and other people there are who use their heads
and think things through, the more our cause will benefit. To make
revolution and build socialism we need large numbers of pathbreakers
who dare to think, explore new ways, and generate new ideas.
Otherwise we won't be able to rid our country of poverty and
backwardness or to catch up with—still less surpass—the advanced
countries. We hope every Party committee and every Party branch will
encourage and support people both inside and outside the Party to dare
to think, explore new paths, and put forward new ideas, and that they
will urge the masses to emancipate their minds and use their heads.
(13 December 1978)

The pragmatic emphasis of this approach disturbed those who
wished to cling to certainties. As late as September 1982 (after
Hua had lost power) he queried the argument that practice is the
only test of truth. Communist society had not yet been tested in
practice, nor could it be, Hua objected. Yet its ultimate realiza-
tion was not only a necessity but also a truth, thus proving that
not all truths had to be tested. (The argument was countered by
the ideologue Hu Qiaomu, who replied that the communist
movement had already been tested in practice by sixty years of
Chinese experience and a century and a half in the whole world.)

The pragmatic emphasis of this approach disturbed those who
Deng's ascendancy was first established at the Third Plenum
in December 1978, which endorsed Seeking Truth from Facts and
criticized the Two Whatevers. It also reversed the verdict on the
Tiananmen demonstration, leading to the dismissal of senior
officials who had suppressed it at the time. It would take another

two and a half years to bring to an end Hua Guofeng's transitional leadership and return a verdict not only on the Gang of Four (who were sentenced in January 1981) but on Mao and the Cultural Revolution. This was achieved at the Sixth Plenum in June 1981, when Hua was finally replaced as Chairman of the Party, and the 'Resolution on Party History (1949–1981)' was adopted. Hua was criticized for allowing the personality cult to continue around him, for his 'Left' economic policies, and for failing to correct past injustices such as the Tiananmen Incident. Deng also claimed that Hua was still being supported by 'the remnants of the Gang of Four and others who have ulterior motives'. Certainly the length of time required to remove Hua indicated the strength of feeling among many Party leaders that Deng's reforms would threaten their own bureaucratic grip on power. At the Twelfth Congress a year later, Hua made a partial self-criticism but claimed he was the victim of slander, including accusations that he had leaked the news of a 'state secret', namely the theft of a television set from his home, and that he was somehow implicated in the suicide of a nurse who had been assigned to his personal staff. Hua remained an important symbol as late as 1987, when to general surprise he was re-elected to the Central Committee at the Thirteenth Party Congress.

Reaching a verdict

'Don't think there can be no more chaos in China', warned Deng Xiaoping in July 1979. 'Those who belong to the factional systems of Lin Biao and the Gang of Four are deaf to the Party's directives and would like nothing better than nationwide confusion.' One-half of the Party membership (35 million in 1980) had joined since 1966; one-third since 1973. Many still believed that while the leadership now stressed material progress, the pendulum would shift again to a renewal of cultural revolution. One young cadre encountered in Shandong province offered a typical rationalization: 'At the moment we are stressing one thing [i.e. materialism]. In the future we shall stress another.' The new resolution on Party history was only approved after two and a half years of argument which muffled the force of its condemnation. The senior leaders, Chen Yun and Deng himself, were anxious to ensure that the resolution did not pass too 'negative' a verdict upon Mao and the Party. It was a document, Deng stressed, which must 'unify thinking and unite our comrades', and he criticized an early version for being too 'depressing'. Two questions were primary: Did Mao's achievements outweigh his mistakes, and did the Party's achievements in the period up to the Cultural Revolution also outweigh its mistakes? To produce negative answers would be 'to discredit the Party and the state'.

The resolution identified three causes behind the Cultural Revolution. First was Mao's 'tragedy'. As he grew older, he no longer made 'a correct analysis' of the situation but 'confused right and wrong and the people with the enemy'. Nor could he bear to accept criticism from far-sighted leaders such as Deng Xiaoping. His 'errors' were taken advantage of by Lin Biao and the Gang of Four, who 'committed many crimes behind his back, bringing disaster to the country and the people'. The resolution still sought to salvage as much as possible of Mao's reputation, arguing that even during the Cultural Revolution he had at times criticized the Gang of Four and had safeguarded China's security by formulating correct principles in foreign policy. The second reason, which made possible Mao's 'tragedy', was the tradition of 'feudal autocracy' in China to which the Party largely succumbed. This was compounded by the influence of 'certain grievous deviations . . . in the history of the international communist movement'—a code-phrase for Stalinism. 'Conditions were present', the resolution cautiously suggested, for the development of arbitrary personal rule which made it hard for the collective leadership to prevent the Cultural Revolution. Third and more convincingly, the resolution argued that the Party's birth and maturation over decades of 'war and fierce class struggle' had made it ill-equipped to deal with the more subtle contradictions of a peaceful society. Its tendency to exaggerate the continued role of 'class struggle' was exacerbated by the split with the Soviet Union. China's legitimate struggle against Soviet 'big-nation chauvinism' abroad led to an internal campaign against 'revisionism'. Normal differences within the Party leadership were presented as a 'struggle between two lines'.

The resolution concluded (as instructed by Deng) that '[Mao's] merits are primary and his errors secondary', even if he had committed 'gross mistakes' in his later years. It distinguished between these mistakes and Mao Zedong Thought, a synthesis of Mao's own ideas and the Party's collective wisdom over the years, which it described as 'Marxism-Leninism applied and developed in China'. Failure to preserve the main elements of Mao Zedong Thought, Deng had argued during the drafting, would undermine all those activists who had struggled in Mao's name to transform the country after 1949.

Deng's second key question—the responsibility of the Party as a whole and leaders of his generation in particular—produced the ritual admission that 'the Central Committee of the Party should be held partly responsible'. There was not a word about the specific responsibility of any leaders, even though Deng had originally instructed that the resolution should contain a 'fair evaluation of the merits and demerits of some leading comrades'. A section claiming that the Party's work in the decade leading up to the Cultural Revolution was 'generally good' had been inserted on Deng's insistence. After all, he argued, 'didn't the rest of us go along with him?' The limits of criticism were set by Deng in a crucial speech just before the resolution was approved:

Why are we now stressing that assessments must be balanced? Because certain recent remarks about some of Mao Zedong's mistakes have gone too far. These excesses should be corrected so that, generally speaking, the assessment will conform to reality and *enhance the image of the country and the Party as a whole* [my emphasis]. Part of the responsibility for some past mistakes should be borne collectively, though the chief responsibility, of course, lay with Chairman Mao. We hold that systems and institutions are the decisive factor, and we all know what they were in those days. At the time, we used to credit everything to one person. It is true that there were certain things which we failed to oppose and for which we should be held partly responsible. Of course, in the circumstances, it was really difficult to express any opposition (22 June 1981).

The need to preserve the Party's authority also made it necessary to insist that it had continued to exist during the Cultural Revolution and that the Politburo and Central Committee had continued to be legitimate organs. Even the October 1968 Plenum which had condemned Liu Shaoqi as a traitor and expelled him from the Party was judged to be constitutional. (Only a bare majority of the Central Committee took part, outnumbered by members of revolutionary committees and army representatives, including one who was not even a Party member.) 'To deny their legitimacy', said Deng, 'would pull the rug out from under us' by conceding that the Party had lost control. Instead, it must be argued that it was only thanks to the Party remaining in existence, and to its use of Mao Zedong Thought, that the Gang of Four were finally defeated!

This insistence upon legitimacy worked against the Party when the Gang of Four went on trial. When the indictment was read to Jiang Qing, she asked the court how it regarded the Party congresses held during the Cultural Revolution. She too was carrying out the instructions of Chairman Mao, she argued defiantly. The difference was that she had remained loyal to the Chairman and to the millions of revolutionary Red Guards. The official media went to some lengths to justify the trial by distinguishing between the 'mistakes' made by the Party and particularly by Mao, and the 'crimes' committed by the Gang of Four and by the Lin Biao group with whom they were tried. The main charges against the Gang were that (1) they had attempted to overthrow the socialist state, (2) they had planned armed rebellion, and (3) they had caused people to be killed and tortured. The first two 'crimes', though regarded officially as the most serious, were not supported fully by the evidence. On the first charge, it could equally be argued that the Gang were seeking to defend their conception of a socialist state against the subversion of their rivals. The evidence of 'armed rebellion' was based upon plans made in Shanghai to arm the militia after Mao's death, which, as we have seen, came to nothing. But evidence supporting the third charge was abundant. Cases of victimization and torture often leading to suicide and death were common knowledge. The most damning piece of evidence was a tape-recording of the brutal questioning of Zhang Zhongyi, a 67-year-old professor who had the misfortune to have had a colleague who was friendly with Liu Shaoqi's wife, Wang Guangmei, before Liberation. His evidence was required to support the charge that she had been a Guomindang agent. Zhang was interrogated as he lay dying from liver cancer. His feeble attempts to parry the questioning had been recorded and were played in court:

Q. What espionage activities was Wang Guangmei engaged in?
A. I hope to get this question clear.

Q. This is your chance. Do you want to take the question along into the coffin with you?

A. No. I am not clear at all about this question . . . I cannot cook up a story, either.

Q. You are making yourself a nuisance. You are resisting to the end.

A. I've never thought about that.

Q. Why don't you confess? Do you want to put yourself against the people to the very end? Who is Wang Guangmei?

A. She is a Communist.

[Professor Zhang at one point did describe Wang as a 'secret agent', but added that he had learnt about this from a 'government communique'.]

Jiang Qing and Zhang Chunqiao (who, suffering from terminal cancer, remained as defiantly silent during the trial as Jiang Qing was defiantly vocal) were sentenced to death but with a two-year stay of execution. Jiang had already dared her captors to have her executed before a mass rally in Tiananmen Square. Two years later, the sentences were commuted to life imprisonment even though there is no evidence that she had shown the required 'signs of repentance'. Yao Wenyuan received a twenty-year prison sentence but Wang Hongwen, whose rapid 'helicopter' promotion in 1973 enraged the veteran cadres, was sentenced to life. Mao's former theoretical adviser Chen Boda, in prison since 1971, was sentenced to eighteen years' gaol. Five senior military officers, also imprisoned since the Lin Biao affair in 1971, received similar sentences. With the trial concluded, many expected a thoroughgoing purge of Gang supporters at lower levels of the Party. But this proved politically delicate, while in the meantime new problems of Party discipline had arisen.

The Party's cancer

By the end of the 1970s, the Chinese Communist Party had reached its lowest point ever in morale and public esteem. Economic reform would be of little value unless the Party could also be reformed. The agenda for rectification was set by Deng Xiaoping in an important speech to the Politburo (18 Aug. 1980). It covered 'bureaucracy, over-concentration of power, patriarchal methods, life tenure in leading posts, and privileges of various kinds'. In Mao's classic metaphor, the Party depended upon popular approbation just as the fish requires water to survive. In a later speech Deng gave the phrase a new gloss, quoting the proverb that 'water can keep a boat afloat, but it can also sink it' (12 Nov. 1981). If there was no improvement in Party discipline within a couple of years, he said, it could become an incurable disease. The Party had 39 million members and 2 million grassroots organizations. One could not stand idly by while the cancer spread until whole sections were 'paralysed or even completely rotted'.

The official catalogue of Party failings could not have been worse if it had been invented by China's enemies. (In fact western comment, by now universally favourable to the open-door reforms, tended to minimize the extent of China's internal disarray or to regard it as a necessary price to pay for developing a market economy.) On the Party's July 1982 anniversary, its propaganda head Wang Renzhong produced the following list of manifestations of 'individualist thought':

1. 'An ardent quest for individual ease, comfort, reputation, and position.'
2. Putting 'personal benefit' before service to Party and people.
3. Arrogance and self-righteousness, 'refusing to submit' to Party directives.
4. 'Striving for power, position, reputation, and pay', and sulking when these could not be obtained.
5. Using one's office for private advantage, choosing the best housing, placing one's children in the best jobs, and so on.
6. Nepotism, forming small groups and cliques.
7. Preferring the interests of one's own unit to those of the community.
8. Protecting one's friends and being reluctant to go after 'bad people'.
9. Looking for money in everything, and taking bribes.
10. Infatuation with a capitalist life-style, falling into 'corruption and decadence'.

Perhaps even worse, there were many who took the view that 'selfishness is human nature' and made no effort to struggle against these deviations from communist morality. At the other extreme, there were those, especially former supporters of the Cultural Revolution, who wrote off the Party, saying that 'it has already degenerated ... and a new dynasty has been established in its place'. Even honest Party officials were often unwilling to investigate internal misdeeds (especially when committed by their friends), or did so reluctantly, as if 'trying to catch a sparrow with their eyes closed'. This particular phrase had been Mao's, and there was no shortage of pithy sayings to dramatize the Party's crisis. Too many Party members, said Wang, were like 'pleasure-seekers who want to enjoy the cool shade but are unwilling to plant trees'.

How had the Party got into such a mess? As the austere Chen Yun (head of the Party's new Discipline Commission) remarked, 'Ice which is three inches thick was not formed in a day.' Part of the explanation lay in the fertile ground provided by the Cultural Revolution for authoritarian attitudes which were loosely labelled as 'feudal'. In the absence of normal political rules, it was the strongest individuals who usually survived, only paying lip-service to Party discipline. 'At what time in the past', complained Deng Xiaoping in November 1979, 'did a Party committee secretary—a secretary of a county or commune Party committee, say—have as much power as he has today? Never!' Discipline had declined even in the armed forces, where officers sometimes simply refused to take up new appointments, obliging Deng to say that 'when a cadre is reassigned, he must change his residence' (June 1978). The acquisition of privilege also became more blatantly feudal, and so did its loss:

During the 'Cultural Revolution,' when someone got to the top, even his dogs and chickens got there too; likewise, when someone got into trouble, even his distant relatives were dragged down with him. This situation became very serious. Even now, the abominable practice of appointing people through favouritism and factionalism continues unchecked in some regions, departments, and units. There are quite a few instances where cadres abuse their power so as to enable their friends and relations to move to the cities or to obtain jobs or promotions (Deng, 18 Aug. 1980).

The loosening effect of the new reforms quickly added another layer of indiscipline and corruption. It was no longer just a question of the traditional need to entertain officials (especially when they were paying visits of inspection to subordinate units) with banquets, cigarettes, wines, and rare local produce. A report from the Discipline Inspection Commission in 1981 said that the Party's standing had been seriously damaged by speculation, profiteering, and the misuse of state funds which caused 'hundreds of millions of yuan to flow into the hands of small collectives and individuals through hundreds of thousands of loopholes'. Such bribery was often conducted as much for the benefit of the factory or enterprise as for the individual (although he would share through bonuses in the resulting profits). Contracts were now regularly negotiated on the basis of what were called 'under-the-table relations' in which gifts or cash rebates were expected. As central planning began to loosen, local officials now had the new freedom to do business directly. The restoration to favour of the archetypal 'national bourgeois' businessman, who now enjoyed the use of private cars and luxury accommodation, also offered a tempting example. So did the opportunity to secure goods such as cameras, TV sets, and calculators from visits abroad or from foreign businessmen. One small drama group on tour to Japan was said to have returned with sixty-nine colour TVs and 138 watches.

By the mid-1980s corruption had grown considerably, and was now said to involve a number of 'veteran cadres and Party members' either directly or through their families. The *People's Daily* felt obliged to warn (11 Mar. 1985) that one reason why the Guomindang fell in 1949 was that 'officials were engaged in business and used their special powers to make large fortunes'. *Party Branch Life* (No. 5, 1985) carefully distinguished between 'old and new malpractices'. The former were the familiar types of activity over housing, jobs, college places for children, and changing the residence status for relatives from rural to urban areas. The latter involved economic activities carried out in the name of reform, and led to unjustified price increases, wasteful production of goods, and huge bonuses.

Some Party members ... believe that 'reform means contracts and contracts means fishing for money', and they see reform purely as the reallocation of profit. In order to make money, they use any means they can to evade taxes, make false reports of profits, seize any opportunity to sell anything, raise prices at random, and engage in other illegal activities which undermine the foundations of society, harm consumers, and will lead to disorder and anarchy.

Party misbehaviour was tackled by the Central Discipline Inspection Commission, which carried out a three-tier 'rectification' of the membership between the 1982 and 1987 Party congresses. It reported to the 1987 congress that more than 650,000 members had been disciplined, including over 150,000 who had been expelled. But it was evident from an earlier report by its president, the veteran leader Bo Yibo (in May 1987), that these figures were only achieved by counting in a large number of Party members who had supported the Gang of Four and had been 'ferreted out' in 1982–3 before the rectification began. The 1987 report admitted that the problem of 'unhealthy practices' was still acute and had seriously damaged popular trust in the Party.

Much was made of a small number of cases where high-ranking Party officials had been disciplined or expelled. The highest were the Minister of Forestry Yang Zhong, held responsible for the incompetent handling of a disastrous forest fire earlier in 1987 in the north-east, and a Central Committee member and director of Chinese civil aviation, Shen Du, who had mishandled funds. A few provincial officials were also exposed, as well as the unfortunate writer Zhou Erfu, who had watched pornographic films on a visit to Japan (this was described as 'seriously contravening discipline in foreign affairs'). Several other notorious cases, though not mentioned in the report, concerned the children of senior cadres who had been exposed and in at least two cases executed for rape. (This followed an instruction by Deng Xiaoping that an example should be made of such 'glaring cases'.)

But whatever would be claimed at the 1987 Party Congress, the lack of results had prompted the setting up of a new Party task force in the hands of the reformers in January 1986, after a meeting of 8,000 government and state cadres. This amounted to a challenge to the Discipline Inspection Commission, which claimed exclusive rights. The more conservative Commission also offended by arguing that economic reform was the main source of corruption. The reformers replied that, in the words of Hu Qili, 'we should not give up eating for fear of choking'. They also sought to shift the emphasis of rectification towards the more traditional 'feudal tendencies', especially in high places. When a year later the conservatives took the offensive in the anti-bourgeois liberalization campaign, back-street gossip in Beijing claimed that it was because they had been touched too closely by recent attempts to rout out the 'little tigers'—their own sons and daughters. Corruption at this level faced the conservatives with a dilemma: they realized that it should be exposed to protect the reputation of the Party, but feared that exposure of its full extent would provide more ammunition for those who held the Party in increasingly open contempt. The veteran army leader Nie Rongzhen, in an open letter published in the army newspaper (25 Apr. 1987), instructed the Political Department of the armed forces to promote 'family education' among its senior cadres:

A small number of children of senior cadres have indeed done evil and perpetrated outrages by relying on their powerful family connections, or have lined their pockets or obtained official positions through the influence of their parents. Such things will certainly cause popular indignation and disgust. As a popular saying goes: 'A piece of rotten meat may ruin the whole pot of soup.' We should handle these cases impartially: those who are not promoted or appointed through regular organizational procedures should be demoted and dismissed; those who have committed crimes should be arrested and executed according to the law ...

On the other hand, it is also necessary resolutely to expose the sinister plots of a small number of people who viciously slander cadres' children in an attempt to evoke a grievance from the masses and stir up trouble in society.

Towards political reform

If modernization was the magic weapon of the first decade after Mao, then 'political reform' became the new weapon of the late 1980s without which economic reform would not succeed. It was approached cautiously by those in the Party who saw it as a threat to their own status and the Party's prestige, but enthusiastically by those who wanted to reduce the Party's dominating role. (Deng Xiaoping's own position was somewhere in between.)

The failure of the rectification process to tackle seriously Party abuse breathed new life into the demand for political reform early in 1986. The need for it had been diagnosed several years before. The main problems in the Party and state leadership, Deng Xiaoping had said in August 1980, could only be overcome through reforms which would make people 'trust our leadership,

our Party, and socialism'. Party reformers were already arguing in
favour of the election of cadres, a proper system of supervision
and removal, improvements in the legal system so that the Party
would not be above the law, and the separation of the Party and
state apparatus. Feng Wenbin, deputy director of the Central
Party School, asked outright in the *People's Daily*: 'Why does the
political system of our socialist country have so many defects?'
His answer was a combination of 'feudal autocracy' (the
relationship between the leader and his subordinates, Feng
commented, had become like that 'between the cat and
the rat'), excessive emphasis upon 'class struggle', and 'over-
centralization'.

Six years later Deng returned to the theme, explaining that in
1980 nothing concrete had been done to put it on to the agenda.
The press was dominated now by reformist arguments: Party
malpractices, said the *People's Daily* (5 May 1986), could only
be cured through political democracy including 'the right to
criticize and supervise'. The greatest obstacle to economic
reform, judged the *Workers' Daily* (30 May 1986), lay in 'serious
abuses in the political system, feudal vestiges . . . the patriarchal
system'. In July 1986 the Central Committee's Party School for
cadres held an unprecedented seminar, which included academic
reformers from outside the Party propaganda and theoretical
establishment. One young scholar even suggested a multi-party
system.

It could fairly be said that since 1976 some progress had been
made in overhauling the political machine. The achievements
were listed by the Party propaganda head, Zhu Houze, and other
speakers. They included:

- a return to more normal political life with the arrest or
  dismissal of Gang of Four supporters;
- the re-establishment of central control over wayward provinces;
- strengthening of state control over the armed forces;
- greater autonomy for trade unions, professional groups, and
  the small 'democratic parties';
- the beginnings of a legal system, with codified laws and
  regular courts under a judiciary with a degree of autonomy;
- abolition in principle of life tenure for Party and government
  cadres;

- direct elections at the county level and below for people's congress delegates;
- restoration of the rural townships, separating out Party, government, and economic authority in the countryside, which had previously been combined on the 'one man wearing three pairs of trousers' principle.

Conservatives were happy with reforms which returned to the more 'normal' practices of the mid-1950s, but reformers argued that China had to move on. If socialism has not yet reached its highest stage, said the *Guangming Daily* (7 June 1986), then neither has democracy. Besides, even today there are places 'where even formal democracy does not exist, the will of the people cannot be expressed, and the views of the leader are not transmitted downwards'. Political reform, the Party seminar was told, should follow the development of the economy, according to the law that the 'superstructure' should conform to changes in the 'economic base'. The new reforms required the services of talented managers who were held back by the current cadre system. The Party secretariat leader Wang Zhaoguo, himself talent-spotted a few years before by Deng Xiaoping as a successful factory manager at the Second Automobile Factory in Harbin, told the seminar that cadres from now on should become 'Marxist theorists, excellent political leaders, and social-ist entrepreneurs'.

Deng's support was vital for the reformers. A quotation in which he had talked of 'comprehensive economic restructuring' as also affecting the political field gave them the authority to proceed. The journal *Social Sciences in China* (Mar. 1986) admitted that some people thought that 'political restructuring' should be postponed to the 1990s. But others quoted Engels: when state power moves in the opposite direction to economic development, it can do great damage and cause enormous waste of energy and material. In a crucial passage, the journal extended the frontier of political reform to the verge of creating a classless society:

The socialist state should mark the transition from a state based on class to one based on society, and from primarily direct control to primarily indirect control, and become a democratized and socialized state.

Deng soon gave a more direct testimonial to political reform: 'In the final analysis,' he said, 'all our other reforms depend on the success of the political reform, because it is human beings who will—or will not—carry them out' (28 June 1986). But Deng also set limits which should have warned the academic reformers that they were in danger of going too far. The separation of Party and government had already been forecast in his August 1980 speech. His other main requirements were for the devolution of some powers to local authorities, and the streamlining of administration. But he added soon afterwards (13 Sept. 1986) that the present structure of leadership had some advantages: 'For example, it enables us to make quick decisions, while if we place too much emphasis upon checks and balances, problems may arise.' More explicitly, he stipulated on 12 June 1987, after the campaign against bourgeois liberalism, that 'we should neither copy western democracy nor introduce the system of a balance of three powers'.

Deng's position flowed from his desire to fashion not a weaker but a stronger Party which would be capable of modernizing China where it had previously failed. The Cultural Revolution had come about because the Party in 1966 failed to use its theoretical majority to vote down Mao's plans and press ahead instead with the Four Modernizations. Nor had it been able to prevent the alienation of public opinion which resulted from the Cultural Revolutionary excesses. Deng sought a responsible and responsive Party, but not a Party which allowed a dilution of its leading role. No one should be interested, said the *China Daily* (17 July 1987), in 'a separate purely political effort to reform the political structure'.

The conservative reaction

A Chinese cadre with many years of experience abroad laments in conversation the declining morale among youth which he discovered on returning home in 1985. For example: his nephew had turned up from the countryside, seeking his advice. Where could he buy a foreign-made refrigerator? The cadre advised him to hang around outside the shop where Chinese workers who have earned money abroad can purchase such goods—which are then resold on the street at a profit. The nephew took his advice. But instead of just purchasing one for his own use, he bought four, took them all home, and sold them to rich peasants! How could such things have been imagined only a few years ago?

Another cadre worries about his eldest son. Instead of working hard for college, he watches foreign videos on subjects which could not be shown publicly. He belongs to the Youth League, but says quite openly that it is only for the purpose of getting recommended to a good job. Worse still, he has been reading Jean-Paul Sartre and other favourite authors of those who espouse 'bourgeois liberalism'. The cadre explains the Party position on Sartre: he made a very good stand in the Spanish Civil War. But the Party cannot accept his existentialism: it does not reflect socialist reality.

Party support for what is generally labelled the 'conservative' reaction to reform and change, expressed notably in the campaigns against spiritual pollution (1983) and bourgeois liberalism (1987), was fuelled by an instinctive disquiet among large numbers of lower- or middle-level cadres at the way things were going. A generation brought up to be wary of 'the sugar-coated bullets of the bourgeoisie' against which Mao had warned after Liberation found that its own children enjoyed the taste. Such cadres had often acquiesced or benefited from the small-scale privileges which came their way 'through the backdoor' during the years of hardship. Now they balked at the enormous profits made by the new 'suitcase businesses', paper companies set up by the families of senior cadres taking advantage of their official connections. Ideologically, the conservatives still saw nothing wrong in asking people to show a proper 'communist spirit' and to practise the 'hard struggle' style of Lei Feng, the model soldier of the 1960s.

The five years between the Twelfth and Thirteenth Party Congresses (1982–7) was a period of uneven transition in which Chinese society changed more rapidly than at any time since 1949. The most senior conservative leaders had themselves been targets of the Cultural Revolution (Peng Zhen) or advocates of reform in the 1950s (Chen Yun). Their strongest political weapon was that while they were still in office, the rejuvenation of the leadership regarded as essential by the reformers could only proceed lamely. A dominant political theme during these five years was the step-by-step easing out of the 'old bosses' into the newly set up Central Advisory Commission. It was also a period of uneven transition in the style of political argument. The reformers deployed their views at conferences and seminars, sometimes with foreign participation, or in new journals like the *World Economic Herald* (which has a contents page in English). The conservatives relied on more traditional organs such as the Party monthly *Red Flag* (whose circulation had slumped and was now hard to find on sale, even at post offices which were supposed to stock it). Their arguments had a leftist tinge, often resorting to selective quotes and to accusations of lack of patriotism which carried an ugly echo of past rhetoric. Their theoretical chief Deng Liqun had been Liu Shaoqi's secretary, but several among his team of ideological hacks had ultra-left connections with the Cultural Revolution. Personal prejudice and ambition played a part in the reaction. The veterans resented the assurance of a clique of younger leaders around Hu Yaobang (most of whom had worked with him when he ran the Youth League). They complained that Hu had not properly consulted them—just as Mao once complained that Deng Xiaoping ignored him. Deng Liqun had resisted the Gang of Four campaign against Deng Xiaoping in 1976, and wished to be rewarded with Hu's post of General Secretary. But these factional motives were intertwined with serious ideological objections. The conservatives still asserted the validity of the central core of post-1949 doctrine: the necessity of Party leadership, the primacy of the state in the economy, and the dominance of a socialist spirit. The reformers did not openly dissent, but diluted these principles in practice, and tolerated or encouraged reform-minded economists and social scientists to go much further. Hu Yaobang's famous statement in December 1984 that Marxism could not solve 'all of China's problems' was in principle not much different from Mao's sinification of Marxism in the 1940s, but it was viewed correctly by the conservatives as a green light for ideological revision.

The People's Liberation Army adopted a left-of-conservative position. Although the target of the Gang of Four in 1975–6 (and, under Marshal Ye Jianying, the guarantor of the anti-Gang coup after Mao's death), it had been politically moulded by a decade of Lin Biao's 'politics in command'—the Little Red

Book was originally compiled as an army manual. During the Cultural Revolution army units had worked hard to carry out Mao's instruction to 'support the left', seeking to keep essential communications going and to encourage the less extreme rebel groups. Many now failed to see why all their efforts should be written off as 'negative'. In essence, the PLA resented the loss of its shining vanguard role and a fall in prestige which meant that military service was no longer so socially desirable. (The new economic policies now offered career opportunities which at one time were only available through the PLA.) Nor was the PLA sufficiently compensated by new military technology. Defence spending was cut—to 10 per cent of the budget by 1987—and defence was the least prominent of the Four Modernizations. Throughout the 1982–7 period Deng Xiaoping found it necessary to retain control of the chairmanship of the Party's Military Commission and (from 1983) of the new State Military Commission which had been intended to provide a separate source of civilian authority over the PLA. Finally, soldiers were still fighting and dying on the Vietnamese border, living examples of self-sacrifice and the Lei Feng spirit. Why should they continue to do so if the rest of society turned its back on socialist hard struggle?

The ambiguous feelings of many Chinese leaders towards reform were summed up most influentially in the person of Deng Xiaoping himself. Every bout of conservative reaction had been licensed by Deng, although he withdrew the licence when it had served his purpose. Some reformers claimed he was acting for reasons of tactical necessity, but he drew a firm and consistent line which was not to be crossed. This had been defined first at the height of the Democracy Movement when in March 1979 he proclaimed the Four Principles:

1. We must keep to the socialist road.
2. We must uphold the dictatorship of the proletariat.
3. We must uphold the leadership of the Communist Party.
4. We must uphold Marxism-Leninism and Mao Zedong Thought.

It was Deng who had insisted on the punishment of the dissident Wei Jingsheng. Seven years later he still argued defensively that it was justified, linking Wei with those now calling for 'bourgeois liberalism'. In October 1983 Deng endorsed the criticism of 'spiritual pollution' already raised tentatively by Deng Liqun. People working in the ideological field, he said, 'must not spread spiritual pollution . . . They have engaged in discussions of the value of the human being, humanism, and alienation, and have only been interested in criticizing socialism, not capitalism.' Many believe that Deng was forced to sanction the campaign after private pressure from his veteran colleagues, who had pointedly asked him to 'pay attention to the nation's state of health'. But Deng's speech of 12 October 1983 shows the same hurt bafflement shared by many senior cadres. Why is it, he asked, that China had allowed 'harmful elements of bourgeois culture to be introduced without impediment', including the import of material which was regarded even in the west as 'pernicious junk'? Deng also criticized the reform-minded intellectuals—at this stage still only venturing their views with circumspection—for objecting to conservative censure. Real Marxists should be allowed to step forward and speak up against wrong ideas without people complaining that the big stick of the Cultural Revolution was being wielded again. The same resentment at what conservatives regarded as modish reformism which cried foul when it was criticized would be voiced in the 1987 campaign against bourgeois liberalism.

The campaign against spiritual pollution betrayed the obsession of old men and jealous cadres with the trivia of daily life and a nostalgia for earlier simplicity. The reformist Party secretariat was soon able to compile a dossier of absurdities: women had been told not to let their hair descend below the shoulders; soldiers had been ordered to hand over photographs of their girl-friends; the Beijing Party Committee posted a notice banning long hair and high-heeled shoes; young people had their sun-glasses confiscated in the street. More seriously, some newly rich peasants committed suicide because their bank accounts were frozen; cadres and soldiers from the countryside were forbidden to seek spouses in the towns; and foreign investors were post-poning signature of contracts. At a critical Politburo meeting, Premier Zhao Ziyang produced a letter from Japan asking for a postponement of loan negotiations, and threatened to resign. In the resulting compromise, a limit was set on the campaign, notably excluding the rural population as well as interference with clothing and hairstyles. The Chinese working class regarded the campaign with amused contempt—'I think I'll buy a tube of spiritual pollution', said fashion-minded girls as they purchased lipstick and make-up. Teachers and intellectuals, who had destroyed lecture notes and manuscripts or paintings in the first days of panic, felt less confident. The ultra-left ideologues waited for another chance to ally with party conservatism.

The Party style

Only the first of the three targets set at the 1982 Party congress—to 'bring about an all-round upsurge' of the economy—had been achieved. Progress towards the other two goals, to fundamentally improve 'standards of social conduct' and 'the working style of the Party', was slower and in the view of many non-Party people almost non-existent. It was supposed to be helped by the selection of more responsive and younger leaders. By the late 1980s cadres at the most senior level often showed a degree of informality and initiative which was refreshingly new. At local levels, the new economic policies also favoured younger people with entrepreneurial talents. The main problem lay at the intermediate level, the thick 'filling' in the bureaucratic sandwich which was most resistant to change. 'It is not the new policies I find difficult,' said the Mayor of Shanghai in 1984, 'it is finding good people to carry them out.'

The transformation of *dangfeng*—the Party's style of work—was slow and still heavily influenced by past political culture. It is doubtful whether any of the younger generation of leaders now in their late forties or fifties could have reached their present office without the sponsorship of senior leaders. Potential successors from existing cadre families would start with an advantage, and those with real talent who lacked family connections usually needed to catch the personal attention of leaders from the 'higher level' in order to make their way.

When in January 1987 Premier Zhao Ziyang took over as acting Party Secretary-General from the disgraced Hu Yaobang, two names were immediately mentioned as likely successors to his own post of premiership. These were the two Lis, Vice-Premier Li Peng and Mayor of Tianjin Li Ruihuan, men of widely contrasting background who nevertheless had both been 'fostered'.

Li Ruihuan, born in 1934, was a self-educated carpenter who caught the Party leadership's eye in 1959 when he was working on construction of the Great Hall of the People in Beijing. In keeping with the Great Leap spirit of technological short-cuts, he proposed to eliminate the need for detail mock-ups by master craftsmen. As a result, the time taken to lay the flooring in the Great Hall was cut from an estimated one month to sixteen days. Later he wrote an article in the *China Youth* magazine using carpentry technique to demonstrate the truth of Mao's dialectical argument that 'One Divides into Two'. Li achieved further merit after Mao's death as deputy manager of the construction of the Mao Zedong Mausoleum, another rush job which was finished in six months. He came to the attention of the reforming Vice-Premier Wan Li, and was sent to Tianjin where he solved the problem of temporary housing for victims of the 1976 Tangshan earthquake within a year. He was promoted to become Mayor in 1981, replacing Hu Qili (a protege of Hu Yaobang who moved to the Party secretariat in Beijing). He rapidly acquired a national reputation for tackling Tianjin's run-down urban environment. A scheme to arrange for workers to swap flats so that long hours of commuting to their jobs could be saved was particularly admired. Li became known as the 'darling' of the national leadership. Although he was not the eventual choice for Premier, he joined the Politburo in 1988.

Li Peng, born in 1928, the son of the 'revolutionary martyr' Li Shuoxun, was informally adopted by Zhou Enlai at the age of 11. He spent the war years in Yanan, and was sent to the Soviet Union in 1948, graduating with honours six years later from the Institute of Dynamics. Protected by Zhou during the Cultural Revolution, Li became responsible for energy policy in the late 1970s, tackling this crucial area of the economic superstructure with enthusiasm. He joined the Party Politburo and Secretariat in 1985, having visited both the Soviet Union (for the Chernenko funeral) and the US, where he studied nuclear and other energy projects, in the same year. Li became Premier in 1988, but was not a popular choice. His careful avoidance of difficult political issues pleased the Party's conservatives but was judged colour-less and disappointing by public opinion. Although fairly able, his rapid promotion was not so dissimilar from the 'helicopter' elevations for which the Cultural Revolution leaders had been criticized.

The mythology of self-sacrifice on the part of Party leaders survived in the 1980s but was greeted with growing cynicism outside. At the top they were still conventionally described as working late into the night with little regard for their personal comfort, in the tradition of the late Premier Zhou Enlai. At lower levels, they still sought merit by going on tours of inspection to 'listen to the opinions' of the masses, braving bad weather, missing meals, and rolling up their sleeves to join in hard work. In 1986 Hu Qili, then head of the Party secretariat, described the selflessness of the leadership (and in particular of his patron, Secretary-General Hu Yaobang) in these terms:

The central leaders working on the front line handle a host of things every day as regards domestic and international affairs, but they still keep in contact with the broad masses of the people through different channels. Our leaders do not have spare time and a day off is, of course, out of the question. Moreover, in order to read documents and letters from the people, they often have to work late into the night . . . Every year, the central leaders try and find time to go down to factories and the countryside in order to make investigations and studies. There are more than 2,200 counties through the country. Secretary-General Hu Yaobang has been to at least 1,500.

Total Party membership in 1988 was 47.75 million. There was still a steady flow of applicants to join. Two million were accepted in 1987 out of eight million applicants, according to the Party's Organization Department. Yet the assumption that one only joined the Party in order to secure personal advantage was widespread, and the reformist leaders recognized the gap which had to be bridged. Political reform, said the *People's Daily* (1 July 1987), was

a gigantic social systems engineering project, which involves straightening out the relationships between the Party and the government, power and judicial organs, mass organizations, enterprises, and institutions, and between central, local, and grassroots organizations; it concerns hundreds of millions of people. This is an arduous and protracted task.

CHAPTER TEN

The Scholars Speak Out

HUMANISM OR BOURGEOIS LIBERALISM?

In November 1985, a year before he became known as 'China's Sakharov', the astrophysicist Fang Lizhi had given a speech to students at the Department of Wireless Electronics at Beijing University (Beida). Fang argued that Chinese intellectuals should be concerned with society as a whole, and should be encouraged by the Communist Party to do so. Instead the leadership had tried to solve the current crisis in education by simply inviting a few notable professors to 'come and have a meal'. Intellectuals in China, Fang complained, had for too long been marginalized from political life. 'Take care of pulling the cart,' said the authorities, and 'never mind anything else.' How different this was from the West where, in spite of the hollowness of much of its society, many intellectuals had a real sense of social responsibility which was lacking in China.

Perhaps Fang's speech would have been overlooked, but he broke the rule strictly observed by more cautious reform-minded scholars in China of the 1980s: He named names. If there was a crisis of ideals as the present leadership lamented, he said, then it started at the top—and he offered a 'practical example':

Recently an academic seminar on acceleration equipment was held in the US, with both Taiwan and the mainland participating. I naturally assumed that experts and specialists in this field would go. However . . . many of those who went were not even physicists and had nothing to do with acceleration equipment. Is this how we abide by our rules and regulations? Among those who went was the vice-mayor of Beijing, Zhang Baifa [applause]. I don't know what he was doing there! [loud laughter]. If you're talking about lack of discipline and breaking rules, here is a flagrant example! . . . (China Spring, Feb. 1987)

The next day, Fang received a message from the Academy of

Sciences, parent body of his own college, ordering him to apologize to the Beijing Party Committee. He refused to do so and thereby gave offence to one of the senior Academy officials, Gu Yu, the wife of the conservative ideologue Hu Qiaomu (once Mao's secretary). He soon had to apply to her office for his passport to leave the country for another conference in the US. It was withheld until he 'recognized his mistake'. In Anhui province where he worked, the top-ranking Party leader came personally with the same request: Everyone else did what the 'high-ups' asked. Why couldn't he? Eventually, Fang spent half a day talking with Hu Qili, one of the leading Politburo reformers. At last he got his passport, but he would soon be in trouble again.

The scholars' licence

Chinese scholars have traditionally played a validating role for those in power, whether rewriting history to prove the iniquities of a fallen dynasty or demonstrating the Confucian propriety of the new emperor's edicts. The obligation to validate may be accompanied by a degree of licence to enquire beyond the established frontiers. During the Cultural Revolution, such liberty was available only to the committed or opportunistic. (The most famous was the *Liang Xiao*—a homonym for 'Two Schools' because it was drawn from Beida and Qinghua universities—Big Criticism Group organized by Jiang Qing in 1973 to renew the attack on 'bourgeois ideology'. It was housed in a lakeside guest-house with private rooms and access to foodstuffs in short supply elsewhere.) For the rest, as one scholar later recalled, 'when someone above says you are right, then you are right. Otherwise, you are wrong.' The story of intellectual activity since the Cultural Revolution is largely that of the struggle by a growing number of reform-minded intellectuals to broaden this licence, particularly in the sensitive fields of political and social science. A few of them would go beyond the bounds, denying (to the disapproval of some of their more cautious colleagues) that a licence was needed at all, and falling foul of the campaign against bourgeois liberalism in winter 1986. Party Secretary-General Hu Yaobang, who had greatly widened the scope of permissible intellectual enquiry in the previous two years, was forced to resign. Within another two years, the licence had been renewed under the new Party leader Zhao Ziyang, although with important provisos.

Intellectuals had been regarded with mixed feelings by the Party after it took power in 1949. Distinguished artists and scholars were personally honoured by Mao, whose own scholarly pretensions were far from modest, but many Party cadres were suspicious of those with a better and often foreign education. Mao himself periodically accused intellectuals of taking too tender a view of past Chinese history. The origins of the Cultural Revolution would later be traced back to these earlier interventions, starting with his denunciation in 1951 of a film, *The Life of Wu Hsun*, which presented an overly favourable view of a poor peasant in the mid-nineteenth century who became a wealthy philanthropist. 'Our writers', he said, 'do not bother to study Chinese history and learn who were the enemies oppressing the Chinese people.' By the mid-1950s the intellectuals appeared to have won the leadership's confidence. Bracketed until then as part of the bourgeoisie, their social status was reclassified during the Hundred Flowers campaign by Zhou Enlai. 'The overwhelming majority of the intellectuals', he said, 'have become government workers in the service of socialism and are already part of the working class.' Living conditions at Beijing University were improved, recalls Yue Daiyun, then a young teacher. 'Everybody was excited in 1956; we thought the fight had finished and that we could concentrate finally on building our country.' But Mao took a more critical view as the wave of scholarly criticism broke over the Party during the campaign. Most intellectuals, he concluded, had not yet managed to shed their 'bourgeois world outlook . . . and unite with the workers and peasants'.

As many as 200,000 intellectuals were labelled as 'rightists' in the reaction to the Hundred Flowers, prevented from teaching or writing, and sent to work for long periods in the countryside. Conditions for many improved again in the early 1960s, but they remained easy targets for denunciation in the Cultural Revolution. Paradoxically the old 'rightists' often suffered less, physically, than the newly identified 'black elements' in the Party, but the physical and psychological toll was still enormous. (Out of a group of ten Chinese students in Britain who returned home after

Liberation, two committed suicide during the Cultural Revolution, and one had his back broken by the Red Guards.)

From 1978 onwards China's intellectuals gained new confidence from the Party's new policies of reform. Sometimes they
even received an apology for past mistreatment. In spring 1983
Lu Dingyi, once head of the Communist Party's Propaganda
Department, sent a self-criticism to Hu Yaobang on 'the question of knowledge and intellectuals'. (It was Lu who in May
1956 had launched the Hundred Flowers.) Lu wrote that,
although a graduate himself, he had 'failed to take note of the
particular importance of knowledge and intellectuals during the
period of socialist construction'. An army without culture was a
dull-witted army, he continued. The Party leadership and its
poorly educated cadres shared the weakness of ignorance, which
led 'those without knowledge to look down upon those with
knowledge'. Intellectuals had been subjected to oppression 'and
were even listed as the "target of dictatorship" during the
Cultural Revolution'.

In spite of such admissions, the intellectuals' position was still
vulnerable. They could reasonably complain that they were the
first to suffer when the political wind blew from the conservative
quarter and the last to benefit from its easing. They felt the chill
in 1980, after the army writer Bai Hua was criticized for his film-
script *Bitter Love*. The film's hero was an intellectual who
returned home to help China and was victimized. 'You love the
motherland, but does the motherland love you?', it asked. It
portrayed Mao too openly as an idol 'blackened by the smoke of
burning joss-sticks and candles of faithful believers'. The literary
and art worlds were among the first targets in the 1983 campaign
against 'spiritual pollution', accused of promoting modern-
ism, abstract humanitarianism, pessimism, egoism, and sexual
liberation. A depressing feature of every conservative backlash
was the willingness of more than one radical figure from the past
to side with the critics. In 1983 this included the feminist Ding
Ling, who had been purged from 1958 to 1978, spending five of
those years in prison and three more raising chickens and pigs in
a Shanxi village. Perhaps disturbed by the bolder ideas of
younger writers, she now wrote censoriously:

If light music is played in the theatres, everyone applauds, but when
they hear serious music, no one does. It has even got to the point that

when someone sings 'Without the Communist Party there would be no New China', people laugh. Another peculiar thing is that, because some foreign scholars praise certain works, our people say they are good. Young people like liberalism too much.

Yet overall the intellectuals' licence to enquire and explore continued to broaden. In part this was a response to market pressures: writers and film-makers were now supposed to be entrepreneurial and provide saleable books or films, reducing the need for state subsidy. The interest of the outside world in Chinese intellectual activity also provided some security. Political and social scientists were more directly involved in providing the intellectual back-up for the Party reformers while depending on their patronage. This relationship of mutual dependence would directly provoke the next conservative backlash, the 1987 campaign against bourgeois liberalism.

Opening the debate

Chinese scholars—'theoretical workers' in Marxism and economics—established an informal alliance with the reform wing of the Party leadership to prepare the ideological ground for change. Over ten years they shifted official thinking from the repetition of the dogmas of the Cultural Revolution to the acceptance of market socialism and the separation of Party and state powers. The scholars were not tame ideologues, and sometimes moved ahead of their political backers, almost disastrously in 1986–7 when several heads were sacrificed to the conservatives, but although always cautious about public expression of their ideas, they gained a degree of intellectual autonomy unthinkable a decade before. As the *People's Daily* observed (21 July 1986):

Encouraging the people to speak their minds is not easy, because once in our country there prevailed a political atmosphere of not allowing them to say what they really think and also of being unwilling to listen to their innermost thoughts and feelings ... In those days, to speak one's mind was to invite an unexpected calamity; without feigning politeness and compliance, it was hardly possible to live a peaceful life. But those who were willing to kiss the feet of some people would be in their good graces ... Such a situation was completely abnormal ... To encourage people to speak their minds, we must first and foremost adhere to the principle of freedom of speech as stipulated in the Constitution and we should not infringe on the right of the people to state their views.

In May 1977 a small group of scholars were brought together by Hu Yaobang to discuss the proposition that 'Practice is the only criterion of truth'. This apparently innocuous statement, which echoed Mao's earlier teachings ('No right to speak without investigation'), was in fact a direct theoretical challenge to the mainstream Maoist view that socialist truth was self-evident and enshrined in Mao Zedong's policies and directives (the 'Two Whatevers'). Politically it meant an offensive by Hu on Deng Xiaoping's behalf against the leadership known as the 'Small Gang of Four' under Hua Guofeng (Beijing Mayor Wu De, Mao's former bodyguard Wang Dongxing, Beijing regional commander Chen Xilian, and Politburo member Ji Dengkui). By February 1978 the power struggle had begun to shift in Deng's favour. Li Xin, the conservative historian who had drafted the 'Two Whatevers', failed to enter the Politburo and the Small Gang of Four began to lose influence. In May 1978 the proposition that 'Practice is the only criterion for truth' was published in an article in the *Guangming Daily*, then known as the intellectuals' newspaper. This opened the way for public discussion and was shortly followed by speeches in which both Deng and Hu attacked the 'Two Whatevers'. The significance of this theoretical argument is stressed in official Party histories which say that it provided a 'good preparation' for the Third Plenum in December 1978 which approved Deng's new course of reform. The *Guangming Daily* article argued that even when a theory had been tested in practice, it must be tested again, and altered if necessary, as circumstances changed. Its appeal for a scientific approach was central to the reformers' attack upon dogma:

In theory or in practical work, the Gang of Four set many 'forbidden zones' which fettered people's minds. We must dare to investigate these 'forbidden zones' and dare to correct them because in fact there are no forbidden zones in real science. Wherever there is a 'forbidden zone' which transcends practice and styles itself as absolute, there is no science of real Marxism-Leninism-Mao Zedong Thought; there is only obscurantism, idealism, and cultural despotism . . .

Immediately after the Third Plenum the discussion group was enlarged to form the nucleus of a running internal 'Seminar on the ideological principles of theoretical work' which is treated as another landmark in Party history. But on this occasion the reformist scholars discovered the point at which Deng Xiaoping would draw the line, and divisions began to appear within their ranks. In the phrase much used to indicate the rejection of dogma, those who attended had 'liberated minds' and put forward proposals which would not be aired publicly for several more years. These included the abolition of lifelong tenure for Party and government leaders, the concept that socialism should be divided into different stages, and the proposal that more than one candidate should stand in elections.

After more than two months of discussion, Deng Xiaoping returned from the United States and (at the same time as the first arrests were made on Democracy Wall) set a firm limit on the scholars' debate. China's long-term task, he said, was to modernize, and politics was now above all about modernization. But it could only be achieved on the basis of the 'Four Principles' which Deng now enunciated for the first time: 'To keep to the Socialist Road, to uphold the Dictatorship of the Proletariat, the Leadership of the Communist Party, Marxism-Leninism and Mao Zedong Thought.' At this point the more orthodox theoreticians led by Deng Liqun detached themselves from the reformers, seeing the Four Principles as a weapon against too radical change. The more outspoken reformers regarded the Four Principles as contrary to the spirit of testing theory in practice, but the formula could not be directly opposed, particularly after it was incorporated into the Constitution.

Extending the frontiers

Reformist scholars provided much of the intellectual groundwork for the 1981 Party Resolution, although the leadership and particularly Deng had the last word. The Resolution included the crucial sentence that 'China's socialist system remains at its initial stage', a formulation originated by neo-Marxist Professor Su Shaozhi, which would legitimize further enquiries. Before and after the Resolution, the frontiers of debate were steadily extended against conservative opposition.

Class struggle

The December 1978 Plenum had marked the initial victory of the reformers by saying that the Party could now 'shift the focus of work' from class struggle to economic construction. But the 1981 Resolution still said that 'class struggle will continue to exist within certain limits for a long time to come and may even grow acute under certain conditions'. This provided a reserve weapon for leftist critics to employ when they had the opportunity. In December 1981 the Party reformer Liao Gailong spoke on 'the problem of class struggle in socialist society', returning to Mao's view during the Hundred Flowers period (1956–7) that this had been 'basically resolved' in China. Su Shaozhi had already gone further, suggesting that the term was either out of date or to the extent that it was still used meant something different. Mao's formulation in 1957 had allowed that 'class struggle within the ranks of the people' could, if handled properly, remain 'non-antagonistic' and susceptible to being resolved peacefully. Su said that it would be more sensible to rename this as 'ideological remoulding' to avoid the term being abused by those who, like Lin Biao, had wished to widen the struggle. The real effect of this argument was to empty the term 'class struggle' of its previous connotations while preserving it as a concession to the Party purists. Su similarly sought to redefine the 'dictatorship of the proletariat', which had been used to justify the deprivation of many people's most basic rights during the Cultural Revolution and was still insisted upon by official post-Mao dogma. Yes, it still existed under socialism, Su conceded, but as a means of exercising political leadership rather than ruling by force.

Alienation

The 1981 Resolution on Party history had accounted for the Cultural Revolution largely in terms of a historic failure 'to handle the relationship between the Party and its leader correctly'. Wang Ruoshui, deputy editor-in-chief of the *People's Daily*, wrote that the problem was not just the relationship between the Party and its leader, but that between the Party, the leader, and the people. 'Not only did the Party and state find it hard to prevent the initiation of the Cultural Revolution, but also the people did not have the strength to prevent that disaster'—nor indeed, he added, had they necessarily wanted to. The relationship between the leader and the masses was a form of alienation in which the people who had made the revolution and from whom the Party and its leader emerged transferred the power which they had won to those in authority. He compared the near-deification of Mao with man's attribution of his own wisdom and nature to God. It was the people, not Mao, who were the life-giving 'sun', and the people, not the Party, who should be compared to the 'mother'. The problem was not merely how to avoid the return of plotters like the Gang of Four, but how to prevent 'public servants of society transferring themselves to masters of society':

Once a Party which was formerly under oppression comes into power, its position is changed. There is the danger that it will cut itself off from the masses and become alienated; there is the possibility for it to become alienated. When a Party, which formerly served the people and was a tool and servant of the people, is divorced from the people and becomes an aristocratic overlord, it no longer belongs to the working class but has become an alienated force ...

This problem exists at all levels of our leadership and has not yet been solved. The Party Central Committee has taken notice of it. Promoting democracy, perfecting the legal system, laying down the rules governing life in the Party, and abolishing the system of life-long appointment of cadres—we may say these are all measures for preventing alienation ('*On Alienation*', May 1981).

Democracy

The concept of democracy as the 'fifth modernization', first put forward by the Democracy Wall dissident leader Wei Jingsheng, was applied concretely by the neo-Marxist scholars to the drive for economic rationality and efficiency. It could be argued that the Chinese economy had made its best progress when there was a relatively more democratic atmosphere (the mid-1950s, early 1960s, and post-1978). 'Without democracy', Su Shaozhi had written in a paper for an international conference in Yugoslavia (Sept. 1980), 'there are no Four Modernizations ... The masses of the working people are the masters of the country and of the enterprises. It is therefore important to ensure that the people truly have the power to manage the affairs of the state and of the enterprises. It is an important factor for preventing the evils of bureaucracy.'

Party traditionalists have always reacted to calls for democracy with the warning that this could lead to a collapse of the Party's leadership. This argument was countered by the director of the Fujian Academy of Sciences Li Honglin, who wrote in March 1982 that the opposite of democracy is not 'authority' but 'autocracy', and that the real opposition is between 'the authority of democracy and the authority of autocracy'. He also rejected the claim that too much talk about democracy led to social disorder, arguing that on the contrary it was the lack of publicity in favour of democracy which fostered the survival of the kind of 'feudal autocracy' that had led to the 'anarchy' of the Cultural Revolution.

Early in 1983, the scholars' enquiry reached a new high point at a conference called to celebrate the anniversary of Marx's death. Su Shaozhi argued that Marxism was often accused of being out of date but had only itself to blame for treating new questions in a dogmatic manner. He called for a fresh analysis of advanced capitalist society and a scientific study of the errors committed by Stalin and Mao Zedong, while looking again at the ideas of Rosa Luxembourg and Bukharin. The veteran Party ideologue Zhou Yang, known in the past as a conformist who was willing to denounce his colleagues, now spoke positively on the concept of alienation in analysing socialist society. His speech created a sensation, but the conference was instantly adjourned for two days to give the conservatives time to organize criticism of Zhou. Led by Hu Qiaomu, another veteran ideologue whose thought had not moved with the times, they would prevail upon Deng Xiaoping to endorse the autumn campaign against spiritual pollution, closely identified with the concept of alienation.

The failure of this short-lived period of reaction underlined the essential weakness of the conservative-left critique—its lack of a coherent intellectual alternative other than to warn that the *political* effects of reformist argument might be dangerous. Even Hu Qiaomu did not deny that the concept of 'Marxist humanism' was valid, but he warned that even 'well-intentioned' discussion of it would encourage anarchist and individualist

tendencies of thought. With remarkable speed the reform argument was resumed, encouraged once again by Hu Yaobang, who
warned sharply against 'residual leftist poison' which had pene-
trated the Party very deeply. In December 1984 Hu dramatically
extended further the terms of the scholars' licence in a manner
which attracted international attention:

[Marx's] works were written more than a hundred years ago. Some were
his tentative ideas at that time, and things have changed greatly since
then. Some of his tentative ideas were not necessarily very appropriate.
Many things have happened which Marx and Engels did not experience, and which even Lenin did not experience, so they had no
contact with them. We cannot expect the writings of Marx and Lenin
at that time to provide solutions to our current problems (7 Dec.).

In the storm (fanned by the foreign press) which followed, the
People's Daily quickly published a correction: the last sentence
should read 'We cannot expect the writings of Marx and Lenin
at that time to provide solutions to *all* our current problems.' It
was explained unofficially that the commentary had been based
on notes taken at a briefing by Hu Yaobang, and that the
qualifying adjective had been omitted. Even with this proviso,
the way was now cleared to discard openly some elements of
traditional doctrine: 'We must study Marxism in close connec-
tion with realities,' explained the Party journal *Red Flag* (No. 3,
1985), '. . . and distinguish clearly what is still applicable from
what is not.'

The Great Debate

In 1986 Deng Xiaoping, by now convinced that economic reform
would not succeed without the reformation of the political
structures which still dominated the economy, granted a new
licence, although in somewhat limited terms. The initial quote
on which the reformers relied merely said that 'During this time
[the Seventh Five Year Plan] comprehensive economic restructuring will affect every field: politics, education, science.' Deng
spoke more clearly later on, but always presenting political
reform in a wholly utilitarian context:

As economic reform progresses, we deeply feel the necessity for changes
in the political structure. The absence of such changes will hamper the

development of productive forces and the success of the Four Modernizations.

The summer of 1986 saw the most lively and varied intellectual movement that China had known since the Hundred
Flowers. Suddenly there was a rash of seminars, often with
innocuous-sounding titles: 'The Chinese Import of Culture' or
Historical Aspects of Western Democracy'. The subject-matter
was far from historical. In July 1986, at an important seminar on
theoretical work which was fully reported in the Party journal
Red Flag, social scientists called for a new democratic spirit of
scientific enquiry. 'Without a spirit of democracy', said Su
Shaozhi, 'there will be no spirit of science':

Theoretical workers must have real courage and boldness of vision, and
must ponder questions independently rather than mechanically following the instructions of higher authorities and books. They must not be
afraid of being regarded as advocators of 'unorthodox opinions'. Many
such opinions were later proved correct through scientific experiments.
Our theoretical workers must have such courage in the course of
promoting our socialist spiritual civilization.

Su demonstrated his own boldness by talking of the persistence of 'feudalist autocracy' among the leadership and its
corrosive influence on the economic reforms. For example, the
development of widespread commerce (the 'commodity economy') was being undermined by the phenomenon of the children
of senior cadres 'engaging in commercial activities'. He also cited
opposition to 'bourgeois democracy' in the past as an example
of dogmatism. Had it not been advocated during the French
Revolution, and was it not valid to discuss the issues of universal
suffrage and checks and balances of power? 'The real situation at
present is very complicated', said You Lin, another participant in
the 1986 seminar. 'There is neither pure capitalist society nor pure
socialist society in this world. The situation is especially complicated when socialism is in its primary stage.'
Other speakers criticized the lack of a tradition of free
intellectual discussion. China should follow Lenin's example,
argued Lin Jizhou, and allow policies to be debated in the press
before being decided by the Party Congress.

If our theoretical workers cannot make daring explorations and cannot
air their views freely, it will be harmful to our socialist construction.

The abnormal phenomenon of regarding all articles published by newspapers and magazines as a reflection of the will of the central authorities should be changed.

Many scholars called for an end to 'old idols' and the development of a real scientific spirit. Gao Fang criticized the view that veteran Party cadres necessarily understood Marxism. On the contrary, they had been affected by many 'non-Marxist or semi-Marxist theories'. A scientific spirit meant three things, said Jin Guantao: first, the principle on which modern science had developed ever since the Renaissance, that 'practice is the criterion of truth'; second, an attitude of 'conditioned scepticism', in support of which he quoted T. H. Huxley; and third, the creation of a friendly and tolerant atmosphere in academic circles, where people would no longer be criticized over 'a single source or a single sentence'. The events of the next few months showed that this atmosphere was still some way off. As the argument for political reform came closer to a call for real internal Party democracy (even though no one in the debates yet mentioned pluralism), it began to be echoed in the official press to the alarm of the conservatives. Li Honglin demanded democracy 'even if it grates on the ears of the leaders'. His article in the pace-setting Shanghai *World Economic Herald* was quickly followed by a *People's Daily* commentary with the title, 'There can be no socialist modernization without socialist democracy':

The people are the masters of a socialist state, and their initiative can only be brought into play and turned ultimately into material force if they indeed play their role as masters of the house in political, economic, and all social life . . . Socialist democracy also confers on the masses the right to criticize and supervise, thus ensuring the flourishing vitality of the cause of socialist modernization . . . Malpractices such as abusing power for private purposes, and persistent ailments such as bureaucracy must, in the final analysis, be solved through relying on political democratization. The most elementary thing here is to allow the masses to speak out and to listen to their views (8 May 1986).

Three who went too far

Dissenting scholars in China who go too far have traditionally expected punishment. In imperial days it used to be banishment or even decapitation. In the milder atmosphere of Deng's China it meant expulsion from the Communist Party. The student demonstrations of winter 1986/7 gave the conservatives the pretext they needed to attack the reform-minded scholars with, for the time being, Deng's approval. Three leading critics were singled out by Deng himself. In the Chinese idiom he 'marked their names' as surely as the emperor had once circled the names of those meriting punishment with his vermilion pen. Each of them had already made many enemies, and had shown a deliberate impatience with the slow pace of democratic reform.

Fang Lizhi

Born in 1936, Fang had drawn attention to himself as a Beijing University physics student in 1956 by interrupting a Youth League meeting to suggest that it should discuss 'what kind of person is education supposed to develop?' He was later named as a rightist and expelled for the first time from the Party. During the Cultural Revolution, he took up the study of astrophysics while doing labour in the countryside. Returning to the Chinese College of Science and Technology in Anhui, he soon became internationally known, but did not confine himself to cosmology. In speeches and interviews on Chinese university campuses, he stressed his two favourite themes: the role of the intellectual as an independent force for social reform, and the need to consider democracy 'as a right and not a gift from above'. In both respects he regarded the West as much more advanced. When appointed vice-president of the college, he had pledged to make 'freedom of thought' one of the principles of university education. His handling of administration and finance, where he encouraged internal staff elections and open budgeting, was praised in a series of articles in the *People's Daily* only weeks before his second dismissal from the Party.

Fang's stress on proper recognition of the intellectual's contribution to society led him to propose not just that class labels traditionally applied to the intellectual were outdated but, much more heretically, that the intellectual constituted a new and more dynamic class than the traditional working class.

Marx classified people into different groups according to the means of production they owned. In my view, this was tenable in the last century and the beginning of this. However, in modern society, the development of science and technology, knowledge, and information, including high-tech and soft science, has become an important force propelling society forward, and is bound to involve a change in the concept of who leads in the political and economic fields. *Intellectuals, who own and create information and knowledge, are the most dynamic component of the productive forces, and this is what determines their social status (Beijing Review, 15 Dec. 1986) (my italics).*

Fang also spoke of the need to substitute a sense of 'intellectual consciousness' for the old concept of 'class consciousness'. It was hardly surprising that he should be accused of 'exalting the role of intellectuals while sowing discord between them and the Party', and of 'instigating trouble by saying that Chinese intellectuals . . . ought to constitute an independent force'. There was indeed an élitist tinge to Fang's ideas which the professional theorists disliked, although it appealed to a new, less political generation of students.

Wang Ruowang

Wang belongs to an earlier tradition of outspoken scholarship. He joined the Communist Youth League in Shanghai in 1933, was thrown into prison by the Nationalist government, and moved in 1937 to Yanan where he joined the Communist Party. He wrote one of the first biographical articles on Mao, and edited cultural journals in the liberated areas. In Shanghai after the war, he was criticized even before the anti-right campaign as an editor of the *Literary Monthly*. The campaign labelled him a 'right-wing element' for his articles attacking dogmatism and expelled him from the Party, but his membership was restored in 1962. Imprisoned for four years in the Cultural Revolution, he emerged swearing to devote the rest of his life 'to struggle with those false Marxists who accuse people unjustly and inhumanly of crimes'. Wang had long possessed a reputation for fearless criticism. When the rural co-operative movement was stepped up in 1955 and led to a vogue for collectivizing everything, Wang wrote a sharp critique for which he was later accused of 'rejecting the Party's leadership'.

It seems that when the trend was towards the collective feeding of livestock in the co-operatives, various theatrical groups and publications in Shanghai were also in the process of being collectivized . . .

One could hardly escape being branded as a conservative if one failed to support the movement. None the less, the facts have shown that when both cattle and men were collectivized, the cattle became scrawny, the arts became scrawny, the theatrical troupes and publishing houses became scrawny. This . . . does not reveal the superiority of socialism; on the contrary, it reveals our blindness (*Literary Gazette*, No. 21, 1957).

By 1985 Wang's increasingly libertarian views had already led to renewed calls for his expulsion from the Party. He also caused offence by circulating an open letter calling for a national conference to commemorate the 30th anniversary of the 1957 Hundred Flowers movement. An article 'Zest for life', written for the popular magazine *Youth Generation* (No. 4, 1986), reflects his eclectic approach: he recommended a sense of optimism, humour, and a willingness to express one's innermost feelings as characteristics which were far superior to the traditional virtues of Chinese sobriety and reticence. He cited with approval President Reagan's ability to joke about an operation, and asked why people should always ascribe credit for their achievements to 'the Party and the government', quoting instead the Argentinian footballer Maradona who had acknowledged the support of his family and girl-friend! Wang showed his own zest for life by writing his autobiography under the provisional title 'I Feel Good about Myself'. Criticized for behaving like 'a trolleybus without a line', he retorted that Mao Zedong's trolleybus, by keeping to its line, had led China straight into the Huangpu River.

Wang caused maximum offence late in 1986 by publicly taking issue with some remarks by Deng Xiaoping about the need for economic reforms to avoid the polarization of incomes. Wang's argument—that relative differentials between rich and poor were a necessary part of economic development—was not so different from the official justification for allowing some entrepreneurs to 'get rich first', but his real offence was to criticize Deng by name. 'Can the common people carry on a public discussion with the leaders of our country?', he asked in his article, published provocatively in the Shenzhen Special Economic Zone (*The Worker*, 5 Nov. 1986). He was expelled from the Party for errors including 'distortion and denial of its leading role'.

Liu Binyan

'Wherever he writes something, chaos ensues', complained Party bureaucrats in Shaanxi province after the investigative journalist Liu Binyan had exposed corruption in the province. When he was expelled from the Party in January 1987, there were threats of libel action from the administrations which he had offended. Using the device of *baogao wenxue* (reportage literature), Liu had begun his writing career with articles on bureaucratic bungling at a bridge construction site and in a local newspaper, which earned him a 'rightist' label in 1957. He was only rehabilitated as a journalist in 1979, having spent over twenty years either in the countryside or as a proof-reader or translator. Writing for the *People's Daily*, he quickly made his reputation with 'Between Men and Monsters', the story of a county Party secretary in Heilongjiang province who made a fortune by taking bribes. The official concerned was later sentenced to death for embezzlement. His next major work, 'A Second Kind of Loyalty', praised the supreme loyalty of those who dare criticize the Party when it does wrong. In 1985 he was elected vice-chairman of the Chinese Writers' Association, declining nomination for chairman, which he would easily have won.

Liu gave particular offence by consistently focusing his attack upon the 'left' in the Party, which he blamed for twenty years of misrule. From the 1950s onwards, he observed, the Chinese train had 'raced towards the Cultural Revolution' uncontrollably, and even today 'the main danger still comes from the left'. After his second expulsion from the Party in January 1987, the *People's Daily* accused him of painting a picture of 'utter darkness' in which the Party was 'corrupt from top to bottom'. Liu was also accused of 'vilifying the broad masses of intellectuals' by saying that many of them took the safe way out, and joined the 'going-with-the-wind faction'. Liu certainly upset many colleagues by refusing to exempt them from responsibility for what he regarded as intellectual timidity. People in their thirties, he observed, 'generally hate politics, are uninterested in Marxism-Leninism, and disillusioned about China's future'. But he urged them to write about the political struggle: after all, it was extremely dramatic, 'which should be an advantage for artistic creation!'

Liu regarded the post-Mao claim that ultra-leftism could be

blamed on a 'small handful' of careerists around Mao Zedong as a shameful alibi. Its roots lay deep in China's 'great ocean of small scale farmers', and were overlaid even today by a strong tinge of anarchism which easily degenerated into oppression of a wholly unpolitical and gangsterist nature. The brutality which he had witnessed in the land reform campaign before 1949, when minor landlords were cruelly tortured, even when this had been explicitly forbidden by the leadership, had its counterpart in Heilongjiang during the Cultural Revolution:

A platform inspector, Liu Shulan, was brutally attacked because she would not let the friends of a leading official board a train without a ticket. Several times, to make fun of her diseased womb, Zhao Yufeng [the local Party boss] forced her to take down her trousers at meetings. When it became serious she went into the hospital, womb and anus swollen together; they sent people to the hospital to drag her back on a truck, without trousers, for more struggle.

The conservative reaction

The reaction was bound to come. Party scholars who had been 'formed' as a new generation of 'ideological workers' in the 1950s felt themselves to be ridiculed by a coalition of old and new rightists who unaccountably enjoyed both the support of foreign friends and domestic Party reformers. Backed by the Party conservatives, they found their voice again with a real sense of grievance when Hu Yaobang was forced to step down in January 1987. The world of Marxist theory, they complained, had been turned upside down. Those who dared to criticize Marxism were regarded as having 'liberated their thought' and were well received, but those comrades who persisted in their correct opinions were suppressed. 'Marxists should be full of courage and have the confidence to speak out.'

Everyone sees clearly that for some time the ideological trend of bourgeois liberalization has spread unchecked, and a few people have been busy writing articles and delivering reports that negate the Four Basic Principles and advocate Total Westernization, while not allowing others to say No. Some papers, journals, and platforms controlled by them have refused to give the slightest space to Marxists, and even the Central Committee's opinion that 'Marxists should stand out and speak' has been mocked. Comrades who adhere to the Party's stand have been isolated and subjected to joint attacks ... they have been labelled as 'ultra-leftists,' 'ossified' and 'purgers'. (*Xinhua*, 28 Jan. 1987.)

Simple truths were reasserted with an unashamed chauvinism. 'Socialism is good!', proclaimed the people of Henan province, according to a commentary on their radio station. 'It is socialism that has made China, a poverty-stricken and backward country that allowed itself to be bullied and trampled on ... stand proudly among the nations of the world' (Shenyang radio, 2 Feb. 1987). The social evils of western society were highlighted by the *Beijing Daily*: 'drugs, alcohol abuse, violent murder, suicide, divorce, prostitution, homosexuality, and AIDS.' The conservative *Guangming Daily* asserted in a barely disguised critique of the open door policy that 'even if the Chinese people intend to study and learn from the Western system, the result can only be to become a semi-feudal and semi-colonial society and the object of imperialist designs' (5 Feb.). 'Do not forget the spirit of hard work and plain living; persist in building China frugally', wrote Bo Yibo, one of the veteran conservative patrons, in an inscription for the new Tianjin Development Zone. The glossy face of western-style consumerism was condemned: 'All over the country', said the *People's Daily*, 'people with money in their pockets are spending it on building high-class hotels, shopping malls, theme parks, sports grounds, commemoration halls, "centres" for this and that, repairing temples and travel and entertainment at public expense' (22 Jan.).

The weakness of traditional theory was its failure to transcend old-fashioned leftist arguments and produce coherent alternatives. A conference of conservative ideologues was convened in April 1987 at Zhuozhou, Hebei province. It was hoped that this would lead to production of several hundred articles by well-known theorists for publication in the next three years. (Contributors, gossip had it, would be paid 90 yuan per thousand characters or nearly ten times the usual rate.) Yao Xueyin, author of a famous trilogy on the Taiping Revolution, returned to print to urge Chinese writers not to abandon China's 'brilliant tradition of revolutionary literature'. The Maoist poet He Jingzhi argued for the suppression of 'unhealthy works'. Yet the conference produced only a handful of passable articles, and one episode which delighted progressive scholars: a professor of

Chinese from the leftist province of Hunan had denounced the publication of a book which he referred to as *Lady Thatcher's Lover*. 'Besides corrupting the morals of our youth', he declaimed, 'would not this spoil our relations with Britain?' The right-wing offensive demonstrated once again how factionalism and chauvinism undermined the conservative critique. It gave Zhao Ziyang much-needed ammunition: only four or five of the articles passed muster, he said. Some echoed the Cultural Revolution and most failed to convince. The futility of it reminded him of a Cantonese saying: 'Water has been poured over the duck, but its feathers are still dry.'

Reform had also weakened the intimidatory effect of yet another conservative campaign. Deng Xiaoping himself lamented that only a few intellectuals could be found to speak up against 'bourgeois liberalization'. They included the novelist Wang Meng, now Minister of Culture, who judged it prudent to give his lukewarm approval to the campaign rather than run the risk of replacement by a leftist. Distressingly, the elderly sociologist Fei Xiaotong, who thirty years before had called courageously for a real spring thaw at the time of the Hundred Flowers, now spoke in favour of the winter clamp-down. Many scholars, summoned to meetings to denounce the three heretics, pleaded illness or came only to sit in silence. Yet another device was to link criticism of bourgeois liberalization with an attack upon 'feudalism'—the mentality of those who were running the conservative campaign. Among cadres and students, the reading out of selective quotations from Fang Lizhi and Liu Binyan often had the opposite effect from that intended. Extracts from Liu condemning ultra-leftism as 'against humanity and despising man', and from Fang insisting that it was 'better to study socialism than to Love Socialism' were greeted with appreciative laughter.

Another weakness of the conservatives was that they kept company with activists of the Cultural Revolution. The editor of the *Beijing Daily*, which denounced the student demonstrations, deputy Party Secretary Xu Weicheng, had been active in the Gang of Four's 'Two Schools' Writing Group. When the conservatives sought to make him the Party's new propaganda head, the widows of four Party leaders persecuted in the Cultural Revolution wrote to Deng Xiaoping denouncing him. Xu caused alarm in the first weeks of the anti-bourgeois liberalization campaign by compiling blacklists, but within the year he had been demoted to work far away from Beijing in Guizhou province.

Compromise

At 8 a.m. on 1 August 1987, while the Party leadership was meeting by the seaside at Beidaihe to resolve the argument between conservatives and reformers, the playwright Wu Zuguang heard someone coming laboriously up three flights of stairs to his Beijing apartment. It was the Politburo ideologue, 75-year-old Hu Qiaomu, bringing a verbal message from the Central Disciplinary Commission urging Wu to resign from the Party. The charges ranged from Wu's alleged 'rightist' activities in 1957 to a recent speech arguing against play censorship. Touched, Wu said, by Hu's personal attention, and not wishing to embarrass the Party, he agreed to resign quietly (but a full account of the visit and of Wu's subsequent letter to the Disciplinary Commission was leaked shortly afterwards in the Hong Kong press). Wu then circulated to his friends a proposal to compile a collection of essays on the pleasures of drinking. Four other prominent intellectuals, including Su Shaozhi and Wang Ruoshui, also received visits that day in what became known as the 'Incident of the Five Gentlemen'.

Fellow-intellectuals were briefly alarmed, but the incident was soon seen as a last token gesture to the conservatives, necessary in order to save face for Deng Liqun and the leftist ideologues who had compiled much longer lists of suspect scholars after the spring offensive against Fang, Wang, and Liu, and who would shortly be isolated at the Thirteenth Party Congress. Far from winning a post on the Politburo (he had even hoped at one stage to become Party Secretary-General), Deng did not even remain in the Central Committee. The weight of official condemnation of 'ossified thinking' fell heavily on his shoulders. Su Shaozhi and others on the original list reappeared after the Congress, quoted extensively on the theory of reform. Nevertheless, their statements reflected the price which had to be paid for the curtailment of the leftist campaign. Once again Chinese intellectuals were required not to cross a line drawn by others. The first neo-Marxist scholar to reappear, Yan Jiaqi, author (with his wife) of the frowned-upon history of the Cultural Revolution, set the limit:

Yan Jiaqi stressed that the next five to ten years would be a crucial period of China's political structural reform. He said: Building democratic politics to a higher degree than in other developed countries will be a long-term process ... At present, any social unrest might lead to the rise of ultra-'leftist' ideology. People must bear in mind the historical lesson as regards this issue. *Political structural reform must be carried out step by step, in an orderly way, under the leadership of the Party* (my italics) (*China News Service*, 29 Oct. 1987).

The same phrase (adapted from Zhao's report to the Congress) was repeated by Ma Hong, head of the Chinese Academy of Sciences, where Su and so many of the reformers worked. 'The method of a political movement and of "great democracy" will not be adopted', said Ma, stressing that the 'ultimate purpose of political reform is to promote the development of the social productive forces' (*Guangming Daily*, 29 Oct.). The novelist Wang Meng continued to play his delicate bridging role, warning the scholars not to expect too much from reform nor be depressed at the need for cautious advance. Many men of letters, he said, had 'gone ahead of their times' in calling for reform. Yet when they met with setbacks or 'complex situations', they easily became downcast and sighed in despair. They should realize that the situation was rich with hope as well as with 'troublesome issues'. Wang also expressed the view of many of his older generation of intellectuals that some reformers were publicity-seekers: he spoke of people who were 'cheer-leaders' rather than practical reformers, and who copied western styles and 'indulged in narcissism' (*People's Daily*, 17 Nov.).

CHAPTER ELEVEN

The Door Opens Wide

CHINA AND THE WORLD ECONOMY

The new hotel opposite the foreigners' apartment blocks in north-east Beijing was ready to celebrate its opening. It was near the Sheraton Great Wall, but it was a joint venture not with the Americans but with an extremely patriotic—and wealthy— Chinese, Mr Y. K. Pao from Hong Kong. The hotel was named after his father—the Zhaolong Hotel—and Mr Deng Xiaoping himself had agreed both to open it and, in a further 'generous gesture', to pen the calligraphy for its neon sign. One day in October 1985, the main road outside was cordoned off several hours before the event. The stalls selling clothing and fruit on the other side were thoroughly searched and closed for the day. Finally a convoy of Mercedes swept through the gates. They contained Mr Deng, Vice-Premiers Wan Li and Xi Zhongxun, the deputy head of the Military Affairs Commission Yang Shangkun, the minister in charge of China's 'open door' policy Mr Gu Mu—and Mr Pao.

Mr Deng entered the foyer to the applause of the hotel staff, lined up smartly in their uniforms (and many of them the sons or daughters of officials who had secured these desirable jobs for their offspring 'through the back door'). He glanced appreciatively at the hotel fountain and hanging chandelier, and then unveiled a plaque which recorded the patriotic intentions of Mr Pao:

... in a dedicated effort to help promote the tourist industry of his mother country, he proposed to the Central Leadership his preparedness to contribute US $10 million to build a hotel in filial memory of his father ...

Tourism to China had increased by more than 20 per cent in the years 1982-5. One and a half million foreign nationals would visit in 1986, of whom half a million came from Japan and nearly 300,000 from the US. (The total figure for tourism was much higher—over 21 million: the remainder were overseas Chinese who would not usually stay in the Zhaolong or Sheraton Great Wall.) Foreign currency income was in excess of one and a half billion US dollars.

The foreign businessman no longer brought his own bottle of Scotch to China or spent long evenings reading China Pictorial *by low wattage bulbs. There were now joint venture hotels in all the main cities, with late-night coffee shops, in-house videos, and air conditioning. The cisterns flushed and the staff were taught to say 'Good Morning, Sir (or Madam)'. The flask of hot water and packets of green tea had been replaced by a drinks cabinet.*

The new patriotism

China's new opening to the West in the 1980s would have been instantly denounced by the ultra-left ten years before as capitulationism or 'national betrayal'. (Only a few remnant Maoist sympathizers outside China now used such terms.) Certainly it contained elements of what Mao once condemned as the tendency to believe that 'foreign farts smell sweeter' or, more decorously, that 'the moon shines brighter in the West'. But to limit an analysis of the Open Door policy to the importation into China of the Holiday Inn culture of international tourism, the establishment of Colonel Saunders' Kentucky Fried Chicken in Tiananmen Square, and the pursuit of imported videos and computer technology, is to miss the policy's main thrust. This was concerned with the central theme of Chinese nationalism for a hundred years: how to Revive the Country and make it Strong. Woven into the Open Door was a strong thread of 'patriotic' sentiment, often expressed in language which could have been used by Sun Yatsen. It shaded into a more sophisticated form of international *realpolitik* in which China's role as a potential superpower (although still formally denied in the formula that 'China will never be a superpower') was quietly taken for granted. A less chauvinistic form of nationalism was expressed by younger intellectuals, especially those who had studied abroad, who viewed China as interdependent with the rest of the world, participating in a global economy and culture. The Party leadership accepted such participation in economic terms but balked at cultural universality. For the 'socialist system', although less well defined than in the past, was now subsumed into a definition of Chinese nationhood—'socialism with Chinese characteristics'—which must be defended. Complicated by these more and less modern strands of thought, the Open Door by the late 1980s had nevertheless become the concept most capable of unifying the country. After the Thirteenth Party Congress it was inseparable from the concept of reform, almost wholly replacing the earlier mobilizing concepts of Revolution and Socialism. Through the 1984 agreement with Britain on Hong Kong, the Open Door policy also sought to restore the integrity of the Chinese nation, regaining the first territory to be lost to Western 'semi-colonialism' and offering a model for the eventual reintegration of Taiwan.

The Chinese word for patriotism, 'love-countryism', is explicit, as is the word for native land, 'land-of-our-ancestors', whose long civilization, say all the school textbooks, dates back nearly four millennia. The chronology is extended further by a succession of legendary rulers, popularly spoken of as if they were historical figures. The very first ancestor was the Yellow Emperor, who ascended to heaven from a small town which still bears his name in present-day Shaanxi province, in the year 2697 BC. When Deng Xiaoping in 1984 appealed to the rulers of Taiwan to follow Hong Kong's example and return to the ancestral land, his exact words were an invitation to rejoin the descendants of the Yellow Emperor. Chairman Hu Yaobang had made a similar appeal to the President of Taiwan:

'A tree may grow ten thousand feet high, but its leaves fall back to its roots.' Does Mr Chiang Ching-kuo not love his native land? Doesn't he want to have Mr Chiang Kai-shek's remains moved back and buried in the cemetery of the Chiang family in Fenghua? ... Foreign aid is important, but what is most important, most reliable and most powerful is the great patriotic unity of the 1,000 million people of our own country.

When Mao Zedong wrote in 1939 jointly with some of his colleagues a textbook to educate Communist Party members on the significance and strategy of the Chinese revolution, he began by describing Chinese history as extending back a full five thousand years (later corrected to 'nearly 4,000 years'). Sun Yatsen had lamented the tragedy that, in spite of its long history, China occupied the lowest position in international affairs. 'The rest of mankind', said Sun in discussing the principle of nationalism, 'is the carving knife and the serving dish, while we are the fish and the meat . . .' Paying tribute to Sun in 1956, Mao echoed his regrets. With its vast population and territory, he said, 'China . . . ought to make a greater contribution to humanity. But for a long time in the past its contribution was far too small. For this we are regretful.' Deng Xiaoping also regretted that progress since 1949 had been too slow, even though (and partly because) he and his colleagues had been so anxious not to waste time. China would have to work hard for another fifty or sixty years, he said (30 Apr. 1987), to demonstrate 'the superiority of socialism over capitalism'. The proof would come when China had reached a figure of US $4,000 billion GNP and occupied a position 'among the advanced countries of the world'. Patriotism was compatible not only with socialism but with the concept of 'proletarian internationalism' which China had once reproached the Soviet Union for abandoning. An official of the All-China Federation of Trade Unions explained:

Patriotism is unfortunately not possible for workers under capitalism, but under socialism one can be both patriotic and internationalist. After all, to love one's own country and to build socialism in it is what the proletariat of the whole world want. So for the Chinese worker today, the most practical task is to build one's own country. Only then can we make our contribution to the world, otherwise we have no strength and can do nothing.

But Deng Xiaoping's thoroughly traditional desire to Revive the Nation was transformed by his refusal to do so behind closed doors, or to accept the equally traditional Maoist explanation for China's weakness. China had suffered in the past, Deng told the Party's Advisory Commission in October 1984, from the withdrawal of the Qing dynasty into isolationism. 'As a result, China fell into poverty and ignorance.' Chinese historians elaborated on the theme: the emperor Qian Long, wrote a professor from Beijing University, was wrong to reject the British envoy Lord Macartney's mission in 1793. By refusing to open up China's ports to trade, and limiting foreign commerce to Guangzhou

(Canton), the Manchus 'confined the economic and cultural exchanges between China and foreign countries to a very narrow scale. . . . In short, during this time China underwent a change from progress to backwardness.' This was a total reversal of the standard view that the Manchus, while acting in part out of straightforward fear that their own domination would be threatened by the westerners, also displayed what the Party historian Hu Sheng had called 'a natural reaction to the lawless conduct of the marauding European merchants'. Deng Xiaoping also dismissed fears that the European merchants of the 1980s would be marauders. Some veteran comrades, he told the Advisory Commission (largely composed of such veterans), feared that 'undesirable things may happen' if the door was opened. They should not be afraid: the negative consequences could be contained. It was the country and the people who would benefit most from opening up to foreign investment and participation in joint ventures, not the capitalists. It was on this argument that Deng effectively staked his political reputation in the last years of his life.

Rethinking self-reliance

The Open Door policy in the late nineteenth century had been inflicted upon China by the great powers to provide equal access to China's markets and to ensure (unsuccessfully in reality) that no one power gained special privileges from which the others were excluded. It was aptly described by President Wilson as 'not the open door to the rights of China but the open door to the goods of America'. Both sorts of doors had closed after 1949, when China was largely excluded from significant trade with the West under pressure of a US embargo, and obliged to enter an unequal relationship with the Soviet Union which broke down within ten years. China's new Open Door policy in the late 1970s was initiated by the post-Mao leadership, as a reaction against two decades during which the door had been closed, and as an assertion of China's right to participate in the international market. Post-Mao reformers now looked back, arguing that Mao had gone too far in making a virtue of self-reliant necessity. It had been elevated into 'closed-doorism', a refusal to countenance anything beyond minimum contact with the outside world, which had strong overtones of the chauvinism of the feudal empire. A country such as China should still be self-reliant in the sense that its progress ultimately depended upon its own economic resources and moral/political commitment, but it should not exclude the outside world and attempt to go it alone. The Party journal *Red Flag* (16 Apr. 1982) argued for steering a middle path:

> In our history, there were two kinds of people. One kind of people worshipped and had blind faith in foreign things and was subservient to foreigners. As a result these people humiliated the nation and forfeited its sovereignty. Whether it was the Empress Dowager Cixi, Yuan Shikai [first president of the Republic, who capitulated to Japan's '21 demands' in 1915] or Chiang Kai-shek, they were without exception cast aside by the people. The other kind of people upheld closing the country to international exchange . . . [such as] the diehards at the end of the Qing dynasty who regarded China as the 'heavenly kingdom' and treated all foreign countries as 'uncivilized nations' . . .
>
> These two tendencies are still to some extent reflected in the minds of some of our Party members and cadres. This may perhaps be regarded as a kind of historical legacy. Some people feel ashamed before foreigners and that everything is good in other countries and bad in ours. Others are very apprehensive about opening up to the outside world and are of the opinion that there will be no peace and security if we do so . . .

But the new Open Door involved basic questions not only of policy but of theory towards the outside world which challenged accepted truths on the relationship of socialism to capitalism. Deng Xiaoping's advisers now credited the capitalist system with vitality and the ability to adjust for a long period to come, during which it would 'coexist' with socialism. The old view that 'imperialism will soon die out and socialism will soon win a total victory', said Huan Xiang (vice-president of the Academy of Social Sciences), was 'at odds with reality'. So was Mao's doctrine that world war was inevitable and that socialism would survive it, which had so shocked Khrushchev at the 1957 Moscow Conference and helped create the 1960s image of China as a 'bellicose' nation. (It took time to discard an argument which had led the entire Chinese urban population in the early 1970s to dig air-raid shelters to 'prepare against war'. Hu Yaobang in November 1980 was the first to say that an imperialist war could be 'postponed or even prevented'.)

How China, and indeed all socialist countries, should relate to the world market was also radically rethought. In the early 1950s China had accepted the Soviet 'two bloc' view that there were two separate markets, capitalist and socialist, and that the latter was the stronger. A decade later Soviet attempts to enforce an 'international division of labour' in the socialist market were regarded as a form of covert imperialism and the bloc was rejected. 'The correct method', wrote Mao, was for every country to strive for 'regeneration' as independently as possible. Chinese economists argued that foreign trade and economic relations must play only a subsidiary role. 'The people of every country', wrote one advocate of self-reliance, 'have for hundreds and thousands of years depended on their own hard toil.' In the early 1980s Chinese thought now adopted a 'one world' view of the international economy which had been rejected ever since Liberation (although during the revolution Mao had sought to tempt visiting Americans with a vision of Sino-American economic co-operation). Not only was there a single economic world system, said Huan Xiang, but 'both capitalism and imperialism occupy a dominant position' in such a 'unified market'. The first issue of the new journal *Social Sciences in China* (Mar. 1980) carried a pioneering article on the international division of labour. China could only avoid a 'lopsided economy', it argued, if it removed both internal and external obstacles to its development and 'established foreign economic relations based on equality and mutual benefit'. The fact that it was a socialist country, capable of 'highly social large-scale production', made it even more necessary to join the world market. To confine economic activity to national boundaries would, in a Marxist sense, become 'a fetter upon the productive process' (just as private enterprise under capitalism became a fetter on production).

Younger Chinese economists and sociologists showed less interest in whether or not China was a socialist country, basing their analysis rather on the relationship between the developing nations (among whom they counted China) and the developed world.

The developing countries, when they began to take their first steps, were faced with advanced industrial nations which were well beyond the pre-industrialization stages and were absolutely pre-eminent in technology and wealth ... Confronted with a fully developed world market, it is impossible for a country which cuts itself off and relies on the spontaneous role of its home market to catch up, let alone surpass the economically advanced countries (*Beijing Review*, 2–8 Nov. 1987).

There was a degree of ambivalence in this classification of China as a 'developing country'. It was at the same time the largest and most populous of the developing group, and the strategy proclaimed in the mid-1980s was that it should have attained or neared the level of the world's most developed nations by the middle of the twenty-first century. Sometimes different categories were used: Huan Xiang spoke of the 'great trilateral relationship' between China, the USSR, and the USA, which was linked to two sets of four-cornered relationships (China, USSR, USA, and Japan in Asia, and USA, USSR, and Western and Eastern Europe on the European continent). For a long period to come, he said, it was the great trilateral relationship which would 'truly determine' the international scene. But however the analysis was framed, China was definitely cast in a global economic role far removed from its 1960s role as a self-sufficient exemplar for the revolutionary people of Africa, Asia, and Latin America.

Reshaping foreign trade

'There are still some comrades', wrote the economist Ji Chong-wei in the *People's Daily* (6 Nov. 1981), 'who insist that the fewer exports the better and the fewer imports the better.' Until recently there had been little choice. For more than twenty years China had maintained a low level of balanced trade, unable even if it had so desired to enter the Western market for technology and investment on any significant scale. This policy of restraint began to come under pressure in the early 1970s as US–Chinese relations improved, but a careful line was drawn. 'China will never try to attract foreign capital or exploit domestic or foreign natural resources in conjunction with other countries', said the Minister of Foreign Trade Li Qiang in June 1974.

She [China] will never go in for joint-management with foreign countries, still less grovel for foreign loans as does that superpower [the Soviet Union]. China welcomes technical interchange with other countries and imports essential equipment on a planned and selective basis according to the needs of socialist construction. Methods of payment are arranged through negotiation by the two business parties in the light of common international trade practice.

At first after Mao's death these principles were reaffirmed. The increased imports of foreign technology were laboriously rationalized with the argument that by the process of adaptation to Chinese conditions they became a Chinese-developed technology. But Chinese financial experts quietly complained that valuable foreign currency was being wasted by a refusal to take advantage of normal commercial credits. Chinese oil surpluses were also reaching their peak, available for financing export growth, and justifying the Deng Xiaoping plan for mortgaging Chinese fossil fuels resources against imports of new technology which had ignited the great 1975 controversy. Before long Minister Li Qiang reversed his position entirely, announcing that 'by and large we now accept all the common practices known to world trade'. It was argued that China's historic share of the world market—about 1 per cent—was far too low and should be quadrupled by the end of the century. A theoretical balance between exports and imports was still asserted, but with the important qualification that it should be calculated over a longer period than one year.

Not surprisingly the shift of policy led to a splurge of buying complete turn-key plants and new technology which caused three successive trade deficits in 1978–80. In the flush of modernization, factory directors competed to order new plant from abroad, which in some cases ended up deteriorating in its packing cases. Though the buying spree stemmed from Deng's policies, he was able neatly to off-load responsibility on to Hua Guofeng. In the 'readjustment' of 1979–80, a moratorium was declared on new contracts and more than two-and-a-half billion dollars' worth of contracts with Japanese firms were temporarily suspended. Traders with China, long accustomed to regard a handshake as sufficient guarantee, now discovered that increased volume led to increased uncertainty. It also became more difficult to establish where the ultimate power of decision-making lay. A new tension arose in the mid-1980s between the desire to increase local initiative in promoting foreign trade, which implied decentralization, and fears that the process would get out of hand, which prompted new moves to concentrate power at the centre. Over the single year 1984–5, policy shifted three times. In March 1984 the Ministry of Foreign Economic Relations and Trade announced plans to tighten control, re-establishing the authority of the six great foreign trade corporations which had begun to lose ground to local export promotion, fixing prices and quotas, and increasing commodities subject to export licence. In September the policy was reversed as part of the new package of 'urban reform' promoted by Zhao Ziyang. Accountability was to be devolved to the actual importers and exporters, operating through a total of more than 900 specialized foreign trade companies. In reality most staff in these local bodies lacked the experience to hold their own with foreign negotiators, or were easily subverted by bribes and kickbacks, while the lack of central control allowed an unrestrained import boom. Within months control was reimposed following a disastrous fall in China's foreign exchange reserves. Once again many contracts were cancelled or deferred, causing further loss to China's traditional business reputation.

Control of foreign trade, whether at the centre or locally, could still be regarded as control by the socialist state. More difficult problems were raised by inviting foreign capital to participate in *production* by investing in the new joint venture companies. The reformers relied on Lenin, painting an exaggerated picture of the scope of foreign concessions allowed in the Soviet Union under his New Economic Policy. (*Red Flag* said there had been more than two hundred such concessions, but as Alec Nove has written, the policy 'came to very little', accounting for only 0.6 per cent of industrial output by 1928.) Chinese writers also blamed Stalin for concentrating on 'building socialism in one country surrounded by the capitalist world', and for failing to elevate the question of 'opening to the outside world' to the level of theory. The new joint ventures in China were now defined as a form of 'state capitalism' which was analogous to the jointly owned state–private industries allowed in China in the early 1950s.

Joint venture controls were indeed sufficiently strict to provoke many complaints from foreign businesses accustomed to easier terms in other Third World countries. By 1987, out of a total of 9,000 joint ventures licenced to operate, less than 3,500 were actually operating—one-third of these still at a loss. More than half of them functioned in the four Special Economic Zones (Shenzhen, Zhuhai, Shantou in Guangdong province, and Xiamen in Fujian). Complaints included excessive taxation and charges for labour, of which the greater part did not benefit the individual worker, and lack of access to the domestic market or payment in non-convertible Chinese currency where access was allowed. In November 1987 new regulations allowed some joint ventures to sell their goods within China as import substitutes and to be paid in foreign exchange. Admitting that China fell short of foreign capitalists' aspirations, the State Councillor chiefly responsible, Gu Mu, asked them 'to take a dynamic perspective with regard to investment in China—a long-term point of view which puts greater stress on the future of China's investment environment'. By 1986 China had made use of over US $20 billion in foreign credits to import technology, although substantial potential credits for another US $7 billion remained unused. More than US $17 billion in investment contracts had been approved, although less than one-third had been taken up. China had also issued what one Western news agency called 'the first international bond under communism'. Fifty million dollars worth of bonds were snapped up, underwritten in an echo of 'semi-colonial' history by a ten-bank international consortium. The 'current West European euphoria for everything Chinese', said the experts, 'had helped brush away any reservations among investors'.

Regional development

By far the greatest part of investment and participation in joint ventures came from 'patriotic' business in Hong Kong. Mainland disapproval of Hong Kong capitalism surfaced occasionally during the Sino-British negotiations (1982–4) but was soon submerged by an appreciation of Hong Kong's usefulness, not just as an existing source of foreign exchange (it continued to furnish about one-third of China's earnings) but as an open window to the world. Leading Hong Kong businesspeople whose families had 'fled' the mainland after 1949 and loudly advertised their fears of a 'communist take-over' during the negotiations were quickly reconciled. (But some quietly made alternative arrangements for the future, while younger Hong Kong professionals expressed open doubts about the agreement and many decided to leave.) In the post-1984 internal argument over democratization of the Hong Kong government, the business community sided with the Beijing view (shared also by the British government) that serious democratic reform—in particular, direct elections to the Legislative Council, which became the central issue—should be undertaken only 'step by step', if at all. Many of them were welcome guests in the Chinese capital, as Deng Xiaoping had promised when he first met a Hong Kong industrial and commercial delegation (22–3 June 1984):

It must be required that patriots form the main body of administrators, that is, of the future government of Hong Kong . . . Who are patriots? The qualifications for a patriot are respect for the Chinese nation, sincere support for the motherland's resumption of sovereignty over Hong Kong, and a desire not to impair Hong Kong's prosperity and stability. Those who meet these requirements are patriots, whether they believe in capitalism or feudalism or even slavery.

Hong Kong now began to play an important role in a new theory of economic development by regional stages. Ever since the First Five Year Plan (1953–7) Chinese planners had viewed their country in terms of three separate regions, divided roughly into north–south segments from the 'western' through the 'central' to the 'eastern' or 'coastal' section. For most of the time the view prevailed that the more advanced eastern region should lead the way, although efforts were made to shift the balance towards the interior, particularly during the Great Leap and in the early 1970s. The Open Door policy strengthened the argument for sequential development from East to West. Not only was Hong Kong to be increasingly associated with the coastal region, but other sub-regional units emerged which would take the lead. The Open Door policy, said Zhao Ziyang in his 1987 Party Report, should be extended 'progressively from the special economic zones and coastal cities, then to coastal economic regions, and finally to interior areas'.

In the Seventh Five Year Plan (1986–90), the east was expected to focus on modernizing old industry and the development of high technology and 'quality consumer goods'. Its four Special Economic Zones and fourteen Open Port Cities would become

China's main base for foreign trade. The central region would serve as China's energy reservoir, stepping up development of electricity, oil, and coal and the production of minerals and building materials. The west would devote its main energy to expanding agriculture, forestry, animal husbandry, and transport. Exposure to foreign economic activity was strictly graded. Conditions in most of the western region, explained the economist Xue Muqiao, 'have not yet matured for the import of foreign funds'.

The Special Economic Zones were originally assigned a special role as 'windows on the world'. The economist Ji Chongwei said that to some extent they would act as 'filters between China's socialist system and the capitalist world, allowing market mechanisms and the law of value to operate under the guidance of socialist planned economy, and taking in positive things and sifting out negative aspects of Western culture'. According to the Deng Xiaoping doctrine of 'One Country Two Systems', the SEZs would thus serve as a controlled conduit between the capitalist economy of Hong Kong (including Macao and eventually, it was hoped, Taiwan) and the socialist economy of the rest of China. Deng insisted that while capitalism in Hong Kong would be guaranteed until the middle of the next century, the same must be true for socialism on the mainland. But by the late 1980s, the pressure for economic change had diffused more widely in the eastern region, leading potentially to a much larger 'window' on the world. In the north, Tianjin emerged to dominate what became known as the 'golden necklace' of fifteen cities and prefectures around the Bohai Basin of North China. Three 'golden triangles' of development were identified, in the Yangtze river delta centred on Shanghai, southern Fujian centred on the Xiamen SEZ, and the Pearl River delta centred on Guangzhou. Neat dividing lines were discarded as the new leaders spoke of development spreading from the coastal areas to the interior 'in a gradual wave-after-wave manner' (Gu Mu). The goal, said Zhao Ziyang, was 'to change from closing various parts of the country from the world to opening them'. A new bout of sub-regional door-opening began immediately after the Thirteenth Party Congress had reaffirmed the reform policy, in an unashamedly competitive mood. The island of Hainan was told to prepare for provincial and special zone status, and its Party secretary Xu Shijie boasted that he had been given the green light by Zhao Ziyang:

Hainan is to implement 'a policy which is more "special" than the present special zones' . . . He [Zhao] also said that Hainan would be given more independent powers and more preferential treatment, greater examining and approving powers, a more extended and less restricted scale of basic construction than in other regions, freer entry and exit policies for foreigners, and a more relaxed foreign exchange administration . . . Ah [exclaimed Xu], with such effective measures Hainan definitely will become the country's biggest special zone!

As a gesture of encouragement for the new coastal entrepreneurs, the man held most responsible for the great Hainan scandal in 1985 was now rehabilitated. Under Party Secretary Lei Yu, the island had imported 79,000 foreign cars and trucks in the space of one year for illegal resale at inflated prices to other provinces and cities in the interior. (Other profitable imports were 347,000 TV sets, and 45,000 motorcycles.) The resale racket brought in vast sums of foreign currency from the purchasers, and allowed pay-offs to local officials of up to one million Yuan (£200,000). In January 1988 Lei Yu was appointed a vice-mayor of Guangzhou, with the citation that he was 'receptive to new things . . . familiar with economic affairs . . . and enjoys considerable prestige among cadres and people'.

Party leaders in Guangdong (who until now had been responsible for Hainan) had their own reasons for optimism, with the expansion of the Guangdong Open Zone to include the Pearl River 'golden triangle'. The party secretary Lin Ruo confessed that the anti-bourgeois liberalization campaign earlier in 1987 had caused alarm: 'Should there be a mere rustle of leaves in the wind, it would make people abroad uneasy.' Now that the Party was committed to speeding up reform and the Open Door, Guangdong was in a position to benefit more than most. Lin forecast that the province would show a 'two-digit' rate of increase in economic output, and that by the end of the century, it should attain the current level of Asia's 'four little dragons' (Hong Kong, Taiwan, Singapore, and South Korea). A former Party secretary, Xi Zhongxun (an old friend of Deng Xiaoping), sitting at Lin's side chipped in: 'We should be a little faster!' The example of Asia's 'economic miracles' had been much discussed in the early 1980s, when it was concluded that their circumstances and experiences were very different from those of China and should not be taken as a model. Yet by the late 1980s the coastal districts of the eastern region were increasingly tempted by their success, and could argue that while China as a whole could not be compared with these relatively small, self-contained, and export-oriented states, their zones had more in common. They too offered a labour surplus capable of learning new technologies for low wages, good communications with South-East Asia, and a positive investment environment under a centralized system of government which minimized the chances of labour unrest. If Hong Kong capitalism had feared that it would be subverted by mainland socialism, it now appeared more likely that Chinese socialism would be subverted in the spearhead sectors of the eastern region.

Across the border from Hong Kong, in the Pearl River delta, more than a million out of a total population of 23 million were already servicing Hong Kong industry by 1988. Lorries with dual Chinese and Hong Kong number plates headed north and south between Shenzhen and Guangzhou (a super-highway was also under construction) carrying in cloth, leather, plastics, and electrical parts, and taking out garments, shoes, toys, and assembled electrical goods and electronics. Deep in the country-side factories sprang up employing local peasant labour at a quarter of the rate paid in Hong Kong and half of that in the Shenzhen Special Economic Zone. Migrants from the interior sat in village squares, hoping to pick up casual work for even lower wages. In the town of Dongguan, a centre of this new industry, 1,800 new cable circuits were installed in 1987 to provide direct telephone links with Hong Kong. (Guangzhou City was spending five times as much as Shanghai on telecommunications.) Hong Kong's own economy was increasingly dominated by mainland investment—at least 30 per cent according to most estimates—and the territory also provided a free management school with several thousand mainland visitors at any one time learning new skills.

Towards an open society?

'The present world is an open one', Deng told a group of Japanese businessmen in June 1984. 'China's past backwardness was due to its closed-door policy ... the experience of the past thirty years or more proves that a closed-door policy would hinder construction and inhibit development.' China was still self-reliant in the sense that a country of such a large size must provide most of its own inputs for development, but Deng looked forward to increased economic interaction with the outside world, with a considerable increase in foreign trade over the next fifty or seventy years. 'If anything, we will only open up still more. Our people would not allow anything else.'

Neo-Marxist scholars attempted to translate this limited and expedient view of the Open Door policy into an operating principle which would open the ideological as well as the economic doors. There was a dangerous flaw in Deng's argument: The Open Door was bound to increase China's prosperity, he said, and therefore the Chinese people would insist that it remained open. But what if the policy produced a negative result in these narrow economic terms when, for example, China found itself adversely affected by foreign competition or a reverse in the international terms of trade? Would not some people insist that the door be shut again?

The Open Door had to be linked to socialism by much more than its presumed economic benefits. An important essay by Li Honglin, published in the *People's Daily* (15 Oct. 1984) with the provocative subtitle 'Socialism should be an open society', tackled this question squarely. Li argued that there was a basic trend not just in economic life but in all social existence to develop 'from ignorance to the nation, and from the nation to the world'. Feudalism relied on and sought to perpetuate a self-contained economy; capitalism broke down the national barriers. It would be nonsensical to suggest that socialism, a more advanced system than capitalism, should seek to restore those barriers. Socialism should start from the high level already reached by capitalism, and not feel obliged to begin all over again.

Facts have proved that in the past we did not have a clear idea of what Marxism and socialism were ... Opening to the outside world gives us an opportunity to know about new situations, new problems, new materials, and new ideas in the world. This will inevitably speed up the course of 'purification' and development. Is this not a more favourable condition for upholding the Marxist scientific truth? ...

Communist society will not flourish in a courtyard behind locked doors. Opening the country to the outside world is not an expedient measure but a fundamental principle for building a socialist society, as well as the only road to a communist society. Let us spare no effort in discarding all outmoded viewpoints which have suppressed us for many years, free ourselves from the parochial concept of small-scale production, and open the doors and windows wide to the world!

CHAPTER TWELVE

China's New Face

THE END OF IDEOLOGY

More Shanghai citizens wed foreigners. In 1986 there were 794 mixed marriages in Shanghai. Most were to Hong Kong or Macao citizens, but eighty-nine were to real foreigners. Some had met through introduction by friends or relatives, others at dancing parties.

Tianjin mayor on housing reform. Tianjin had begun selling apartments, at an average price of 300 yuan (US $81) per square metre. Mayor Li Ruihuan said that 'those who are rich can pay for their flats once and for all', but others could pay in instalments. Residents would be allowed to sell the part of flats they own later in order to purchase larger apartments.

Tiananmen rostrum opens to public. An American tourist was the first foreigner to visit the rostrum where Chairman Mao proclaimed that China had 'stood up' in 1949. Mr Richard Carter paid 30 yuan (US $8) for his ticket, but received a *cloisonné* plaque with dragons painted on it from a vice-mayor of Beijing. Nineteen hundred and eighty-eight was declared China's International Year of the Dragon for foreign tourism.

The first pawnshop starts business. A pawnshop has opened in Chengdu, dealing in household electric appliances, antiques, motorbikes and cycles, watches, etc. The proprietor explained that 'unlike the pawnshops of old' it did not practice usury. Instead it aims to help people or businesses 'who are badly in need of funds but fail to get loans'.

Babies short of iron, survey says. The *Health News* reported deficiency of iron intake among babies under 1 year old ranging from 59 per cent of those surveyed in Yunnan to 40 per cent in Zhejiang. Frank discussion of chronic medical or social problems would have been impossible in the years when socialism was supposed to have transformed everyone's lives.

China decides to abandon 'mu' for measuring land space. The Chinese 'acre'—the *mu*, which is equivalent to two-thirds of a hectare—will be discarded because it is not an international unit of measurement. Besides, its real size may vary by 100 per cent according to local customs.

(Selection of stories from the Xinhua News Agency, 1 Jan. 1988.)

The pace of change

By the late 1980s China was changing visibly, not only year by year but from one season to the next. Villages became towns, towns became cities (thirty new ones in 1987 alone). Tracks became roads, and roads became highways (100,000 new kilometres of new roads in less than a decade). Trucks began to outnumber the horse and cart; young men no longer saved up for the bicycle but for the motorbike. New fashions in clothing and hairstyles rippled outwards from Hong Kong through the south up to Beijing. It was getting harder to tell the difference between the sharply dressed young mainland Chinese and his or her overseas Chinese cousin. By the mid-1980s the boast was that 'There are no patched trousers in Beijing.' The old saying that trousers should be 'worn for three years as new, for three more as old, and then another three as patched-up' was out of date. New telephone exchanges were imported, and Beijing had its first public phone boxes instead of the 'neighbourhood phone' where everyone listened in. More people began to take holidays, finding 'business' reasons to extend the official three days off for the Chinese New Year. Television advertisements were no longer simple written messages and people stopped complaining about them. There were fewer children—5 per cent less of the total population in 1988 than in 1982—and more old people. The number with high school education or above grew by 1 per cent a year. Young people were growing taller, having increased in height by an average of 2 centimetres every ten years. More meat was being consumed—an average of 13 kilos per capita annually in 1983 compared with 8 kilos in 1978. Foreign tourists continued to circulate more widely. Nearly 27 million visited in 1987, over 17 per cent more than the previous year, and could travel without special permission to more than 470 cities, towns, and counties. Venereal disease, believed to have been eradicated in China, began to reappear, especially in Guangdong province adjacent to Hong Kong.

In a political atmosphere where it was right to spend but no longer to make revolution, the official desire for a healthy market economy also meant official approval for a surge in consumerist values. China's need to participate more fully in the world market allowed the door to open ever wider to foreign examples of material progress and consumption. Newspaper kiosks stopped stocking the Communist Party's theoretical journals, selling instead a growing range of magazines with titles (often in English as well as Chinese) such as *Healthy Life* and *Young People*. The December 1986 issue of *Sino-Foreign Consumer* carried a photo supplement on a new shopping arcade in Istanbul, a selection of 'international hairstyles', a profile of an American–Chinese TV presenter (her motto was 'Beauty, Brains, and Breeding'), and a variety of consumer hints. These included articles on what the Queen of England eats, what Prince Charles wears, and whether black is a fashionable colour. An article in the bi-monthly *Knowledge and Living* wrote of the 'white revolution' which had just started to reach China. More than sixty domestic electrical appliances were now produced at home, it said, even though China had a long way to go to catch up with Japan and the US.

Popular culture as reflected in these magazines was almost entirely secular, with little or no expression of political values. Film magazines and romantic fiction were widely sold. The lead short story in the January 1987 issue of *Flower Garden* told the tale of a Chinese soldier on the Vietnam frontier who captures an enemy scout and discovers that she is a young girl. Compassionately, he sets her on her road across the border, but she refuses to leave. 'Please, let me stay with you', she murmurs, 'My heart melted', says the narrator. 'What should I answer in return? Anything would be too much! I quickly gave her my arm . . . Resolutely we turned and headed for the dark woods . . .' Police and detective novels also sold well. They contained factual information on legal problems as well as 'real life' stories of crime and disaster from home and abroad, and a new genre of shocking tales about the behaviour of the Gang of Four. Other popular themes in street-corner kiosk displays included motorcycling, foreign films and theatre, sports (with double-page spreads on scantily clad female body builders), and popular medicine. The medical advice covered general hygiene and diet as well as illnesses and, increasingly, sexual techniques.

The baby booms of the mid-1950s and 1960s put increasing pressure on China's stock of urban housing, most of which had not received even a lick of new paint during the Cultural Revolution. Many existing units had been subdivided until no more families could be squeezed in, with the exception of a small number of courtyards and villas, often confiscated from the 'class enemies', which were reserved for high-level use. Faceless high-rise blocks began to encircle Beijing in the mid-1970s and multiplied in the 1980s to most other urban centres. The goal was to achieve an average space of 8 square metres per person by the year 2000. In Beijing this figure had not risen much above 6 square metres for the past thirty years. In 1981–6 China built 800 million square metres of urban housing, but this still could not match demand. Many municipal tenants complained of poor fittings and services or of preferential treatment in the allocation of apartments. The rural areas suffered from a different problem—extravagant use of capital and land to build new housing of brick or stone, often replacing quite adequate thatched adobe dwellings which could have been more easily modernized. In the same five years 4 billion square metres of living space were built in the countryside. City dwellers said enviously that the peasants now lived in greater comfort than they did.

Family planning, neglected in the 1960s when population was believed to present no problem for socialism, had been official policy since the early 1970s and was effective in reducing the rate of population increase. Beijing's original population more than doubled from 4.1 million in 1949 to 8.3 million in 1986 plus a further 1.3 million as the result of migration into the city. Family planning meant that the increase from 1970 was 'restrained' to 1.8 million instead of a theoretically probable increase of over 4 million! In the countryside attempts to enforce the one-child-family had sometimes involved measures of coercion—compulsory abortion and punishment—which attracted international criticism. The target for the whole nation was 1,200 million by the year 2000. However, the economic reforms and greater social mobility now weakened the effectiveness of official deterrents. Peasant families were prepared to pay large fines in order to

increase their 'labour power' for the future. The transient portion
of the urban population in the big cities where resident controls
were no longer strictly enforced also had a higher-than-average
birth rate. Premarital sex and early marriage further undermined
the birth-control campaign. The forecast for the year 2000 was
revised upwards in 1988 by an extra 84 million.

Life and love

After years of sexual repression, young Chinese were now
increasingly able to express open interest in questions of love and
marriage. New, more 'modern' attitudes were mixed uneasily
with the revival of older more 'feudal' traditions, in particular
those which treated marriage as an economic institution. In 1988
it was calculated that rural weddings absorbed up to six times
the average annual wage; urban weddings up to ten times. With
the effective privatization of agriculture, marriage renewed its
significance as a formula for creating new units of land and
labour-power, with complex bargaining between the two families on the assets—land, tools, housing, and so on—to be
contributed. Lavish wedding feasts could consume several years
of family income, but served as investments to win favours from
local government and commercial officials. In the towns, the
dowry was likely to consist of expensive consumer durables. The
typical couple expected to be set up with four electrical necessities: a refrigerator, a cassette player and recorder, a washing
machine, and a colour TV. Attitudes towards divorce were also
changing. A 1987 survey showed that 45 per cent favoured
divorce if both sides wished to terminate relations, although
30 per cent remained opposed under any circumstances. The
1980 marriage law provided for divorce if one party alone
insisted, though strong social pressures remained in favour of
'mediation'. Unmarried relationships, extra-marital relations,
and remarriage were often the subject of newspaper articles
and debates, and the role of the 'Third Person' in the break-
up of marriage was vigorously discussed. Official reminders
that, in the words of Zhou Enlai's widow Deng Yingchao
(republished in 1981), 'young men and women should
subordinate their own marriage and lifestyle to political

demands and what benefits the revolution', were increasingly ignored.

Many young Chinese in the 1980s could enjoy pleasures unknown except to a few in the past. They were reasonably well informed through TV, films, and magazines about the outside world. They could dress smartly in copies of Hong Kong fashion, and have their hair cut stylishly without fear of criticism (except briefly during the 1983 campaign against 'spiritual pollution'). Political demands on their time were reduced and there was less scrutiny of their personal behaviour. Yet there were new uncertainties, deriving in large part from the absence of the old political and ethical imperatives. In May 1980 *China Youth* magazine had launched a debate about the meaning of life by publishing a despairing cry from a 23-year-old woman. No one could tell her what life meant, and she could no longer believe that the purpose was 'to live for the revolution'—she had had enough of 'that sort of preaching'.

There isn't a single person who will really act sincerely according to the lofty morals and beliefs he normally mouths. Everyone acts for himself. There is no such thing as a selfless person. . . . Let me ask those great sages, distinguished scholars, honoured teachers, and respected makers of propaganda, if they look at themselves honestly just how many will escape the general rule of struggling for one's own advantage? I used to fervently believe that 'we live to make life better for others', and that 'we do not grudge our own lives for the sake of others'. Now it makes me laugh to think of it!

The mid-1980s created opportunities for some young intellectuals and cadres to commit their energies to the new ideal of 'reform' and make money quite respectably out of it. Some who would have been pace-setters in the Young Communist League or faction leaders in the Red Guards might instead now take over and modernize a collectively owned business, or travel the country trading independently, or perhaps set up office in Shenzhen or Hainan to enter the import–export trade. Yet *China Youth* in January 1987 published a similar lament of 'listlessness' and a sense of futility among young people who found their commitment to reform blocked by older cadres. In February another debate was inspired by the news that when the new Hilton Hotel in Shanghai advertised for junior staff, hundreds of college students and graduates rushed to apply. 'Our country has spent so much on their education', complained a senior cadre, 'and now they are willing to go and be servants for capitalists just to make a bit more money.' A student replied that though the money was important, the real reason was that he preferred to work at a faster rhythm and learn some managerial skills, instead of idling away his time in a Chinese office.

The growing diversity of Chinese life affected the position of women in a number of contradictory ways. Urban society saw the emergence of what has been called by Elisabeth Croll, author of *Chinese Women since Mao*, 'the permed-hair city miss', aware of fashion and her body in a way which had been repressed since 1949 (except in a closed world which served the sexual tastes of high cadres). A very small number of women in the intellectuals' and cadres' strata now had opportunities to travel, meet foreigners, engage in business, and import cosmopolitan values. In literature, a new generation of 'strong women' (*nu qiangzhe*), writers such as Zhang Jie and Zhang Xinxin, showed a robustness (also reflected in their personal lives) which rejected the more usual literary avoidance of conflict and stress. For those with the strength of mind and economic opportunity, traditional social pressures to conform (to remain chaste while single, to marry early, to have children) could now more easily be resisted. The demand for gender equality became more explicit, and was even expressed in popular magazines which criticized women's dependence upon men.

Old ideas such as 'Woman is made from one of man's ribs', and 'If a woman does not have a husband her body does not have an owner', etc., still influence some people. . . . History and present circumstances oppress and constrain many women comrades. This makes it impossible for us to display our talents, intelligence, and creativity. We just become men's servants or their burden. Woman is not the moon. She must rely on herself to shine. These are words that many pioneers of the women's liberation movement, masculine women, and heroines have inscribed with their own actions, tears, and blood. Let us treasure these words, remember them, and implement them. Hopefully each person can find her own path in life and develop her own brilliance.

Post-Mao change, while creating a freer atmosphere for urban women, has restored some aspects of traditional agricultural production to the disadvantage of rural women. During the

Cultural Revolution, the slogan that 'women hold up half the sky' by no means reflected the reality of unequal opportunity, yet many young women did become more mobile, as Red Guards, educated youth sent to the countryside, barefoot doctors, or rural technicians, while 'feudal' traditions affecting courtship and marriage were sharply discouraged. Women's liberation remained more pronounced in the workplace than at home, but official praise for such models as the 'Iron Girls' of Dazhai brigade did encourage a sense that women's roles were not biologically determined. Women who mended high-power lines, drilled for oil, and even (in one of the films by the Belgian film-maker Joris Ivens) crewed fishing trawlers were celebrated in reportage and on propaganda posters. (However, this model, like most other aspects of officially sponsored equality of the sexes, always implied that women could do men's work rather than the reverse.) But in the 1980s, the return to the individual peasant household led to a restoration of old divisions of labour based upon gender. The situation has been summarized by Phyllis Andors, author of *The Unfinished Liberation of Chinese Women*:

The widespread decollectivization of agriculture that occurred between 1981 and 1984 has drastically altered female access to the means of production. The return to the household as the basic unit of production reinforces the traditional, patriarchal family as the institution that controls its members' labour. For women, that means a tightening of control by the family over their production and reproduction. Stories in both the national and regional press describe a decline in the numbers of young girls in rural schools. As the state pushes the one-child-per-family policy female infanticide has reappeared, since peasants want a male child and male labour within the family. Social welfare services have been privatized and access to public medical care reduced. In many areas, agriculture based on family labour has been feminized, especially near the Special Economic Zones and in regions that have opened to foreign investment. Men in these areas leave farming for more profitable construction and industrial jobs created by domestic and foreign investment in these areas.

By the late 1980s there was growing concern about the abduction or sale of young rural women both by professional gangs and families for forced marriage or prostitution. *Women of China* reported (Apr. 1987) that the traditional ceremony of

'Virtuous Wives Day' had been revived, when 'the whole village turns out at the threshing ground, beating drums and gongs, to watch the village leaders pin red flowers on the jackets of virtuous wives and present them with certificates of merit'. Their virtue would have been displayed in helping their husband to make a fortune, or caring for him if he was mentally ill, or 'concentrat[ing] all their affection on their children when they were widowed . . .'. Nearly sixty years before, the young Mao Zedong had published an appeal for the liberation of society including a passage written on behalf of oppressed women which denounced male double standards with this sarcastic remark: 'The "temples to virtuous women" are scattered all over the place, but where are the "pagodas to chaste men?"'

China and the world

A growing number of the educated élite were now able to travel abroad, but it was only a fraction of those who longed to do so. Foreign visitors who asked young Chinese what was their aim in life were likely to receive the answer 'to visit your country'. (Ten years previously it had been 'to serve the people'.) Between 1978 and 1987 about 40,000 Chinese had gone abroad to study at the government's expense. Another 10,000 were allowed to do so on private funds. No more than half had returned. Many decided to 'extend their stay abroad', often a euphemism for a decision never to return, particularly in North America where support for those who stayed behind was readily available in the local Chinese community. Some of these expatriates published a magazine, *China Spring*, which took up the dissident cause, still kept alive abroad while its leaders from the late 1970s were neutralized or imprisoned at home. (Hu Ping, one of the 1980 candidates in the Beijing University election, was an editor of the magazine.) In June 1987 the Ministry of Education announced new regulations for the screening of applicants to go abroad, and promised that they would be given suitable jobs on their return. A government official explained at the start of 1988 that the focus of his work, hitherto to send people abroad, would now be on 'welcoming them to return'. Thousands of other officials and intellectuals took shorter trips. Foreign institutions and businesses quickly learnt that the best way to cement a relationship with a Chinese partner was to offer such trips for the purpose of a 'seminar' or 'training'.

Chinese academic institutions now had access to the international market-place, securing grants and invitations in exchange for providing western scholars with access for research purposes to China. This process had begun modestly in the late 1970s when some Chinese universities exchanged language students with the West, but developed into a high-level traffic. New institutes were set up in China, often competing for foreign custom. These included the China International Culture Exchange Centre in Beijing, whose brochure promised 'a modern, multifunctional, comprehensive building', complete with a bowling alley and beauty parlour as well as halls and seminar rooms, offering itself for international conferences and performances. Chinese scholars were also able to seek foreign aid in order to develop or reopen areas which had been previously blank. In 1984 the North-East Normal University at Changchun set up the Institute for the History of Ancient Civilizations, offering tuition in Greek and Latin, hieroglyphic Egyptian, Sumerian, Akkadian, and Hittite. It was supported by leading Chinese historians who rejected a long tradition of sinocentric scholarship, arguing instead that the study of other ancient civilizations would be an 'inspiration' to the study of Chinese history. Though initially funded by the state, the Institute's future depended on foreign backing.

Attitudes towards the outside world were still complicated, oscillating unpredictably between admiration and patriotic contempt. The mix was as unassimilated as in the television news programmes. Foreign news arrived on the same day by satellite from western networks, offering a hotchpotch of significant political events, international sports, fashion shows, or humorous items about animals. Domestic news, contained in the same programme, was frequently still several days out of date and often ignored the main political story of the day, showing instead stereotyped economic success stories and pictures of people with bored faces at meetings. Sports events in which China was competing could easily erupt into chauvinistic demonstrations—the old slogan of 'Friendship First, Competition Second' had long been forgotten. In November 1981 the Chinese women's volleyball team won the world tournament in Tokyo, causing an explosion of pride and nation-wide pledges to learn from their 'fighting style'. Of course China had frequently swept international competitions in table tennis, but this was the first ever Chinese victory—people explained—with a 'big ball'. In 1985 foreigners were assaulted outside the Beijing Workers' Stadium after China had lost at football. These outbursts were censured, but conservative Party leaders are believed to have quietly encouraged Beijing University students in their first demonstrations in September 1985 denouncing 'Japanese militarism' and calling for a boycott of Japanese goods. The 1987 campaign against 'bourgeois liberalism' displayed a strong streak of old-fashioned chauvinism. It only took China a little more than three decades after 1949 to increase its steel production to fifty million tons, argued one polemical attack on those who allegedly wished to save China by 'Westernization'. It had taken the United States more than 150 years to reach the same level of output. Was that not evidence of the superiority of socialism, which would enable China to catch up with the capitalist world? Such attitudes had a familiar ring from the past, as one young Chinese teacher argued privately:

The present leadership is showing the same kind of psychology that has been demonstrated by the Chinese ruling class for over a hundred years. They regard Western capitalism as an attractive lady whom they want to kiss. So they say 'bastard' immediately after they have kissed the foreign devil, to prove that they are Chinese and that the westerners should not be taken into consideration. . . . The students write slogans and organize demonstrations, shouting 'revive China' and 'long live China'. It is apparently thought that patriotism is the only medicine which the people will not refuse to drink.

New art, new attitudes

In film, prose, and poetry, dozens—if not yet a hundred—of new flowers began to bloom. In the first post-Mao decade there was a general artistic progression away from the overtly political towards less easily labelled social and, later, entirely personal themes. At first those writers who had been branded as 'rightist' and had suffered for several decades emerged with a determination to set the record straight and revive standards of political morality. The writer Wang Meng described his main theme as 'a land stretching eight thousand *li*; thirty stormy years', referring to the distance from Beijing which he travelled to do physical labour in Xinjiang, and the great changes over time. Lu Wenfu, another casualty of 1957, spoke of his 'historic responsibility' to his friends who had lost their lives or talents in those 'painful years'. Younger writers sought to expunge the pain of the Cultural Revolution through what was called 'the literature of the wounded', encouraged nervously by the authorities who before long claimed that the scars had been healed and writers should now sing of new achievements. Although the social setting of many successful stories of the 1980s still centred on the workplace, new writers emerged who shifted the focus to the individual and his or her feelings. In a metaphor for her creative writing, Zhang Jie wrote that 'like a boat drifting about on the waves, I have cast aside my self-control and let myself be buoyed along in a state of happy abandon. I have taken the sea to my bosom, let the waves lap at my feeble heart.' Dai Houying's *Stones of the Wall* describes a group of university teachers trying to rebuild their personal lives after the Cultural Revolution. Part two is subtitled 'Each heart is looking for a home. Each one is different.' By the late 1980s, a new generation of writers no longer sought to relate the individual to society but simply to portray the individual in his or her existentialist being.

Film-making, an art which provides possibilities both for mass commercialism and for the utterance of powerful statements, demonstrated most clearly the diverse forms of expression now sanctioned by the post-Mao reforms. On the one hand, the great majority of the approximately 130 films produced annually catered for mass tastes, offering Kung-Fu pictures, melodramas, urban comedies, and war films (especially on tales of heroism at the Vietnam front). On the other, the so-called 'fifth generation' of young film-makers produced films which won foreign awards while provoking internal controversy. Working in provincial studios (where funds could more easily be allocated to young directors and the Party's hand was less heavy), Chen Kaige (*Yellow Earth* and *The Big Parade*), Huang Jianxin (*The Black Cannon Incident*), Zhang Zimou (*The Old Well* and *Red Sorghum*), Zhang Junzhao (*One and Eight*), and Wu Ziniu (*The Last Day of Winter*), made their names in the mid-1980s. All of these films in different ways could be seen as allegories dealing with alienation and authority in contemporary China, the very same themes with which the reformist scholars were grappling. Controversy was first stirred up by *Yellow Earth*, a film which showed the relationship between a young Red Army cadre and a backward peasant community in 1939. Chen Kaige was accused of distorting the Communist spirit (the cadre fails to save a young girl from forced marriage) and of using art to portray 'the backward and ignorant aspect of the Chinese peasantry' (the film ends with a superstitious rain ceremony). 'The peasant who sings the folk songs in the film is very ugly', complained one cultural bureaucrat; '. . . we must not encourage naturalism, nor let our film-makers waste their energies by indulging in voyeurism and the depiction of the remnants of the primitive past . . .' Others, including the veteran film-maker Xia Yan, argued that films should be made for mass audiences, otherwise 'there will be an unconscious drift towards "art for art's sake"'. Speaking an entirely different language, Chen's cinematographer Zhang Zimou explained:

We wanted to express a number of things in *Yellow Earth*: the boundless magnificence of the heavens; the supporting vastness of the earth. The racing flow of the Yellow River; the sustaining strength and endurance of a nation. The cry of a people from the depths of primitive obscurity, and their strength; the resonant paean that issues forth from the impoverished yellow land. The fate of a people, their feelings, loves and hates, strengths and weaknesses.

And Chen added:

In a more sombre mood, if we meditate on the fact that this river gives life to all things, but by the same token can destroy all things, then we realize that the fate of Cuiqiao [the young bride who drowns in the river while trying to escape to join the Red Army], who lived among the people of old China, had an inevitably tragic cast. The road she chooses is a very hard one. Hard, because she is not simply confronted by the malign forces of society in any narrow sense, but rather by the tranquil, even well-meaning, ignorance of the people who raised her . . .

The leadership continued to be upset by challenging artistic statements. In November 1988 Xia Yan told a congress of writers and artists that they should be aware of their 'solemn historical responsibilities'. In a message to the congress, the Party urged them not only to 'ponder over the past', but to 'praise heroic deeds' and 'look towards the future'.

Chinese art also moved in the post-Mao decade from a conscious but still collective reaction to the recent past to a broader, more personal search for diverse forms of expression. At first many older painters had returned to painting what they did best—landscapes, chrysanthemums, pines and bamboos, donkeys and small children. The ubiquitous propaganda posters (*xuanchuanhua*) simply shifted theme. The atomic symbol replaced the Red Lantern; revolutionary youth no longer marched into the countryside. Instead they contemplated a sky filled with logarithmic signs under the Leninist slogan: 'Study, Study, Yet More Study.' Peasant painters stopped portraying collective endeavours—the digging of a new well or enthusiastic attendance at a rural night school. Instead they showed the benefits of modernization reaching their nearest county town—hairdressers, furniture shops, and new houses— and hoped that their paintings might be sold to foreign tourists.

During the 1979 Democracy Movement a group of young and mostly non-professional artists named themselves the Single Spark (which, Mao once said, can Start a Prairie Fire). Their first show was broken up by the police, but in 1980 they were allowed to exhibit in the Beijing Art Gallery. Much of the new art was derivative. Picasso, Munch, Léger, and Klee, to which these young artists had only recently been exposed, were clearly visible. But there were powerful woodcuts and other graphics which stemmed directly from the political art tradition of the 1930s. In 'Breath', a woodcut by Ma Desheng, a Chinese peasant is shown driving his wooden plough across the chest of a sleeping man. Ma explained his intention:

Whenever I go to the countryside, I see how the peasant pursues his heavy and primitive work, so far behind the city in his material and cultural life, yet carrying on silently without a word of complaint. Yet it is quite the reverse back in the city, where some cadres talk about the poverty of our country and how we must tighten our belts, but build great mansions for themselves while other people have no houses.

The very first abstracts made a daring public appearance. The young sculptor Wang Keping posted a set of gently mocking questions and answers at the entrance to the exhibition:

Q. What is this sculpture about? I can't tell what it's meant to be.
A. It is itself. It doesn't have to be like something else in order to be worthwhile.

Q. I can't understand this picture. All I can see are some colours
leaping about.
A. You have understood it correctly.

By the mid-1980s the propaganda poster had almost disappeared (except for appeals for traffic safety and planned parent-
hood), to be replaced on the hoardings by advertisements, which
often showed young ladies of vaguely Eurasian appearance
fondling pots of face cream or brandishing badminton rackets, or
the kindly faces of traditional Chinese doctors with wispy
beards. The Single Spark group had dissolved, as many of its
members won foreign backing or scholarships abroad. Young
painters in Beijing now staged 'salons'—showings by invitation
to Chinese intellectuals and foreign friends who might publicize
or purchase their works. Having rediscovered modern western art
from the Expressionists onwards, many young artists returned to
earlier native traditions, borrowing primitive motifs and themes
from minority folk art. They included Chen Dehong, who based
his art on Chinese characters, making the most of their own
pictographic origins, and Yuan Yunsheng, who developed the
impressionist potential of Chinese ink on rice paper. In 1987 the
Shanghai Art Exhibition gave awards for the first time to nude
and abstract paintings. None of the works on show conveyed
overt political or moral messages, not so much because it would
be frowned upon but because most artists no longer wished to
make explicit statements through their art.

The end of ideology?

By the late 1980s '-isms' had been almost entirely replaced by
'-izes' for the visitor to China. In the 1960s and 1970s one
heard about socialism, capitalism, revisionism, and imperialism,
and more exotic ones such as idealistic apriorism (the charge
against Chen Boda in 1971). The emphasis has now shifted to
concrete activity—modernize, decentralize, and enterprise—
stressing the organizational and entrepreneurial talent which is
now so highly regarded. So does ideology still matter? It is less
talked about (particularly with foreign visitors of a new generation, who ask fewer questions about it anyhow). Its role as
arbiter of policy has sharply diminished as politics itself is
replaced by economics in command, and it provides ever more

hesitant answers about the nature of change in Chinese society. Yet it continues to play an important symbolic role in political culture, and to legitimize changes in policy.

'Who says that a chicken feather can't fly up to heaven?' asked Mao in 1955, deriding those who lacked faith in the ability of the Chinese people to transcend objective difficulties and build a brave new socialist world. Today's leaders no longer believe it can be done, and regret that it has taken so long, in the words of the *People's Daily*, to 'come down from heaven to earth'. Whether or not what Mao had in mind was right for China, it served for many years as a mobilizing concept. This has now been dismantled, and the question for all those concerned with China's future is 'What has been put in its place?' After the 1987 Party Congress, a great shift took place in what was said about socialism, capitalism, and China's role in the world market. By contrast with the past, the statement was clearest about the world market, relatively clear about capitalism, and most ambiguous about socialism.

What is socialism? The official answer today—'socialism with Chinese characteristics'—has very little to do with the old idea of socialism which lasted for three decades (1949–78). This was based upon two assumptions: first, that China was embarked upon a transition which, sooner rather than later, would lead to communism; and second, that one could fairly clearly define the criteria by which progress would be measured—that is, expanding state ownership, reducing differences between town and country, relying more on moral and less upon material incentives. This was to go along with (and was not regarded as in any way incompatible with) the steady increase in the country's productive capacity and modernization and a steady improvement in standards of living. How does China now regard the transition? In theory it still exists, but no longer as a real measure of progress. In its place there is the 'initial stage of socialism', which will last well beyond the lifetime of most people. In the famous formula of Zhao Ziyang's report to the 1987 Congress:

What, then, is this historic stage, the primary stage of socialism in China? It is not the initial phase in a general sense, a phase that every country goes through in the process of building socialism. Rather it is, in a particular sense, the specific stage China must necessarily go through while building socialism under conditions of backward productive forces and an underdeveloped commodity economy. It will be at least 100 years from the 1950s, when the socialist transformation of private ownership was basically completed, to the time when socialist modernization will have been in the main accomplished, and all these years belong to the primary stage of socialism.

There is little interest in what will come after, and why should there be? The sequel is briefly though tautologically described as 'the stage in which socialist modernization will have been achieved', without any further definition. The criterion for progress in socialism (even the word 'transition' is rarely used), then, is modernization. Although this does include cultural and political as well as economic modernization, everything said in the late 1980s indicates that the economic yardstick is the most important. 'The fundamental task of a socialist society', said Zhao, 'is to expand the productive forces', and similarly economic development is described as 'the central task'.

How is that task to be achieved? The answer is, through 'reform'—a word which has now become the new mobilizing concept, no longer used with a qualifying adjective (economic reform, political reform) but by itself to denote the most dynamic element in human progress. 'Socialist society', said Zhao, 'is a society that advances through reform. . . . Reform is a process by which the socialist relations of production and the socialist superstructure improve themselves [not 'advance themselves'], and it is also a force that pushes all work forward.' The concept is also used to reassure western friends: 'Of one thing you may be sure', said a Chinese academic during the anti-bourgeois liberalism campaign in 1987, 'the reform will continue.' It is reasonable to assume from all this that reform has replaced 'class struggle' as the motive force for human progress, while economic modernization has replaced socialism. This is summed up in the phrase expounded by the *People's Daily* (19 Nov. 1987), that China should focus for the next hundred years upon 'One Centre and Two Points', that is, development of the productive forces as the central task, and the reform and opening up to the outside world as the two main points.

To what is said publicly one has to add what is said in private. Deng Xiaoping has declared that he does not know what socialism is, and indeed has openly urged Chinese Marxist scholars, still addressing them as 'theoretical workers', to start investigating the question. Young Chinese researchers usually show impatience with questions about socialism, which they regard as not their concern. Their task, explained a young economist from one of Zhao Ziyang's think-tanks, is to 'find out ways of promoting China's development. We leave it to the older generation to talk about socialism.' (A more cynical view, expressed after the 1987 Congress by a group of Chinese postgraduates studying abroad, is that 'socialism just means the leadership of the Chinese Communist Party'—the Four Principles of Deng Xiaoping.)

While socialism was being demobilized as an operational concept in China of the late 1980s, capitalism assumed a new vitality. It was now taken for granted that the 'economic ingredients of this historical period would be a mix of capitalist and socialist methods' (*Da Gong Bao*, 7 Jan. 1988), and that a measure of what Lenin called 'state capitalism' was entirely acceptable in China. (Although public ownership was supposed to remain in the dominant position, this seemed likely to become notional in many areas as management was separated from ownership and decision-making was privatized.) The precedent for such coexistence was already established in the formula 'one country, two systems', which guaranteed Hong Kong's capitalist system for the same period of time as the 'initial stage of socialism'. The two systems were also seen as coexisting internationally: the economist Xue Muqiao now called for a new understanding of the changes in capitalism brought about by the enormous progress world-wide of science and technology. 'The masses of workers under the capitalist system', wrote Xue, 'have been able to improve their lives to a fairly great extent.' The capitalist countries had changed not only internally but in their foreign policies. There was only one global market, in which China should participate, and socialism and capitalism should 'mutually rely and co-operate with each other'.

Participation in this market was the key to Zhao Ziyang's expanded definition of the 'Open Door'. The argument was that China had missed its first chance in the 1960s, when the four 'little dragons' of Asia began their economic take-off, but that a new opportunity now presented itself, although it needed to be seized before the arrival of the robot age reduced the competitive value of China's cheap labour market. Zhao's new concept of an 'outward oriented economy' meant promoting the policy of letting some people 'get rich first' to the status of China's principal development strategy. He forecast that before very long the coastal population of about 120 million people would be able to achieve the standard of living of Taiwan (*Economic Daily*, 14 Jan. and 12 Feb. 1988). The effect was to commit China for the first time to seeking an export-led economy, thus completing the shift from the 1970s policy of 'self-reliance'.

Whatever may be said about socialism or capitalism, does there still exist a social ethic which may ensure that Chinese development avoids the gross inequalities and the humiliating forms of dependence which characterize many other Third World economies? Certainly the visitor to China will still not find the extremes of wealth and privilege encountered, say, in Brazil, nor is there urban poverty anywhere in China comparable to that in, say, Bombay. Chinese society, some argue, does still place a high value on concepts of 'fairness', social responsibility, and justice. Chinese reformers claim to be pursuing an enlightened development strategy very different from that of the West, as in this idealized account by the economist Liu Guoguang:

While paying attention to economic growth, it also defers to the people's livelihood. While encouraging people to get rich through honest labour, it prevents the polarization of the rich and the poor. While opening the door to the outside world and actively making use of foreign funds, it ensures that the nation does not get bogged down in the quagmire of debts.

Further, there is more to the 'comparatively well-off' idea we have proposed than just to meet the basic needs of life. The idea also calls for reasonably full employment, stable prices and proper environmental protection. All are problems which many of the developing countries have not yet been able to tackle succesfully.

China's new development strategy is entirely different from the economic growth strategy as practised in the developed countries in that what we advocate is 'proper consumption', not the 'high consumption' of the West which is in essence a great waste. What we emphasize is man's value, a higher level of cultural civilization, and a greater sense of security (a much lower rate of crime).

Yet these concerns are not exclusively socialist—they are found in other societies with different systems—and they are also being eroded by more individualistic and acquisitive attitudes. This has led, for example, to declining attention to health, welfare, and education in parts of the countryside. It is also easy to point to areas of Chinese life in the late 1980s where the ideal is very far from the reality, starting with the crime figures. China had 120,000 serious criminal cases in 1987, a 25 per cent increase over the previous year. The increase in corruption is a matter of everyday comment, and is publicly admitted by senior Party officials. Social discontent is more widespread or at least more widely visible. To some extent this may be healthy in the long run, allowing a society where normal political expression of differences was repressed for decades to develop ways of openly mediating social conflict. But the mechanisms for doing this are still fragile and vulnerable to the Party's need to show a firm hand. Many thousands of criminals have been shot in exemplary executions, and the bloody suppression of the Lhasa demonstrations of October 1987 and March 1988 has marred the image of a peaceful society. The largely unconscious racism of many ethnic Han Chinese towards the country's more than fifty 'national minorities' is still clearly visible. The smaller minorities benefit from an indulgence towards their colourful customs and life-styles. (Until recently, the only acceptable way of painting or sculpting a semi-nude female was to choose a 'minority' subject.) But serious trouble must lie ahead with the largely alienated second-class communities of Tibetans and Uighurs in the Autonomous Regions of Tibet and Xinjiang.

Two questions above all will be answered in the 1990s. The Soviet Union of the late 1980s under Gorbachev stresses political reform as the key to economic change. The Chinese leaders present their reforms in the reverse order, arguing that democratization is a slow process which must first be underpinned by the spread of substantial economic prosperity. Can a more appropriate balance be struck between the two strategies which will reverse the political demoralization of recent years? Second, China and the Soviet Union both now accept the concept of 'interdependence' with the West, and participation in a single world economy. Can they do so, and still develop their societies along different lines from that of the dominant Western culture? The sheet of paper has been wiped clean of the bold, dogmatic, but sometimes visionary characters inscribed by Chairman Mao. Is it now being replaced by familiar words from the capitalist West, or are there still beautiful characters to write?

NOTES

ABBREVIATIONS

BR   *Beijing Review* (Beijing, 1979–   )
CD   *China Daily* (Beijing)
CQ   *China Quarterly* (London)
FE   *BBC Summary of World Broadcasts: Part III, The Far East*
FLP   Foreign Languages Press (Beijing)
ICM   *Inside China Mainland* (Taipei: Institute of Current China Studies)
NCNA   New China News Agency (Xinhua News Agency)
PC   *People's China* (Beijing, 1950–8)
PD   *People's Daily (Renmin ribao)*
PR   *Peking Review* (Beijing, 1958–78)
RF   *Red Flag (Hong Qi)* (Beijing, 1958–88)
SW   *Selected Works*

Minor changes have been made in some translations from the Chinese to conform to style or clarify meaning.

1. AFTER THE REVOLUTION

Population statistics: *FE*, 23 Dec. 1987.

Xu Jiatun: in *Wen Wei Po* (Hong Kong), 22 Mar. 1988 (*FE*, 0108).

Xue Muqiao: *PD*, 7 Dec. 1987.

Li Honglin: *Shanghai Shijie Bao*, 11 Apr. 1988 (*FE*, 0139).

Deng on prices: NCNA, 18 May 1988.

Millionaires: *BR*, 21–7 Mar. 1988.

Party corruption: *PD*, 20 May 1988.

Fedor Burlatsky: 'What sort of socialism do people need?', *Literaturnaya Gazeta* (Moscow), 20 Apr. 1988.

Zhao Ziyang on perestroika: Asahi News Service, 29 Feb. 1988.

Cui Naifu on inequality: *FE*, 0158.

'Dream of communism': *PD*, 7 Dec. 1987.

'Capitalist paradise': Jin Ge, *FE*, 0045.

The Times editorial: 3 Nov. 1987.

2. SEARCH FOR SOCIALISM

SKETCH

Secretary Wang: North-west China Party propaganda dept., *Gongchandang-yuan biaozhun de baxiang tiaojian tongsu jianghua* [*Eight Popular Lectures for a Model Communist*], (Xian: North-west People's Press, 1952).

COMMUNIST VISION

Lenin on transition: E. H. Carr, *The Bolshevik Revolution 1917–1923: I* (Harmondsworth: Penguin, 1966), 238–56; Carr, ed., *Bukharin and Preobrazhensky: The ABC of Communism* (Harmondsworth: Penguin, 1969), 16–17.

Great Harmony: Mozi's text in Joseph Needham, *Science and Civilisation in China: II* (Cambridge: Cambridge Univ. Press, 1956), 167–8.

Kang Yu-wei and Mao: Frederic Wakeman, *History and Will* (Berkeley: Univ. of California Press, 1973), 99–102.

PEACH-BLOSSOM SOCIALISM

Soong Ching Ling: 'Shanghai's new day has dawned', 26 May 1950, in *The Struggle for New China* (Beijing: FLP, 1952), 245–9.

Shanghai lanes: Shirley Wood, *A Street in China* (London: Michael Joseph, 1958), 175.

Everyday life: Ralph and Nancy Lapwood, *Through the Chinese Revolution* (London: People's Books Co-operative Society, 1954); Rewi Alley, *You Banfa!* (Beijing: FLP, 1952); Wilfred Burchett, *China's Feet Unbound* (Melbourne: World Unity Publ., 1952).

Chin Chao-yang: *Village Sketches* (Beijing: FLP, 1957), 169–71.

SOCIALISM SOVIET STYLE

Soviet translations: Hu Yu-chih, 'Publications that serve the people', *PC*, 16 Dec. 1952.

P. F. Yudin: Appointment described in Wu Xiuquan, *Eight Years in the Ministry of Foreign Affairs* (Beijing: New World Press, 1985), 40.

Five-Year Plan: See Mark Selden, *The People's Republic of China: A Documentary History of Revolutionary Change* (New York: Monthly Review, 1979), pt. 2.

Chen Han-seng: *China Reconstructs* (Beijing), no. 10 (1955).

THE GRADUAL ROAD

Hinton: Hinton, *Shenfan* (London: Secker and Warburg, 1983), 162–3.

Mao's original Hundred Flowers speech: Michael Schoenhals, 'Original contradictions—on the unrevised text of Mao Zedong's "On the correct handling of contradictions among the people"', *Australian Journal of Chinese Affairs*, no. 16 (July 1986).

Alan Winnington: *Breakfast with Mao* (London: Lawrence and Wishart, 1986), 180.

POOR IS BEAUTIFUL

Mao Zedong: On Confucius, *SW*, v. 273–4; his 'study tour', ibid. 222; his editorial notes to *Socialist Upsurge in China's Countryside* also in *SW*, v., including the reference to 'demons and monsters' 250; 'poor and blank' metaphor in the unofficial Red Guard collection *Mao Zedong sixiang wansui* [*Long live Chairman Mao's thought*] (Beijing, 1969), 34.

Zhou Libo: *Great Changes in a Mountain Village* (Beijing: FLP, 1961), 220–1.

GREAT LEAP SOCIALISM

Water conservancy campaign: *PR*, 4 Mar. and 1 Apr. 1958.

'A Girl's Reply': *Songs of the Red Flag*, compiled by the scholars Guo Moruo and Zhou Yang (Beijing: FLP, 1961), 88.

'The Girl Checker': *PR*, 13 May 1958.

'Great inventors': Ibid. 3 June 1958.

'Introducing a co-operative': Ibid. 10 June 1958.

Chen Boda: On 'brand-new man', *RF*, no. 3 (1958); on the 'primary unit', *RF*, no. 7 (1958) (also probably by Chen).

Anhui photograph: Ministry of Agriculture, *People's Communes in Pictures* (Beijing, 1960).

Wang Meng: 'The Barber's Tale', *Chinese Literature*, July 1980.

RETHINKING THE TRANSITION

Mao's *Notes*: Cited passages found in Moss Roberts, *A Critique of Soviet Economics* (New York: Monthly Review, 1977), sections 14, 23, 25, 29, 32, 41, 43, 49, 66.

Nine Critiques: Trans. as *The Polemic on the General Line of the International Communist Movement* (Beijing: FLP, 1965).

Su Shaozhi: *Democratization and Reform* (Nottingham: Spokesman, 1988), 108.

RETURN TO CLASS STRUGGLE

15-point statement: 'On Khrushchev's phoney communism and its historical lessons for the world', in *The Polemic* . . ., 441–2, 471, 478.

3. LEADERSHIP FROM ABOVE

SKETCH

1967 leadership clashes: Summarized in the important study of Party history since 1949 published by the Central Committee documentary research office, *Guanyu jianguo yilai dang de ruogan lishi wenti de jueyi: zhushi ben* [*Explanatory volume on the [1981] Resolution* . . .] (Beijing: People's Press, 1985), 406–11.

ORIGINS OF THE CULT

Mao in 1965: Edgar Snow, *The Long Revolution* (Harmondsworth: Penguin, 1974), 18; Yan Jiaqi and Gao Gao (his wife), *Zhongguo 'Wen Ge' shinian shi* [*History of the ten years' 'Cultural Revolution'*], 2 vols. (Hong Kong: Dagongbao, 1987).

Mao in wartime: Robert Payne, *China Awake* (London: Heinemann, 1947), 326–7; Edgar Snow, *Journey to the Beginning* (New York: Vintage, 1972), 166–7; Theodore White, *Thunder out of China* (New York: Sloan, 1946), 230.

Early cult: Raymond Wylie, *The Emergence of Maoism* (Stanford: Stanford Univ. Press, 1980), ch. 8; Mao's cult in the late 1950s discussed in the 1985 Party research volume—cited above, 462–8.

Mao on draft constitution: *SW*, v. 141; on airport controversy: ibid. 344–5.

DISCIPLINE AND DISSENT

Rightists: Wang Meng, 'The Young Man who has just arrived at the Organization Department', trans. in Kai-yu Hsu, *Literature of the People's Republic of China* (Bloomington: Indiana Univ. Press, 1980); Liu Binyan, 'On the Bridge Site', ibid. (Liu recalled its fate in a famous speech to the 1979 Writers' Congress).

Bureaucracy: Mao on 'fine comrades', Chi Hsin, *Teng Hsiao-ping* (Hong Kong: Cosmos, 1978), 80–1; on 'bigshots', quoted by *PD*, 16 May 1986.

Foreign Ministry: Take-over, K. S. Karol, *The Second Chinese Revolution* (London: Cape, 1975), 267–9; junior diplomats' complaint, *Survey of the Chinese Mainland Press* (Hong Kong), no. 4004.

ANATOMY OF ULTRA-LEFT

Jiang Qing: Speech of 12 Apr. 1967 in *Hongse Wenyi* [*Red Literature and Art*] (Beijing), 20 May 1967.

THE LOYAL OPPOSITION

Zhou Enlai: 1980s view, Percy and Lucy Fang, *Zhou Enlai—a Profile* (Beijing: FLP, 1986); Deng's praise, *SW*, i. 329–30; reassessment, *PD*, 6 Jan. 1986; Zhou's earlier view of Mao, *SW*, i 370–82.

February Revolt: source as for sketch above.

Deng Xiaoping: Self-criticism, Chi Hsin, *Teng Hsiao-ping*, 54–64; rehabilitation, Chi Hsin, *The Case of the Gang of Four* (Hong Kong: Cosmos, 1977), 146–8, and Yan Jiaqi and Gao Gao, Zhongguo 'Wen Ge . . .', 507–10.

4. THE REBEL ALTERNATIVE

SKETCH

Chen Lining: *Survey of the China Mainland Press (Supplement)*, no. 225; *Survey of China Mainland Press*, no. 4159; *FE*, no. 2765.

MAKING TROUBLE IN HEAVEN

Mao on physical education: Stuart Schram, *Political Thought of Mao Tse-tung* (Harmondsworth: Penguin, 1969), 152–60.

Mao on Hunan peasant movement: Ibid. 250–9; Li Jui, *The Early Revolutionary Activities of Comrade Mao Tse-tung* (New York: M. E. Sharpe, 1977), 30, 84–5.

PEASANT REBELLION

E. J. Hobsbawm: *Social Bandits and Primitive Rebels* (Glencoe: Free Press, 1959).

Mandate of Heaven: Jean Chesneaux, *Peasant Revolts in China 1840–1949* (Thames and Hudson, 1973), 21.

Huifei: Fei-Ling Davis, *Proletarian Culture in China* (London: Association for Radical East Asian Studies, 1974), 39.

Shanxi-Suiyuan peasants: Gittings, *Role of the Chinese Army* (London: Oxford Univ. Press, 1967), 66–7.

Post-1949 campaigns: Rewi Alley, *Man Against Flood* (Beijing: New World Press, 1956); Lapwood, *Through the Chinese Revolution*, ch. 6.

Revival of 'evil tendencies': C. S. Chen (ed.), *Rural People's Communes in Lien-Chiang* (Stanford: Hoover Institution, 1969).

Gu Hua: *A Small Town Called Hibiscus* (Beijing: Panda Books, 1983), 16–17.

THE MAY FOURTH SPIRIT

1957 students' movement: Rene Goldman, 'Rectification Campaign at Peking University', *CQ*, no. 12.

Lin Xiling: In Dennis Doolin, *Communist China: The politics of student opposition* (Stanford: Hoover Institution, 1964), 27, 34–50. Imprisoned 1958–83, Lin has recalled the affair in *Lin Xiling zixuanji* [*Lin Xiling's Selection*] (Hong Kong: Wide Angle, 1985).

Beida's factions: Victor Nee, *The Cultural Revolution at Peking University* (New York: Monthly Review, 1969), 28; Yue Daiyun and Carolyn Wakeman, *To the Storm* (Berkeley: Univ. of Calif. Press, 1985), 120–1, 155; Anna Louise Strong, *Letter from Peking*, no. 49, 30 May 1967.

RED GUARDS AND COMMUNES

John and Elsie Collier, *China's Socialist Revolution* (London: Stage 1, 1973), 87–92; Jean Daubier, *A History of the Chinese Cultural Revolution* (New York: Vintage, 1974), 70–87.

Mao on students: Daubier, 308

Shanghai Commune: Karol, *Second Chinese Revolution*, pt. 3.

WHITHER CHINA?

Shengwulian: Klaus Mehnert, *Peking and the New Left* (Berkeley: Center for Chinese Studies, 1969).

5. SECOND CULTURAL REVOLUTION

SKETCH

Liaoning students: *Liaoning Daily*, 23 Apr. 1975.

THE MAOIST VISION

Mao's talk with Red Guards: 28 July 1968, *Miscellany of Mao Tse-tung Thought* (Arlington: JPRS, 1974), ii. 469–96.

Western views: Peter Worsley, *Inside China* (London: Allen Lane, 1975), 248; Neville Maxwell (ed.), 'China's Road to Development', *World Development*, vol. 3, nos. 7–8, 480 (Chen Yonggui); 'China's Economic Strategy', *Monthly Review*, July–Aug. 1975, 17; Karol, *Second Chinese Revolution*, 141–2; John Gurley, *China's Economy and the Maoist Strategy* (New York: *Monthly Review*, 1976), 5; John Gittings, 'New light on China's political economy', *IDS Bulletin*, vol. 7, no. 2.

Red Guard memories: Mo Bo, 'I was a teenage Red Guard', *New Internationalist*, Apr. 1987.

REVOLUTION IN EDUCATION AND HEALTH

Mao on education: 'Spring Festival remarks' and 'Hangzhou speech', Stuart Schram, *Mao Tse-tung Unrehearsed* (Harmondsworth: Penguin, 1974).

Medical schemes: S. Hillier and J. Jewell, *Health Care and Traditional Medicine in China 1800–1982* (London: Routledge, 1983), 108–11; Qian Xinzhong quoted, 123.

'Spring Shoots': The film was praised in *China Reconstructs*, Aug. 1976, and denounced by Beijing radio, 29 June 1977.

'Loyal Hearts': Text in *Chinese Literature*, no. 10, 1978.

RURAL REVOLUTION

Four conditions: Quoted in H. V. Henle, *Report on China's Agriculture* (Rome: UNFAO, 1974), 180.

Strategy of rural expansion: *Hunan Daily*, 24 Dec. 1974.

REVOLUTION IN LEADERSHIP

1974–5 posters: These have been generally ignored in post-Mao analysis of the Cultural Revolution, rather than attributed to the ultra-left. John Gittings, 'The great walls of China', *Guardian*, 30 July 1974; CQ, no. 59, 626.

Hangzhou strike: Stephen Andors, *China's Industrial Revolution* (New York: Pantheon, 1977), 234–5.

'Going against the tide': *Yao gan yu fan chao liu* [*Dare to go against the tide*] (Beijing: People's Press, 1974).

THE FINAL STRUGGLE

Fengqing affair: Yan Jiaqi and Gao Gao, *Zhongguo 'Wen Ge . . .'*, 499–502.

THE FLAWED DEBATE

Shanghai School: Peter Moller Christensen and Jorgen Delman, 'A theory of transitional society: Mao Zedong and the Shanghai School', *Bulletin of Concerned Asian Scholars*, vol. 13, pt. 2, 1981; Christensen, 'The Shanghai School and its rejection', in Stephan Feuchtwang and Athar Hussain, *The Chinese Economic Reforms* (London: Croom Helm, 1983).

The Tide of History: *Issues and Studies*, no. 3, 1972; Li Chien in *PR*, no. 34, 1976.

Zhang Chunqiao on bourgeois rights: 'On exercising all-round dictatorship over the bourgeoisie', *RF*, no. 4, 1975 (*CQ*, June 1975, 360–3.)

Foreign trade debate: Deng's speech of 18 Aug. 1985 in Chi Hsin, *The Case of the Gang of Four* (Hong Kong: Cosmos, 1977), 273–6; Ultra-left position in *PR*, 27 Aug. 1976, 9.

6. ECONOMICS IN COMMAND

The opening analysis leans heavily on Cyril Lin, 'China's economic reforms II: Western perspectives', *Asian-Pacific Economic Literature*, vol. 2, no. 1 (Mar.), 1988; also Feuchtwang and Hussain (eds.), *The Chinese Economic Reforms*.

THE REFORMS TAKE OFF

Four Modernizations: Problems analysed in Liu Suinian and Wu Qungan (eds.), *China's Socialist Economy, An outline history* (Beijing: Beijing Review, 1986).

Chen Yun on hardship: ICM, Apr. 1980.

Xue Muqiao: *On Socialist Economy* (Beijing: FLP, 1981); addendum in *BR*, no. 49 (1981); 'Socialism and planned commodity economy', *BR*, no. 33 (1987); 'Away with dogmatism and ossified pattern', *BR*, no. 4 (1988).

BONUSES IN COMMAND

Yu Guangyuan (ed.), *China's Socialist Modernization* (Beijing: FLP, 1984), 594–617; Liu Guoguang, 'Socialism is not egalitarianism', *BR*, no. 39 (1987); John Gittings, 'Wages and management in China', *Journal of Contemporary Asia*, vol. 9, no. 1.

DEMOTING THE PLAN

'Bashful' alternatives: Liu Guoguang, 'Unifying planning and marketing', *BR*, no. 41 (1987).

Birdcage theory: David M. Bachman, *Chen Yun and the Chinese Political System* (Berkeley: Center for Chinese Studies, 1985), 152.
Planning defects: Yu (ed.), *China's Socialist Modernization*, 84–101.
Gao Shangquan: *BR*, no. 15 (1988).

THE PROBLEM OF PRICES

Tianjin report: Reuters, 4 June 1977.
Shenzhen experiment: *Ta Kung Pao* (Hong Kong), 17 Sept. 1987.

7. PEASANT CHINA TRANSFORMED

THE FADING OF THE COMMUNES

Fei Xiaotong: *Small Towns in China* (Beijing: New World Press, 1986), 28–36; *Chinese Village Close-up* (Beijing: New World Press, 1983), 200–1.
Origins of responsibility system: *CQ*, no. 81, p. 163, no. 83, p. 615; *BR*, nos. 3, 11, 17, 34 (1981); no. 24 (1982), nos. 4, 7, 22, 33, 44–50 (1983).
Peter Nolan: *China Now*, no. 108.

THE FENGYANG EXPERIMENT

Fengyang County: John Gittings, *Guardian*, 12 and 15 Mar. 1982.
Work-points: Lin Zili in *Social Sciences in China* (1983), i. 65.
Shanxi survey: *BR*, no. 46 (1984).

PRIVATIZATION OF LAND

Further reforms: *FE*, nos. 7576, 7561, 7669, 7671 (1984); *BR* no. 14 (1985), no. 49 (1986).
Hopes for new co-operatives: Deng Xiaoping, *SW*, 297 ff.; speech of 12 Jan. 1983, in *Fundamentals ...*, 13; Fujian view recorded by John Gittings.
Red Flag: Bulletin of 15 Jan. 1983 in *ICM*, Aug. 1983; *Rural Economic Questions*, no. 1 (1984), in *ICM*, Aug. 1984.

RISE OF RURAL INDUSTRY

Rural industrialization: Robert Delfs in *Far Eastern Economic Review*, 4 June 1987.
Labour force statistics: In *Rural Economic Questions*, no. 12, 1985 (*ICM*, Apr. 1986).
Fei Xiaotong: *BR*, nos. 20–2 (1984); nos. 14, 17, 21 (1985).

COSTS OF REFORM

Peasant extravagance: *CD*, 29 June 1987; *Jingji xiaoxi* [*Economic news*], no. 116 (1985), in *ICM*, Apr. 1985; 1987 report: *PD*, 2 Mar. 1987.

THE RURAL ARGUMENT

William Hinton: *Guardian*, 27 Aug. 1984; see also Hinton's detailed argument that the collective achievements of the model Dazhai Brigade were falsely disparaged, *Monthly Review* (New York), March 1988.
Bankrupt households: *CD*, 24 Sept. 1987.

8. THE GROWTH OF DISSENT

THE RED GUARD LEGACY

Gordon Bennett and Ron Montaperto, *Red Guard* (New York: Doubleday, 1971), 215; Liang Heng and Judith Shapiro, *Son of the Revolution* (London: Chatto and Windus), 207; Anita Chan, *Children of Mao* (London: Macmillan, 1985), 187; Yi Ming in Gregor Benton, *Wild Lilies Poisonous Weeds* (London: Pluto, 1982), 44: student's poem recorded at Xiamen University by Charlotte Shalgosky.

POETS WHO DO NOT BELIEVE

Tiananmen poems: Xiao Lan (ed.), *The Tiananmen Poems* (Beijing: FLP, 1979) describes how the poems were hidden; *Tiananmen shichao* [*Copies of Tiananmen Poems*] (Beijing: People's Literature Press, 1978) includes 'We want real Marxism-Leninism', trans. here by Beth McKillop, and carries Chairman Hua's calligraphy; an illustrated volume with the same title (Shanghai: People's Arts Press, 1979), includes 'With head high . . .' and a heroic woodcut of Wang Lishan.

Beijing Spring: [*Beijing zhi chun*]: Texts trans. in Claude Widor (ed.), *Documents on the Chinese Democratic Movement 1978–1980*, vol. 2 (Hong Kong: Observer Publ., 1984), with a well-informed introduction.

Guo Lusheng (pseud. Shi Zhi): Poems in Widor, ii, 233–4 and 348–50; 83 for his membership of United Action group whose attack on Lin Biao is recorded in Jean Daubier, *History of the Chinese Cultural Revolution* (New York: Vintage, 1973), 104; Guo's first poem trans. in David Goodman, *Beijing Street Voices* (London: Boyars, 1981), 130–1.

Bei Dao: 'Answer' in *Shikan* [*Poetry*], Mar. 1979, translation and critical discussion, Bonnie MacDougall (ed.), *Notes from the City of the Sun: Poems by Bei Dao* (Ithaca: Cornell University Press, 1983), and MacDougall (ed.), *Waves* (London: Heinemann, 1983); Ai Qing, 'The Red Flag', in Kai-yu Hsu (ed.), *Literature of the People's Republic of China* (Bloomington: Indiana Univ. Press, 1980), 917–18.

MARTYRS OF THE CULTURAL REVOLUTION

Yu Luoke: Gordon White, *Politics of Class and Class Origin* (Canberra: Australian National Univ., 1976); his sister's novel, *A Chinese Winter's Tale*

(Hong Kong: Renditions, 1986); her article about him in *Siwu Luntan*, Sept. 1979; extract from his diary in *Zhengming* (Hong Kong), no. 3 (1980); poem by Bei Dao is dedicated to Yu (in *Notes from the City of the Sun*, 58–62); a semi-fictional play about Yu by Wang Keping published in *Beijing zhi chun* (Widor, ii. 410–28); the dissidents Xu Wenli ('My self-defence', 9, 16) and Liu Qing ('Prison memoirs', 901) (see below) both take Yu as a model for their own later imprisonments.

Zhang Zhixin: Essay 'My views remain unchanged', in *Beijing zhichun*, no. 8 (1979); prison doctor exposed in *Zhengming*, no. 8 (1979), 32–3: Ren Zhongyi in *BR*, no. 30 (1979).

Wang Shenyou: Mourned in an essay by the Shanghai Democracy Movement activist Fu Shenqi, who himself would be arrested in the great round-up of April 1981. (Benton, *Wild Lilies*, 122–7; Liu Binyan, speech of 4 Nov. 1986.)

THE SEARCH FOR GENUINE MARXISM

Liu Guokai: Anita Chan (ed.), 'A brief analysis of the Cultural Revolution', *Chinese Sociology and Anthropology*, vol. xix, no. 2, 143–5.

Li Yizhe: Document's name from the three principal authors, LI Zhengtian, Chen YIyang, and Wang XiZHE; trans. in Christian Bourgois (ed.), *Chinois, si vous saviez* (Paris: Bibliothèque Asiatique, 1976).

Wang Xizhe: Benton, *Wild Lilies*, 16–38, from which this account is taken.

Chen Erjin: Trans. by Robin Munro as *China: Crossroads Socialism* (London: Verso, 1984) especially 2, 192. See also Munro's 'China's Democracy Movement: a Midwinter Spring', *Survey*, no. 121 (1984).

Fu Yuehua: released from labour camp 1984, still detained 1986.

DEMOCRACY MOVEMENT AND NEW DISSENT

Wei Jingsheng: Texts in Widor, i. Trans. (also Fu Yuehua) in W. Sadane and W. Zafanolli, *Procès politiques a Pékin* (Paris: Maspero, 1981).

Liu Qing: 'Notes from Prison' trans. in *Chinese Sociology and Anthropology*, Autumn–Winter 1982–3.

Xu Wenli: Extracts from his 'Self-defence' published by Amnesty International in Feb. 1986. In November 1988 he was still being kept in solitary confinement in Beijing No. 1 Prison (Reuter, 11 Nov.).

FROM DISSENT TO PROTEST

1980 elections: Full account in Andrew Nathan, *Chinese Democracy* (New York: Knopf, 1985), ch. 10; fate of Hu Ping, in Liang Heng and Judith Shapiro, *Return to China* (London: Chatto and Windus, 1987), 35–55.

1985 demonstrations: See reports in *Zhengming*, Nov. 1985; Bo Yibo called for a stable political environment, complaining that if senior officials had to busy themselves morning, noon, and night dealing with unexpected incidents, the reforms would never take place (Beijing radio, 28 Nov. 1985).

1986 demonstrations: Shanghai quote, *Zhengming*, Jan. 1987; Beijing quotes, *ICM*, Mar. 1987.

9. THE PARTY UNDER PRESSURE

SKETCH

With you in charge: Andres Onate, 'Hua Kuo-feng and the arrest of the "Gang of Four"', *CQ*, no. 75 (Sept. 1978).

THE POST-MAO TRANSITION

Wang Hongwen's challenge: Deng Xiaoping, *SW*, 218, 265–6.

Hua Guofeng: *Hua zhuxi zai Hunan* [*Chairman Hua in Hunan*] (Beijing: People's Press, 1977), a typical hagiographic essay, prefaced by a 'quotation' from Mao: 'We must create public opinion, we must publicize Comrade Hua Guofeng, we must make the whole people gradually get to know him.'

Self-criticism: (3 Aug. 1982) trans. in *ICM*, Dec. 1982.

Argument with Hu Qiaomu: *Zhengming*, Nov. 1982.

REACHING A VERDICT

Deng's comments on drafts of the 1981 Resolution: *SW*, 276–96; see also the lengthy gloss on the Resolution. *Guanyu jianguo yilai dang de ruogan lishi wenti de jueyi* [*On the Resolution on a Number of Historical Questions since 1949*], produced by the Central Committee's Documentary Research Office (Beijing: People's Press, 1985, rev. edn.).

Trial of Gang of Four: *A Great Trial in Chinese History* (Beijing: New World Press, 1971)—torture of Professor Zhang at 45.

THE PARTY'S CANCER

Party problems: Deng's speech of 12 Nov. 1981 in *ICM*, June 1982; Wang Renzhong, *PD*, 1 July 1982.

1986 Party reform: Robert Delfs in *Far Eastern Economic Review*, 29 May 1986.

Origins of political reform campaign: In *Wen Wei Po* (Hong Kong), 21 and 22 July 1986, *FE*, 8320.

THE CONSERVATIVE REACTION

Spiritual pollution: Zhao's complaint in *Zhengming*, Apr. 1984.

THE PARTY STYLE

Li Ruihuan: *BR*, no. 40 (1984); *Jiushi niandai* [*The Nineties*], no. 2 (1987).

Li Peng: *Guangjiaojing* [*The Mirror*], no. 4 (1987).

Hu Qili on hard working: *FE*, 8225.

10. THE SCHOLARS SPEAK OUT

SKETCH

Fang Lizhi's row: Speech of 4 Nov. 1985, summary in *Zhongguo zhichun* [*China Spring*] (New York), Feb. 1987, digest circulated by internal *Cankao xiaoxi* [*Reference News*], trans. in *ICM*, Dec. 1986.

THE SCHOLARS' LICENCE

Yue Daiyun: *To the Storm* (Berkeley: Univ. of California Press, 1985), 23.
Lu Dingyi: Self-criticism in *Minzhu yu fazhi* [*Democracy and the legal system*], no. 4 (1983).

OPENING THE DEBATE

Practice and theory: See *CQ*, Sept. 1978, 694–6.
1979 Seminar: Summarized in *Zhongguo gongchandang liushinian dashi jianjie* [*Introduction to main events in 60 years of the CCP*], (Beijing: National Defence Univ., 1985), 604–6.

EXTENDING THE FRONTIERS

Su Shaozhi on class: *Selected Writings on Studies of Marxism (SWSM)* (Beijing: Institute of Marxism-Leninism-Mao Zedong Thought), no. 6 (Feb. 1981); see generally Stuart Schram, *Ideology and Policy in China since the Third Plenum, 1978–84* (London: School of Oriental and African Studies, 1984).
Wang Ruoshui: 'On estrangement', *SWSM*, i, no. 12 (May 1981).
Li Honglin: 'The authority of democracy', *SWSM*, ii, no. 4.

THE GREAT DEBATE

Deng's licence: 'Political restructuring of socialist states' in *Social Sciences in China*, no. 3 (1988); also *BR*, no. 39 (1987).
Seminars: 'Socialist spiritual civilisation and theoretical work', *Red Flag*, 16 July 1986, trans. *FE*, 8336.
Li Honglin: 'Modernization and democracy', *Shijie jingji dabao* [*World Economic Herald*], (Shanghai), 2 June 1986.

THREE WHO WENT TOO FAR

Fang Lizhi: On intellectuals, *BR*, 5 Dec. 1986.
Wang Ruowang: 1957 criticism, Hualing Nieh, *Literature of the Hundred Flowers* (New York: Columbia Univ. Press, 1981), ii. 385; on zest for life, *Qingnian yidai* [*Youth Generation*], no. 4 (1986); argument with Deng, *Jiushi niandai* [*The Nineties*] (Hong Kong), no. 2 (1987).
Liu Binyan: On the danger from the left, *Jiushi niandai*, no. 2 (1987); remarks at Shanghai conference, *Zhengming*, no. 1 (1987); 1947 recollections, 'The call of our times', *Wenyibao*, nos. 11–12 (1979); Liu Shulan tale, ibid., no. 6

(1979), both trans. in Lee Ou-fan Lee, *Chinese Literature for the 1980s* (Stanford: Stanford Univ. Press, 1985).

CONSERVATIVE REACTION

1987 reaction: Xinhua commentary, 28 Jan. 1987, in *FE*, 8480; *Henan Ribao*, 19 Jan. 1987 (*FE*, 8472); Shenyang radio, 2 Feb. 1987, in *FE*, 8485; *Beijing Daily* on Western evils, 4 Feb. 1987; Bo Yibo, *FE*, 8494; high-class hotels, Xinhua, 21 Jan. 1987 (*FE*, 8474).

Zhuozhou conference: *Guangming Daily*, 21 Apr. 87; *Asiaweek* (Hong Kong), 10 May and 7 June 1987.

COMPROMISE

'Five gentlemen': Wu Zuguang affair in *Jingbao* [*Mirror*] (*Hong Kong*), Sept. 1987.

Limits: Yan Jiaqi, *FE*, 8717; Ma Hong, *FE*, 0003; Wang Meng, *PD*, 17 Nov. 87.

11. THE DOOR OPENS WIDE

THE NEW PATRIOTISM

Deng on Taiwan: Anniversary speech, 1 Oct. 1984, 'The desire for peaceful reunification of the motherland is taking hold in the hearts of all descendants of the Yellow Emperor.'

Hu Yaobang: In *BR*, no. 42 (1981).

China the 'fish and meat': Sun Yatsen, 1924 lecture, in N. Gangulee, *The Teachings of Sun Yat-sen* (London: Sylvan Press, 1945), 65.

Patriotism: Author's interview at ACFTU headquarters, Apr. 1984.

On the Macartney mission: Yue Qingping, 'Opening up: The lessons of history', *BR*, no. 39 (1987).

RETHINKING SELF-RELIANCE

Huan Xiang: Undated speech and 7 June 1984 report, trans. in *ICM*, no. 4 (1983) and no. 2 (1985).

Mao's view: In Moss Roberts, *A Critique of Soviet Economics* (New York: Monthly Review, 1977), 103; Lu Hsin, *Jingji Yanjiu* [*Economic Research*], 20 July 1965, trans. in *Current Background* (Hong Kong), no. 488.

RESHAPING FOREIGN TRADE

See especially Carl Riskin, *China's Political Economy* (Oxford: Oxford Univ. Press, 1987), ch. 13.

Soviet concessions: Alec Nove, *Economic History of the USSR* (Harmondsworth: Penguin, 1969), 89.

Gu Mu: *CD*, 9 Nov. 1987.

Bonds: Reuter, 22 May 1986.

REGIONAL DEVELOPMENT

Xue Muqiao: Symposium on western China, NCNA, 10 Aug. 1984.

Ji Chongwei: *China Reconstructs*, no. 9 (1984).

Gu Mu on wavelike development: *China News Agency*, 24 Feb. 1985 (*FE*, 7886).

Xu Shijie: *FE*, 0017.

Guangdong reports: *FE*, 8717 and 0005.

12. CHINA'S NEW FACE

THE PACE OF CHANGE

Population: *PD*, 14 Jan. 1988; Reuter, 30 May 1988.

LIFE AND LOVE

Women: Elisabeth Croll, *Chinese Women since Mao* (London: Zed, 1984); Emily Hoonig and Gail Hershatter, *Personal Voices: Chinese women in the 1980s* (Stanford: Stanford Univ. Press, 1988), 23–6, on decline of the Iron Girl model, 314, 'woman is not the moon'; Phyllis Andors, 'The incomplete liberation of Chinese women' in *China Now*, no. 113 (Summer 1985); also Shirin Rai, 'Market merry-go-round', in *China Now*, no. 125 (Summer 1988).

Mao on virtuous women: 'The great union of the popular masses', trans. Stuart Schram, *CQ*, no. 49 (Jan.–Mar. 1972).

CHINA AND THE WORLD

Superiority of socialism: Shenyang radio, 2 Feb. 1987, in *FE*, 8485.

NEW ART, NEW ATTITUDES

Wang Meng: 'My exploration', *Chinese Literature*, Jan. 1981.

Lu Wenfu: Preface to *A World of Dreams* (Beijing: Panda Books, 1986).

Zhang Jie: Biographical note, 'My boat', *Love Must Not Be Forgotten* (Beijing: Panda Books, 1987).

Dai Houying: *Stones of the Wall* (London: Michael Joseph, 1985).

Yellow Earth debate: Geramie Barme and John Minford (eds.), *Seeds of Fire* (Hong Kong: Far Eastern Economic Review, 1986), 252–69.

New art: John Gittings, *Guardian*, 12 Apr. 1980; 'Not just a pretty picture', *New Internationalist*, Apr. 1981.

THE END OF IDEOLOGY

Liu Guoguang: With Liang Wensen and others, *China's Economy in 2000* (Beijing: New World Press, 1987), 32.

SELECT BIBLIOGRAPHY

EYEWITNESSES

The reports of two Americans—Edgar Snow and William Hinton—encompass half a century of contemporary China. Snow interviewed Mao and rode with the Red Army in 1936, producing his classic *Red Star Over China* (London: Gollancz, 1937). He saw Mao again in 1960 (*The Other Side of the River* (London: Gollancz, 1963)), and in 1965 and 1972 (*The Long Revolution* (Harmondsworth: Penguin, 1974)). William Hinton observed land reform in Longbow Village, southern Shanxi, in 1948. All his notes were confiscated by the US Customs: *Fanshen* finally appeared in 1966 (New York: Monthly Review). In 1971 he brought the story up to date in *Shenfan* (London: Secker and Warburg, 1983). He will report critically on post-Mao rural reform in *Fenshan* (forthcoming). Other foreign observers, usually friends of China, include Rewi Alley, Wilfred Burchett, Isabel and David Crook, Felix Greene, Han Suyin, Joshua Horn, Ralph and Nancy Lapwood, Jan Myrdal, William Sewell, Alan Winnington, and Shirley Wood. For the Cultural Revolution, K. S. Karol provides a sympathetic socialist viewpoint in *The Second Chinese Revolution* (London: Cape, 1975). Simon Leys presents a dystopia much closer to present Chinese thinking in *The Chairman's New Clothes* (London: Alison and Busby, 1977).

Chinese eyewitness accounts have only been possible since the Cultural Revolution. The Hunanese former student Liang Heng wrote *Son of the Revolution* with Judith Shapiro (London: Chatto and Windus, 1983) followed by *Return to China* (London: Chatto and Windus, 1987). Yue Daiyun wrote her 'odyssey of a revolutionary Chinese woman', *To the Storm*, with Carolyn Wakeman (Berkeley: Univ. of California Press, 1985). The Anglophile businesswoman Nien Cheng wrote *Life and Death in Shanghai* after leaving China (London: Grafton Books, 1986). Yang Jiang gives a more restrained account in *A Cadre School Life* (Hong Kong: Joint Publishing, 1982). Yu Luojin, sister of the Cultural Revolution martyr Yu Luoke, dramatized her

experiences, political and feminist, in *A Chinese Winter's Tale*
(Hong Kong: Renditions, 1986).

TEXTS AND REFERENCE WORKS

The *Cambridge History of China* (16 vols., 1978–) brings
together modern scholarship. Jerome Chen's *China and the West*
(London: Hutchinson, 1979) tells brilliantly the story up to 1937
of this complex and still unfolding relationship. For 1949–76, the
sound China-watching of Jacques Guillermaz, *The Chinese
Communist Party in Power* (Folkestone: Dawson, 1976), con-
trasts with the concerned documentary approach of Mark Selden, *The People's Republic of China: A Documentary History
of Revolutionary Change* (New York: Monthly Review, 1979).
Current research and events are chronicled in the *China Quarterly* (London: Contemporary China Institute), *China Now*
(London: Society for Anglo-Chinese Understanding), and the
Bulletin of Concerned Asian Scholars (Boulder, Colorado).

There are five official volumes of Mao's *Selected Works*. His
unofficial writings are accessible through his best-known West-
ern biographer, Stuart Schram (*Mao Tse-tung* (Harmondsworth:
Penguin, 1966)), with extracts in *The Political Thought of Mao
Tse-tung* (Harmondsworth: Penguin, 1969) and *Mao Tse-tung
Unrehearsed* (Harmondsworth: Penguin, 1974). Deng Xiaoping
has one official volume of *Selected Works, 1975–82* (Beijing: FLP
1984), with more speeches in *Fundamental Issues in Present-Day
China* (Beijing: FLP 1987). Zhou Enlai has one *Selected Works*
(Beijing: FLP 1981) (two in Chinese).

LITERATURE

Novels and short stories, though politically circumscribed, provided vivid insight into the social culture of revolutionary change
before 1966. See *Literature of the People's Republic of China*,
ed. Kai-yu Hsu (Bloomington: Indiana Univ. Press, 1980) and
the monthly *Chinese Literature* (Beijing, 1960–). The Cultural
Revolution eliminated nearly all intermediate shades between
red and black. The output is surveyed in Kai-yu Hsu, *The
Chinese Literary Scene* (Harmondsworth: Penguin, 1976). Hao

Ran's *The Golden Road* (Beijing: FLP, 1981) is one of the brighter examples, taking advantage of the less stereotyped style permissible when writing about peasants. A mostly new generation exposed the scars in *The Wounded: New stories of the Cultural Revolution, 1977-78* (Hong Kong: Joint Publishing, 1979). *Seeds of Fire,* ed. Geramie Barme and John Minford (Hong Kong: Far Eastern Economic Review, 1986), surveys and extracts dissenting Chinese literature (and some political thought) since 1976. By the mid-1980s, realistic writing within broad limits about past and present could be published. Translations in the excellent Panda Books series published by the Chinese Literature Press (Beijing) include Gu Hua's *A Small Town Called Hibiscus* (1983) and *Pagoda Ridge* (1985), Wang Meng's *The Butterfly and other stories* (1983), Lu Wenfu's *A World of Dreams* (1986), and Gladys Yang's selection, *Seven Contemporary Chinese Women Writers* (1982).

POLITICAL ECONOMY

The combined study of Chinese politics and economics has been revitalized by the post-Mao reforms and the retrospective data provided about the past. The best general survey is Carl Riskin's *China's Political Economy* (Oxford: Oxford Univ. Press, 1987). Other works grapple with Chinese thinking on the move: Bill Brugger (ed.), *Chinese Marxism in Flux 1978–84* (London: Croom Helm, 1985); Stephan Feuchtwang and Athar Hussain (eds.), *The Chinese Economic Reforms* (London: Croom Helm, 1983); Elizabeth Perry and Christine Wong (eds.), *The Political Economy of Reform in Post-Mao China* (Cambridge: Harvard Univ. Press, 1985). The most original Chinese thinking is accessible in Chen Erjin, *China: Crossroads Socialism* (trans. Robin Munro) (London: Verso, 1984); Su Shaozhi, *Democratization and Reform* (Nottingham: Spokesman, 1988). Difficult questions of comparison between societies in differing states of change have been opened up by Gordon White in *Revolutionary Socialist Development in the Third World* (Brighton: Wheatsheaf Books, 1983) and *Developmental States in East Asia* (Basingstoke: Macmillan, 1988).

SOCIETY

Chinese Profiles (Beijing: Panda Books, 1986), a path-breaking collection of *vox pop.* interviews by Zhang Xinxin and Sang Ye, typifies a new and franker approach to the description of social relations and everyday life. Lynn Pan's *The New Chinese Revolution* (London: Hamish Hamilton, 1987), provides a good discursive introduction. There are useful essays in Robert Benewick and Paul Wingrove, *Reforming the Revolution: China in Transition* (London: Macmillan, 1988). Post-collective life in a Sichuan village is recorded by Stephen Endicott, *Red Earth* (London: Tauris, 1988). Latest trends in population and family planning are summarized in Penny Kane, *The Second Billion* (Ringwood, Victoria, Australia: Penguin, 1987). Elisabeth Croll does the same for the changing role of women in *Chinese Women since Mao* (London: Zed, 1983). Vaclav Smil, *The Bad Earth* (London: Zed, 1984), discusses China's environmental problems. There are several good travel guides including *China: A Travel Survival Kit* (Victoria, Australia: Lonely Planet, 2nd edn., 1988).

GLOSSARY AND INDEX OF NAMES

CHINESE

OTHERS

GENERAL INDEX

agricultural co-operatives
  low-level, 22–3, 26
  new forms, 139–40
  speed up, xii, 28–33, 215–16
agricultural (rural) responsibility system, xiv, 127–8, 131–3, 135–40
alienation, 208–10, 252, 259
Anti-Duhring (Engels), 19
Anti-Rightist Campaign, xii, 14, 215
April Fifth Movement, 153
April Fifth Tribune, 168
apriorism, idealistic, 254
armed forces, *see* People's Liberation Army
art, 23, 165, 171, 204, 253–4, 259

Beijing Spring, 154–5
Beijing University (Beida), 70–3, 75, 81, 171, 174–5, 201–3, 248, 250
bourgeois liberalization (liberalism), 202, 205, 236, 250, 256
  cadres' disquiet, 194
  conservative campaign, 11, 189–90, 218–21
  Deng's view, 167, 196–7, 220
bourgeoisie, 14, 91, 158, 162
  Mao's view of, 19, 51–2
  national, 20, 188
  'new', 40–1, 99–100, 159
  sugar-coated bullets of, 50, 194
bureaucracy
  analysed by dissidents, 164, 168, 174
  criticized by Deng, 185
  criticized by Mao, xii, 28, 40, 51–2
  denounced by Red Guards, 79–80, 86
  emergence, 69
  in 1980s, 198, 213

cadres, 5, 29, 35, 70, 123, 151, 246
  children of, 38, 89, 189–90, 212, 223

in Cultural Revolution, 94–5, 162
new style of, 198
'old', 43, 197
privileged, 37–8, 79, 107, 186–7
reform of system, 191–2, 209
rural, 136–7
capitalism, 3, 31, 151
  conservative view of, 8, 10
  co-operation with socialism, 5, 111, 228
  new views on, 11, 14, 212, 238, 254–5
  'restoration of', 11, 40–1, 99
  state capitalism, 232, 257
'capitalist road' (and 'roaders'), 41–2, 58, 74–5, 158, 179
Central Advisory Commission, 195, 226–7
Central Discipline Inspection Commission, 187–9, 221
Chengdu Conference (1958), 45
China Spring, 171, 248
China's Destiny (Chiang Kai-shek), 46
class struggle
  mid-50s view of, xii, 27–8
  Mao insists on, xiii, 39–42
  post-Mao view of, 5, 179, 182, 191, 208, 256
communes
  see people's communes; Paris Commune; Shanghai Commune
communism, 4
  a dream, 10, 108
  goal of, 13, 17–18
  and society, 18, 109, 180–1, 238–9
  Soviet view, 25
  transition to, xii, 3, 17–21, 24–5, 34–5
Communist Party (Chinese)
  Congresses/Plenums: Seventh Congress, 46, 51; Eighth Congress,